"In *Archaeology and the Ministry* best option to time travel as he tra..._ Drawing on his decades of scholarship, and with eloquent and jargon-free prose, deSilva tells an exciting story of the 'what, where, and how' of first-century life in the Roman Empire. Beautiful photos illuminate historical settings and invite readers to imagine themselves as travelers with Paul. *Archaeology and the Ministry of Paul* is an essential resource for scholars, pastors, and all curious Bible readers."

—**Lynn H. Cohick**, Houston Christian University

"What a rich source of information! David deSilva provides details and pictures that provoke the imaginations of all New Testament readers. The narratives surrounding the life and ministry of the apostle Paul and his associates come freshly to life with deSilva's discussions and depictions. Archaeological findings can assist our understanding of the Bible. David deSilva interacts with those findings and combines his knowledge of the New Testament to create an indispensable tool for group or individual study."

—**Dennis R. Edwards**, North Park Theological Seminary

"A city name is often just a dot on a map until you visit and experience that place. Most readers of Paul's letters cannot afford to go on a tour of the Roman world, but deSilva has offered the next best thing: an expert guided tour through key locations in Paul's life and ministry. You will see Paul's world come alive in the pages of this book, and it is bound to enrich your reading of Acts and Paul's letters."

—**Nijay K. Gupta**, Northern Seminary

"This carefully researched, lucidly written, richly illustrated, and handsomely produced volume is an essential guide for all who are interested in learning more about the archaeological record of sites associated with the far-flung ministry of Paul. A greater understanding of the varied historical contexts where the apostle conducted his pastoral ministry will greatly enhance one's ability to interpret Paul's letters with both increased precision and enhanced imagination. This is a book I will turn to time and again not only when teaching Paul and his letters but also when leading pilgrims to places where the apostle trod."

—**Todd D. Still**, Baylor's Truett Seminary

ARCHAEOLOGY
AND THE
MINISTRY
OF PAUL

ARCHAEOLOGY
AND THE
MINISTRY
OF PAUL
A VISUAL GUIDE

David A. deSilva

Baker Academic
a division of Baker Publishing Group
Grand Rapids, Michigan

Published by Baker Academic
a division of Baker Publishing Group
Grand Rapids, Michigan
BakerAcademic.com

Printed in the United States of America

Library of Congress Cataloging-in-Publication Data
Names: deSilva, David A., 1967– author.
Title: Archaeology and the ministry of Paul : a visual guide / David deSilva.
Description: Grand Rapids, Michigan : Baker Academic, a division of Baker Publishing Group,
    [2025] | Series: Archaeology and the New Testament | Includes bibliographical references and
    index.
Identifiers: LCCN 2024039002 | ISBN 9781540960955 (paperback) | ISBN 9781493450121 (ebook) |
    ISBN 9781493450138 (pdf)
Subjects: LCSH: Paul, the Apostle, Saint. | Bible. Epistles of Paul—Antiquities.
Classification: LCC BS2506.3 .D47 2025 | DDC 225.92—dc23/eng/20240928
LC record available at https://lccn.loc.gov/2024039002

Cover design by Paula Gibson. Interior book design by Nadine Rewa.

Baker Publishing Group publications use paper produced from sustainable forestry practices and postconsumer waste whenever possible.

25   26   27   28   29   30   31   7   6   5   4   3   2   1

To my first grandson,
Cain Christopher deSilva,
present ever in my heart and thoughts

CONTENTS

INTRODUCTION

Perhaps the most fundamental principle of solid biblical interpretation is "Context is important." A great deal of what I was taught—and what I now endeavor to pass along to my own students—about learning to listen to our Scriptures has to do with immersing ourselves in the various contexts of whatever passage one happens to be studying. How does it relate to its immediate literary context; that is, how do we hear it differently and with greater precision when we consider it not on its own but as part of a larger piece of communication? How does it relate to the context of the shared traditions available to its author and its readers—for example, resonating with or even reciting older texts—and to what end? What is going on historically, what social and cultural circumstances surrounded the audience at the time the work was being composed and heard, and what connections is the audience being asked to make? And of course, what is our own context as readers and interpreters of these ancient texts, and to what extent is *our* context exerting pressure on what we will be able to see in or hear from these texts?

I was a professor of New Testament for almost fifteen years before I began traveling to visit what archaeologists have recovered of the everyday spaces, the material culture, and the monumental architecture of the cities in which these writers and audiences lived and moved and had their being. In retrospect, this should have been an obvious step for me to have taken much earlier, given the importance of context for understanding these texts. It was nothing short of transformative for my engagement with the writings of the New Testament (above all, the letters of Paul) as pastoral addresses and interventions in the collective lives of actual groups of Christ-followers living in the cities of the first-century eastern Roman Empire. These texts moved in a new and dramatic way away from presenting themselves as words on a printed page toward presenting themselves as carefully crafted instructions targeting living Christian communities, whether their members were facing more general challenges shared across the early church or challenges more particular to their own geographic and social locations.

In order for us to enter into these texts more fully as what they are—namely, time-sensitive pastoral interventions—it helps to be able to think in an informed way about questions like: What did these believers see around them? What messages and ideologies were represented in what they saw around themselves every day? What social practices were occurring around them? What tugs (or all-out shoves) did they experience in regard to joining in these practices once again? And how is Paul marshaling the pastoral resources of Scripture, the Spirit, and the community to help them persevere in investing themselves fully in the formation of a *new* social body with *new* practices? The fruits of archaeology, visible for us in well-curated sites and museums, provide us with a great deal of raw material for such reflection.

My goal for this book is to introduce readers to these fruits in regard to the majority of sites associated with the ministry of Paul, as far as this can be known from the Acts of the Apostles and from Paul's own writings. I am particularly interested in helping my readers connect what archaeologists have recovered from these sites with the situations of Paul's churches as reflected in his letters and with the responses Paul urges his converts to embrace in regard to those situations. With such goals in mind, I have sought throughout to focus on what has been recovered of these cities as Paul would have encountered them during his lifetime and only rarely to draw on finds from the late first or early second centuries AD (or beyond). As a result, the reader should not expect a comprehensive guide to these sites but rather a focused exploration of the relevance of these sites for the writings, ministry, and communities of the apostle Paul. We will walk together alongside Paul, as it were, through Philippi, Corinth, and Ephesus as he would have encountered them—and as his converts would have continued to encounter them as they sought to embrace a new way of life in the midst of the old structures and their supporters. I have in mind as my audience primarily those who might never be able to visit the sites firsthand, since travel is expensive and often physically demanding. The book, however, will be of obvious value for those who anticipate visiting some number of these sites—for example, on a "Journeys of Paul" tour.

The book is divided into three unequal parts. Part 1 is devoted to sites connected with the beginning of Paul's preaching ministry, a period during which he is not known to have organized communities of converts into "assemblies" (*ekklēsiai*) or congregations that would persist after his departure. This section includes some of the least well-excavated sites. Part 2, by far the longest, treats cities in which Paul and his team were known to have planted congregations, several of which (Pisidian Antioch, Philippi, Thessalonica, Corinth, Ephesus, and Colossae) were also the recipients of the letters now contained in the New Testament.[1] Connections between artifacts and archaeological remains from these sites, on the one hand, and the contents of those letters, on the other hand, will be a particular focus of the relevant chapters. Part 3 is devoted to the sites connected with the last journeys of Paul recorded in Acts—his journey to Jerusalem to deliver the collection that led, in turn, to his arrest and his eventual journey to Rome in his quest for a resolution of the charges brought against him in Jerusalem.

Individual chapters typically open with a section on the connections between the particular city and Paul's ministry when Paul's engagement with the inhabitants of that site spans more than a single period. The largest share of each chapter explores the archaeological and literary evidence for thinking about the "lived spaces" of a particular city and the ways in which this evidence illumines the situation of the members of the assemblies Paul planted, the challenges they faced, and the instructions Paul gave in his letters. In instances where the sites are stunningly well documented (e.g., Corinth, Ephesus, and Rome), the discussion will be broken up into subsections.

I generally follow the trajectory of Paul's ministry as it has been constructed by the author of the Acts of the Apostles (whom I will refer to as Luke). The reliability of Luke's narrative as a historical source for the life and work of Paul and his team has met with significant challenges from the scholarly community. At the very least, every reader of Acts must acknowledge Luke's selectivity. From Acts we would never guess that Paul wrote letters to his churches, that he had some significantly difficult dealings with his churches in Galatia and Corinth after he moved on from his founding visits, that he conducted missionary work in Illyricum and probably Crete, or that he had an important coworker named Titus. Acts tells us almost nothing about Paul prior to his encounter with the glorified Lord and nothing after his period of house arrest in Rome. Luke is telling the story *his* way for his own purposes, not to satisfy our historical interests and curiosities. There are also significant challenges to reconciling Luke's story of the early part of Paul's postconversion ministry and his interactions with the Jerusalem-based apostles with Paul's own account of the same in Galatians 1–2.

The primary focus of this book, however, is on the archaeology of discrete sites and their relevance for thinking about Paul's missionary activity and,

---

1. Rome and the connections between its lived spaces and Paul's letter to the Roman Christians will be treated in the third part.

above all, his congregations and letters, rather than on the problems with reconciling or otherwise resolving the tensions between the narrative of Acts and the piecemeal data about Paul's movements and mission from his letters. For such a purpose, Acts—consistently tweaked with reference to Paul's own firsthand testimony concerning his activities—provides a sufficiently useful geographic arc to follow.[2]

A book like this would have been impossible to write had I not been able to travel to most of these sites. I want, therefore, to express my deep appreciation to those who helped make such travel possible: Mr. Abdullah Gur of Meander Travel, based in Kuşadası, who arranged for my first extended visit to Ephesus, among other sites; Mr. Levent Oral of Tutku Tours, based in Izmir, who arranged for my most recent visit to multiple sites in Türkiye (and who was a lifeline for me when I fell ill on an earlier solo trip!); and Mr. James Ridgway of Educational Opportunities (EO) Tours, based in Lakeland, Florida, who gave me multiple opportunities by means of EO's "Lands of the Bible" cruises and land-based tours to visit sites in almost all the countries represented herein. A number of the chapters in this book began their lives as presentations I gave to groups traveling on these cruises. Some of these, then, became the basis for essays published in the *Lexham Geographic Commentary on Acts through Revelation* (edited by Barry Beitzel), and I am grateful to Doug Mangum of Lexham Press for securing permission for me to adapt and expand those essays for inclusion here. I wish also to thank Dr. Bryan Dyer, senior acquisitions editor at Baker Academic, for warmly receiving my proposal for this volume and its sequel; Dr. Dustyn Keepers, acquisitions associate, for going above and beyond working with the hundreds of photos that are included in this book, coordinating with the design team, and keeping track of the required permissions; and Ms. Melisa Blok, project editor for this volume, for her meticulous work throughout the copyediting process. It was a joy to work with people of such diligence and competence. Finally, I wish to thank the trustees and administration of Ashland Theological Seminary for study leave opportunities and for professional development funds, which largely subsidized the solo tours of Italy, Greece, Türkiye, and Israel that I have undertaken since I began prioritizing visiting relevant Greco-Roman-period sites in 2011.

---

2. On the historical questions surrounding the presentation of Paul and his mission in Acts, see further deSilva, *Introduction to the New Testament*, 328–32; deSilva, *Letter to the Galatians*, 33–38, 48–58.

ABBREVIATIONS

OLD TESTAMENT

Gen.	Genesis	Eccles.	Ecclesiastes
Exod.	Exodus	Song	Song of Songs
Lev.	Leviticus	Isa.	Isaiah
Num.	Numbers	Jer.	Jeremiah
Deut.	Deuteronomy	Lam.	Lamentations
Josh.	Joshua	Ezek.	Ezekiel
Judg.	Judges	Dan.	Daniel
Ruth	Ruth	Hosea	Hosea
1 Sam.	1 Samuel	Joel	Joel
2 Sam.	2 Samuel	Amos	Amos
1 Kings	1 Kings	Obad.	Obadiah
2 Kings	2 Kings	Jon.	Jonah
1 Chron.	1 Chronicles	Mic.	Micah
2 Chron.	2 Chronicles	Nah.	Nahum
Ezra	Ezra	Hab.	Habakkuk
Neh.	Nehemiah	Zeph.	Zephaniah
Esther	Esther	Hag.	Haggai
Job	Job	Zech.	Zechariah
Ps(s).	Psalm(s)	Mal.	Malachi
Prov.	Proverbs		

NEW TESTAMENT

Matt.	Matthew	Phil.	Philippians
Mark	Mark	Col.	Colossians
Luke	Luke	1 Thess.	1 Thessalonians
John	John	2 Thess.	2 Thessalonians
Acts	Acts	1 Tim.	1 Timothy
Rom.	Romans	2 Tim.	2 Timothy
1 Cor.	1 Corinthians	Titus	Titus
2 Cor.	2 Corinthians	Philem.	Philemon
Gal.	Galatians	Heb.	Hebrews
Eph.	Ephesians	James	James

1 Pet.	1 Peter	3 John	3 John
2 Pet.	2 Peter	Jude	Jude
1 John	1 John	Rev.	Revelation
2 John	2 John		

OLD TESTAMENT APOCRYPHA

1 Macc.	1 Maccabees	3 Macc.	3 Maccabees
2 Macc.	2 Maccabees		

APOSTOLIC FATHERS

1 Clem.   1 Clement

PHILO

Embassy   *On the Embassy to Gaius*   *Spec. Laws*   *On the Special Laws*

JOSEPHUS

Ag. Ap.   *Against Apion*   *J.W.*   *Jewish War*
Ant.   *Jewish Antiquities*

CLASSICAL AUTHORS

Aelius Aristides
Or.   *Orations*

Antipater of Sidon
Anth. Gr.   *Anthologia Graeca* (*Greek Anthology*)

Appian
Bell. civ.   *Bella civilia* (*Civil Wars*)
Mith. Wars   *Mithridatic Wars*

Apuleius
Metam.   *Metamorphoses* (*The Golden Ass*)

Aristophanes
Frag.   *Attributed Fragments*

Athenaeus
Deipn.   *Deipnosophistae* (*Banquet of the Learned*)

Caesar
Bell. civ.   *Bellum civile* (*Civil Wars*)

Cicero
Tusc.   *Tusculan Disputations*

Crinagoras
Anth. Gr.   *Anthologia Graeca* (*Greek Anthology*)

Dio Cassius
Hist. rom.   *Historiae romanae* (*Roman History*)

Dio Chrysostom
Rhod.   *Rhodiaca* (*To the People of Rhodes*)

Herodotus
Hist.   *Historiae*

Horace
Carm.   *Carmina (Odes)*

Martial
Epigr.   *Epigrammaton libri XII*

Minucius Felix
Oct.   *Octavius*

Ovid
Fast.   *Fasti*

Pausanias
Descr.   *Description of Greece*

Philostratus
Vit. Apoll.   *Vita Apollonii*

Plato
Apol.   *Apology of Socrates*
Euthyphr.   *Euthyphro*
Resp.   *Respublica (Republic)*

Pliny the Elder
Nat.   *Natural History*

Plutarch
Mor.   *Moralia (Moral Essays)*
Quaest. conv. *Quaestionum convi-
                 vialum libri IX*

Quaest. rom.   *Quaestiones romanae et
                    graecae (Aetia romana et
                    graeca)*

Strabo
Geogr.   *Geography*

Suetonius
Claud.   *Divus Claudius*
Nero   *Nero*

Tacitus
Ann.   *Annales (Annals)*

Varro
Ling.   *De lingua latina*

Virgil
Aen.   *Aeneid*
Georg.   *Georgica*

Vitruvius
De arch. *De architectura*

Xenophon
Mem.   *Memorabilia*

Xenophon of Ephesus
Eph.   *Ephesiaka (Ephesian Tale)*

PATRISTIC WRITINGS

Eusebius
Chron.   *Chronicon (Chronicle)*
Hist. eccl. *Historia ecclesiastica (Eccle-
               siastical History)*

Orosius
Adv. pag.   *Historiarum adversus paganos
               libri VII (Seven Books of His-
               tories against the Pagans)*

INSCRIPTIONS AND PAPYRI

IGLSyria   *Inscriptions grecques et
              latines de la Syrie*
IGR   *Inscriptiones Graecae ad res
              Romanas pertinentes*

PHerc   *Papyrus Herculanensis*

PART I

BEGINNINGS

According to Luke, Paul encountered the glorified Christ and understood that encounter as his commissioning to announce the deliverance that God had prepared for people from every nation—and to do so without delay. As Paul is remembered to have put it in his hearing before the procurator Porcius Festus and King Agrippa II, "After that, King Agrippa, I was not disobedient to the heavenly vision, but declared first to those in Damascus, then in Jerusalem and throughout the countryside of Judea, and also to the Gentiles, that they should repent and turn to God and do deeds consistent with repentance" (Acts 26:19–20 NRSV). In Paul's own recollection of his activity after that encounter, he speaks of his activity in this regard in Damascus, Arabia, Cilicia, and Syria (2 Cor. 11:32–33; Gal. 1:15–24).

If Paul was able to organize communities of believers during this early period, neither he nor Luke tells us explicitly. There are oblique hints that he did—for example, Paul and Silas returning "through Syria and Cilicia, strengthening the churches" (Acts 15:41 NRSV), concerning which Luke gives his readers no origin stories or specific locations apart from Tarsus and Antioch-on-the-Orontes.[1] This section, therefore, will be necessarily brief, focusing on what archaeological work has revealed of those places specifically

1. There were many cities named Antioch in the eastern Mediterranean, since these were founded (or re-founded) by the rulers of the Seleucid Empire, many of whom bore the name Antiochus. The two of concern in this book are Antioch-on-the-Orontes in the Roman province of Syria and Pisidian Antioch in the Roman province of Galatia.

named in connection with Paul's earliest missionary endeavors—and in the three key cities of Damascus, Tarsus, and Antioch-on-the-Orontes, archaeological work has been terribly disappointing in this regard. Paphos in Cyprus, the first site highlighted by Luke in Paul and Barnabas's first apostolic mission from their base in Antioch-on-the-Orontes, offers a good deal more in the way of archaeological activity. It is included here because, according to Luke, the mission there did not result in the planting of a congregation. Despite the fact that both Luke and Paul attest to some preaching activity on Paul's part in Jerusalem at this earliest stage, exploration of the relevance of the archaeology from Jerusalem for Paul's story is deferred here to part 3 ("Endings"), where the evidence is more directly related to the events.[2]

2. This treatment will be limited since Jerusalem will figure so largely in my forthcoming volume, *Archaeology and the World of Jesus* (Grand Rapids: Baker Academic, 2025).

1

TARSUS

Tarsus in the Ministry of Paul

Although Paul himself never mentions his connection with Tarsus in his letters, Luke pointedly identifies him as "from Tarsus in Cilicia, a citizen of no ordinary city" (Acts 21:39; see also 9:11; 22:3). As a result, Pauline scholars have been keen to learn all they can about Tarsus for the light that Paul's native city might shed on the apostle and his formative upbringing. Luke has Paul returning to Tarsus after his dramatic and course-altering encounter with the glorified Christ and his provocative proclamation about Jesus first in Damascus and then in Jerusalem (9:19–30). We do not hear about him again until Barnabas seeks him out in Tarsus to enlist his help for the work of the gospel in Antioch-on-the-Orontes (11:25). Paul himself recalls how, between the third and fourteenth year after his conversion to faith in Jesus as Israel's Messiah, he "went into the regions of Syria and Cilicia," as a result of which time the churches in Judea "heard it said, 'The one who formerly was persecuting us is now proclaiming the faith he once tried to destroy'" (Gal. 1:21, 23 NRSV). The implication is that Paul was active in evangelistic work throughout both regions, with Tarsus the likely center for his early missionary work in the Roman province of Cilicia (cf. Acts 15:23, 41).[1]

1. See Fairchild, "Paul's Early Ministry in Syria and Cilicia." Fairchild suggests that Paul engaged in a wide-ranging evangelistic ministry both in the eastern lowlands and in the more mountainous western parts of Cilicia, noting that Paul's own account of his ministry, and especially the variety of hardships he endured in the course of his work (2 Cor. 11:23–28), demands a good deal more missionary activity than Acts recounts ("Paul's Early Ministry in Syria and Cilicia,"516). See also Hengel and Schwemer, *Paul between Damascus and Antioch*, 151–77, on Paul's work in Tarsus and Cilicia.

The Archaeology of Tarsus

Ancient Tarsus remains almost entirely inaccessible under modern Tarsus, with the result that very little of Paul's city has been recovered. The foundations of a hippodrome from the first century AD were found on the premises of the Tarsus American College, with the remnants of a Roman theater discovered close by.[2] At Cumhuriyet Square, about 600 yards north of the college, a street from the late Hellenistic or early Roman period, made from basalt paving stones and about 24 feet wide, was uncovered.[3] The remains of the houses and porticoes (column-lined, roofed walkways) flanking the road, however, are from the late Roman period. The so-called Cleopatra Gate, 400 yards west of the college, is a late Roman or Byzantine rebuild of the city's older western gate that would have stood on the site in Paul's time. A late Roman period well, popularly called St. Paul's Well, led archaeologists to first-century Roman remains in its vicinity, 10 to 15 feet below present ground level. Finally, a Roman bridge of uncertain dating marks where a channel of the Cydnus River flowed prior to its being redirected in the Byzantine period to solve issues of flooding.[4]

Nedim Ardoğa / CC BY-SA 3.0 / Wikimedia Commons

The Roman-period road in Tarsus, slightly convex to allow drainage into the gutters on either side.

2. Fant and Reddish, *Biblical Sites*, 325.
3. Fant and Reddish, *Biblical Sites*, 327; Wilson, *Biblical Turkey*, 132.
4. Wilson, *Biblical Turkey*, 132.

A bronze door from a temple in Tarsus from the Hellenistic period
(second century BC). In the ninth century AD, Emperor Theophi-
lus moved the door to Byzantium to grace a side entrance to Hagia
Sophia.

As an important Greek city, Tarsus would have had all the typical structures and institutions appropriate to that status. Strabo (*Geogr.* 14.5.12) mentions a gymnasium—the institution dedicated to the education and physical formation of the next generation of the elite—beside the Cydnus River, which flowed through ancient Tarsus. According to him, Tarsus's elite were so enthusiastic about Tarsus's educational system, extending to the tertiary studies in philosophy and rhetoric, that they rivaled Athens and Alexandria (*Geogr.* 14.5.13). Tarsus would also have had markets, administrative buildings, and temples, though nothing of these from the Hellenistic and early Roman periods has been identified.

Paul was born into Roman citizenship in Tarsus. A good number among the elite of Tarsus might have been awarded with Roman citizenship in connection with the various factions within Rome seeking to consolidate their power during the civil wars that marked the period of transition from the Republic to the Principate. Pompey, Julius Caesar, Antony, and Augustus are all known to have bestowed benefits and granted privileges to Tarsus between 64 and 31 BC.[5] An inscription in the Hatay Archeology Museum (*IGLSyria* 3.1.718) records privileges and honors that Octavian granted to one Seleucus of Rhosos (a city in Roman Syria) in gratitude for his service to Octavian in the war against Sextus Pompeius, son of Pompey the Great (rival of Octavian's adoptive father, Julius Caesar). The privileges included granting Roman citizenship to Seleucus, his family, *and* his descendants. We may never know how Saul of Tarsus acquired Roman citizenship, but a legacy from an ancestor who gained favor with a prominent Roman official is one possibility. At the other end of the social spectrum, slaves of Roman citizens who were manumitted (liberated) as a reward for decades of faithful service also became Roman citizens, a status passed on to their children. It is also possible that Paul received his Roman citizenship in this manner: being born (see Acts 22:28) to Jewish parents (or to the children of Jewish parents) who had been thus enslaved—perhaps in the course of Roman punitive expeditions in response to seditious activity in Galilee or Judea during the period after Rome assumed oversight of the region (63 BC and after)—deported to Tarsus, and later manumitted.[6]

5. Ramsey, *Cities of Saint Paul*, 197–98, 205.
6. Walker, *In the Steps of Saint Paul*, 34–35.

2

DAMASCUS AND ARABIA

Damascus in the Ministry of Paul

According to Luke's reconstruction of the history of the early Jesus movement, Paul's ministry began in Damascus. His goal for his journey there was radically changed by his encounter with the glorified Christ at some point near the end of the 160-mile journey from Jerusalem along the ancient trade route known as the King's Highway. Luke portrays Paul, within days of this encounter, proclaiming Jesus as the Messiah in a number of the Jewish synagogues in Damascus (Acts 9:19–22). That there was a large Jewish presence in an important city located not far north of Israel's historic territory is to be expected. Josephus (*J.W.* 2.559–61) confirms that Damascus had quite a large Jewish population when he writes of the massacre of 10,500 Damascene Jews by their Gentile neighbors in AD 66—in the wake of the activity of the Jews of Judea on the eve of the First Jewish Revolt. We learn, incidentally, that a significant number of the Gentile Damascenes' wives had converted to Judaism (a move that women were understandably readier to make than men). It is possible that Paul's activity in the synagogue had such Gentile converts and God-fearers in particular view from the beginning, in keeping with Paul's commissioning as envoy to the Gentiles (Acts 9:15; Gal. 1:16).

Paul attests firsthand to his presence in Damascus at a very early point in his ministry in connection with a trip "into Arabia" (Gal. 1:17). He also corroborates Luke's claim that he had to make a hasty and rather unconventional departure from Damascus, being lowered in a basket down the outside of the city wall from an aperture (Acts 9:23–25; 2 Cor. 11:32–33). Luke attributes this to the hostility of the Jewish population; Paul names the deputy of Aretas IV (king of Nabatea from 9/8 BC to AD 40/41), who was responsible for regulating the internal affairs of the Nabatean community in Damascus, as the source of the danger.[1] Both parties may have cooperated in the attempt to silence a troublesome and outspoken preacher. The presence of a sufficiently large Nabatean population in Damascus—a fair distance north of Aretas's territory proper—attests both to the importance of Damascus's location at a hub on both north-south and east-west trade routes (the Via Maris and the King's Highway) and to Nabatean interest in this trade at that time.

The Archaeology of Damascus

Damascus has been continuously occupied since antiquity; the Roman-period street lies about 15 feet below the surface of the modern road.[2] If significant excavation of the old city were possible, we could hope to find traces of the temples of Baal and Atargatis—principal Syrian deities featured on the reverses of coins of the Seleucid king Demetrius III (95–88 BC), which were minted in Damascus[3]—as well as remnants of the theater and the gymnasium complex, the construction of which Herod the Great, ever seeking to aggrandize his own reputation and that of his realm, subsidized (Josephus, *J.W.* 1.422). As it is, the only major witness to the Roman period is the Bab Sharqi, a gate on the southeastern side of the old city of Damascus that preserves portions of a third-century AD Roman gate. There are also a number of points at which the Roman-period city wall has been exposed, including a stretch that is traditionally associated with the location of Paul's escape from the city.

The streets of Damascus appear to have been laid out in a grid pattern that was very common in cities throughout the Greek and Roman world—though it is difficult to square this with the fact that one street, in particular, would become known as the "street called Straight" (Acts 9:11). The most common explanation is that this street was the main east-west thoroughfare

---

1. Some scholars regard 2 Cor. 11:32–33 as evidence that Damascus was under Nabatean control during Paul's lifetime, as it had been for a short period in the late Roman Republic (Josephus, *Ant.* 13.391–92), but the majority favor the view that the city merely had a Nabatean *politeuma*, a sizable Nabatean population under the jurisdiction of one of their own (an ethnarch). See Kennedy, "Syria," esp. 734–35; Graf, "Aretas," esp. 375.

2. Walker, *In the Steps of Saint Paul*, 26.

3. Negev, *Archaeological Encyclopedia of the Holy Land*, 95–96.

The Bab Sharqi, the gate on the southeastern side of the old city of Damascus that opens onto Straight Street.

(thus, the principal *decumanus*). It is still visible in the street plan of Old Damascus today.[4]

Arabia in the Ministry of Paul

Paul does not specify his purpose for going "into Arabia" immediately after his encounter with the glorified Lord (Gal. 1:17). It has been common in the history of interpretation to infer that Paul took that time—perhaps the greater part of the "three years" between that encounter and his first visit to Jerusalem to make Peter's acquaintance (1:18–20)—for personal reflection on his changed assessment of Jesus and his own role in the messianic era. It is equally possible, however, to infer that he went "into Arabia" to act immediately on the divine commission to proclaim God's Son to the Gentiles (1:16).[5] While much of the territory referred to in the first century as "Arabia"

---

4. As in McRay, *Archaeology and the New Testament*, 233–34, though he calls this a cardo—the more typical name for north-south streets.
5. So Murphy-O'Connor, "Paul in Arabia"; Hengel and Schwemer, *Paul between Damascus and Antioch*, 106–20; Schnabel, *Early Christian Mission*, 2:1032–38; deSilva, *Letter to the Galatians*, 157–58.

A beautiful example of a winepress from the late Hellenistic / early Roman period. The higher, square section on the right was for pressing the grapes, the lower cistern to the left for collecting the juice.

was deserted or only sparsely populated, it also encompassed, and thus was frequently used to refer to, the Nabatean Kingdom, a people group the Israelites believed to be descended from Ishmael and their closest neighbors to the east and southeast of Judea.[6] The Nabateans had frequent interactions with Judea and Galilee throughout the Hasmonean and Herodian periods through trade, intermarriage at the uppermost echelons, and military conflict. Their cities represented a sensible first step for the apostle to the Gentiles as he set off to fulfill his new commission.

It is, of course, impossible to say which Nabatean city or cities Paul would have visited, if the latter view is correct. One's thoughts almost automatically go to Petra, the Nabatean capital (Josephus, *Ant.* 14.14–16) and the most impressive—and impressively excavated—Nabatean site. It might be more plausible to imagine Paul working in Nabatean cities further north than Petra, though such notable scholars as Martin Hengel and Anna Maria Schwemer believe that Paul not only spent significant time in Petra but traveled even further south into Nabatean territory to the city at Hegra.[7]

---

6. This is frequently the case in Josephus. See also Strabo, *Geogr.* 17.1.21; Beitzel, "Meaning of 'Arabia,'" esp. 528.

7. Hengel and Schwemer, *Paul between Damascus and Antioch*, 113–18. Paul's familiarity with the site of Hegra (and its traditional, though almost certainly incorrect, association with Mount Sinai) is suggested by Gal. 4:25.

The Archaeology of Nabatean Arabia

The ornately carved monumental rock tombs of the Nabatean royalty and nobility are the most iconic images from Petra, but Petra was a city for the living as well. A theater was built during the reign of Aretas IV but was significantly expanded after Rome annexed Nabatea and created the province of Arabia Felix in AD 106.[8] A colonnaded east-west street, showing the marks of the citywide facelift given to Petra by Trajan in the form visible today, was already a main thoroughfare in the time of Aretas IV.[9] Two or three commercial forums were located alongside the south side of the street (the middle "forum" may have served a different function, possibly as a parking lot for traders' camels and other mounts).[10] To the west of these markets sat the Great Temple, erected by the middle of the first century AD and showing a blend of Hellenistic and Nabatean architectural styles.[11] The temple complex occupies an area 180 feet wide and 420 feet deep from the *cardo* (a north-south street); a forecourt takes up the northern half of this area, the temple and its surrounding porticoes the southern (rear) half.

The theater of Petra. In its present form it shows the expansion of the cavea in the early second century AD that resulted in the elimination of the front areas of several rock-carved houses and tombs.

8. Bourbon, *Petra*, 56.
9. Browning, *Petra*, 138; Bourbon, *Petra*, 74.
10. Browning, *Petra*, 137.
11. Bourbon, *Petra*, 77.

The remains of the Great Temple, dating from the first century AD.

A carved relief of Atargatis, an important fertility goddess worshiped throughout Syria and Nabatea, that once adorned the space above an entrance to the Nabatean temple of Atargatis at Khirbet et-Tannur in Jordan (Jordan Archaeological Museum).

North of the cardo sat the so-called Temple of the Winged Lions (so named for decorative blocks found on the premises featuring the common griffin motif). It is thought to have been a temple to the Syrian fertility goddess, Atargatis, often identified with Aphrodite in the Greek pantheon.[12]

12. Browning, *Petra*, 139.

The west end of the colonnaded street terminated at a gate that gave access to the sacred precincts of the temple known as the Qasr al-Bint, plausibly identified as the temple dedicated to Dusares, the principal deity of the Nabatean pantheon. The temple itself is estimated to have once stood 95 feet tall, 100 feet wide, and 105 feet deep. An inscription naming Aretas IV suggests that it was constructed during his reign or that of his predecessor, Obodas III (30–9 BC).[13] As is typical throughout the Mediterranean, the altar stood on a platform erected some distance in front of the temple proper. The decorations are again an interesting mix of Greek and Nabatean features. It is believed that the deity, in more typical Nabatean fashion, was represented by something more like a block or an obelisk than a statue.[14] A sacred place overlooking Petra appears to have been dedicated to Al Uzza, the principal goddess of the Nabateans, in conjunction with Dusares—both represented there by two obelisks, each 20 feet tall.[15] These are remarkable for having been created by leveling the mesa and *leaving* the obelisks rather than erecting them.

Daniel Case / CC BY-SA 3.0 / Wikimedia Commons

The so-called Qasr al-Bint, a massive temple to Dusares, the principal Nabatean deity.

13. Bourbon, *Petra*, 81; Browning, *Petra*, 153.
14. Browning, *Petra*, 159.
15. Browning, *Petra*, 207.

Paul's evangelistic activity somewhere in the Nabatean heartland, where his call to abandon the indigenous gods represented everywhere by idols would have been as unpopular as anywhere in Türkiye or Greece, also helps to explain why the deputy of Aretas IV in Damascus would take a personal interest in hunting him down when he showed up there after causing a stir in "Arabia" (2 Cor. 11:32–33; Gal. 1:17).

3

ANTIOCH-ON-THE-ORONTES

Antioch in the Ministry of Paul

Antioch is remembered as the city in which Greek-speaking Jewish Christians began to announce the good news in Christ to Gentiles as well as to their fellow Jews (Acts 11:19–20). This might have been a consequence of the fact that Antioch was notable for the number of Gentiles attracted to Judaism (Josephus, *J.W.* 7.45). The city became the focus first of Barnabas's church planting and nurturing work and then of Paul's after Barnabas fetched him from Tarsus to join him (Acts 11:22–26). Luke asserts that Christ-followers were first labeled *Christianoi*—"Christ-lackeys," "Christ-partisans"—there (11:26). It was a mission-minded Christian community, commissioning and sending Barnabas and Paul off on their apostolic journey to Cyprus and Southern Galatia (13:1–4) and receiving them again after this particular mission had been completed (14:26–28). Antioch was targeted by Jewish Christians apparently more conservative than Paul and Barnabas on more than one occasion (Acts 15:1–2; Gal. 2:11–14), the occasion in Acts prompting the so-called Apostolic Conference or Jerusalem Council, which was convened to settle the matter of what would be required of Gentile converts to join the people of God in Christ.[1] Paul would return to Antioch to communicate the consensus decision of that council (Acts 15:22–35) and visit the assemblies there once again between his mission work in Achaia and Ephesus (18:22–23).

---

1. On the complexities of reconciling Paul's narrative in Gal. 1:11–2:14 with the narrative of Acts 9–15, see deSilva, *Letter to the Galatians*, 48–58, and the literature discussed and cited therein.

The Archaeology of Antioch

The archaeological remains of Antioch in modern Antakya are disappointingly small compared to the importance of the city in the Greek and Roman periods. It was the capital first of the Seleucid Empire and then of the Roman province of Syria; it was also the location of a vibrant, missional Christian community that was a touchstone for Paul's ministry. The late Hellenistic and early Roman city is estimated to lie between 9 and 12 yards below the surface,[2] sitting below many layers of continuous settlement and building activity. The comparatively little excavation that has been done here and there throughout the modern city of Antakya, which sits atop every previous period's remains, has tended to reach only as far as the late Roman period.

Literary sources and smaller finds do provide some insight into the city's landscape. Antioch sits about 400 miles from Jerusalem by way of the King's Highway. The city was founded by Seleucus I Nicator in or around 300 BC alongside the Orontes River and was laid out in the by then customary grid pattern (Strabo, *Geogr.* 16.2.4). Seleucus I had intended the port city of Seleucia Pieria, a harbor on the Mediterranean some 20 miles west of Antioch, to serve as his capital. His son, Antiochus I Soter, however, moved the capital to Antioch, which was more strategically located on a major east-west land route (commonly referred to as the Silk Road) as well as north-south routes during a time when the Orontes River was still easily navigable for most ships moving to and from the Mediterranean at Seleucia.[3] Seleucus I built an agora (commercial market) for Antioch on the banks of the Orontes within easy reach of the river and the warehouses that no doubt lined its quays. Between 187 and 175 BC, Seleucus IV built a temple in honor of Isis.[4] Around 175 BC, Antiochus IV provided the city with a new council hall and agora while also expanding the residential capacity of Antioch

A first-century representation of the Orontes River personified as a deity.

2. Lassus, "Antioche à l'époque romaine," 58.
3. Hansen, *Silk Road*, 6–8.
4. Wilson, *Biblical Turkey*, 74.

by adding a new quarter, the Epiphania.[5] He also built a monumental temple in honor of Zeus in the guise of Jupiter Capitolinus, a sign of his hearty embrace of the Roman culture in which he was raised while a hostage in Rome to ensure the good behavior of his father, Antiochus III. Dionysus, Pan, Artemis, Ares, Hercules, and Tyche—the city's guardian goddess—also had sacred sites throughout Antioch.[6]

The Seleucid Empire declined significantly in the second half of the second century BC. Antioch was annexed by Tigranes, king of Armenia (83–69 BC). His gains would prove to be short-lived, as Pompey the Great arrived in the region in the mid-60s BC, brought the Seleucid Empire to a complete end, and created the Roman province of Syria, with Antioch as its capital.[7] Anywhere between two and four legions were then stationed in this province on the eastern frontier. By

An early Roman-period statue of Tyche of Antioch (Vatican Museums).

that time it had become the third most populous city in the Roman Empire, after Rome itself and Alexandria, Egypt. Estimates run from three hundred thousand to as high as a half million inhabitants.[8] As such, Antioch—the "metropolis of Syria" (Strabo, *Geogr.* 16.2.5)—could be expected to have all the typical structures of a major city.[9]

Julius Caesar gifted the city with a new aqueduct, an amphitheater (suggesting the introduction of Roman-style entertainment, like gladiatorial combat), a theater, a bathhouse, and a basilica—a large columned hall that typically served judicial functions in Roman cities.[10] Such celebrities of the late Republic as Antony, Cleopatra, and Octavian all visited the city, with

5. Phillips, "Geographic Importance of Antioch," 272.

6. Lassus, "Antioche à l'époque romaine," 69; Wilson, *Biblical Turkey*, 73.

7. Wilson, *Biblical Turkey*, 72–73.

8. Kraeling, "Jewish Community," 136; McRay, *Archaeology and the New Testament*, 227; Longenecker, "Antioch of Syria," 9.

9. Translations of ancient sources are the author's own unless otherwise indicated.

10. Longenecker, "Antioch of Syria," 12–13.

A tetrapylon from Jerash, suggestive of the sort of monumental structures with which Tiberius graced several intersections in Antioch.

Octavian (as Augustus) bestowing significant public works on the city. Herod the Great paved Antioch's principal street—which was a width of about 30 feet and a length of almost 2 miles—with marble (Josephus, *Ant.* 16.148; *J.W.* 1.425). Either Herod or Tiberius provided colonnades on either side of the thoroughfare, a gift that required 3,200 columns.[11] Tiberius also furnished the funds for several bathhouses and for decorative tetrapylons (quadruple-gated structures) at the city's major intersections.[12] Caligula helped the city to rebuild after a devastating earthquake. All this suggests that the city would have had a positive view of Rome's emperors and client kings, many of whom took an interest in benefiting the city.

A large Jewish community existed in Antioch from its beginnings under Seleucus I (Josephus, *Ag. Ap.* 2.39; *Ant.* 12.119). These early settlers were largely veteran soldiers and their families, who would have been given land grants upon being discharged. Jews generally enjoyed significant privileges under the Seleucids and then under Roman rule, no doubt including the right

11. Longenecker, "Antioch of Syria," 13; Fant and Reddish, *Guide to Biblical Sites*, 148.
12. McRay, *Archaeology and the New Testament*, 230.

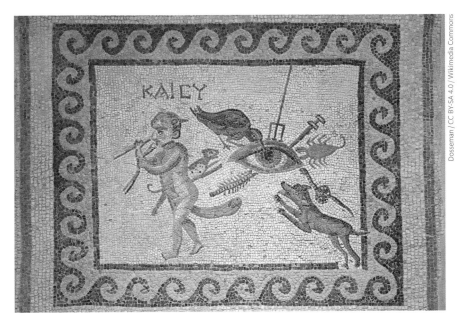

A mosaic designed to ward off the evil eye. Note the many forces attacking the eyeball—the dog, snake, scorpion, sword, trident, bird, cat, and centipede—as well as the goblin's erect phallus working its countermagic.

to regulate their own community life in accordance with their ancestral law, and thus Antioch was an attractive center for diaspora Jews (Josephus, *J.W.* 7.43–45). The Jewish community may have reached a population of forty-five thousand by the time of Augustus.[13] Prior to Paul's activity, Jews demonstrated en masse in Antioch before the Roman governor Petronius. Caligula had ordered that a statue of himself be placed in the temple of Jerusalem. This was not merely an act of megalomania (though that no doubt played a part) but also a specific reprisal for the actions of the Jews in Jamnia against a locally erected shrine to Caligula. Petronius, faced with an impossible task, was eventually persuaded to intervene on the Jews' behalf, but only after the Jews had made it clear that they were prepared to die rather than see their temple thus desecrated. A little more than two decades after Paul's early activity in Antioch, brutal and devastating anti-Jewish pogroms would erupt in the city in connection with the later years of the First Jewish Revolt (Josephus, *J.W.* 7.46–62)—instigated by an apostate Jew.

---

13. Kraeling, "Jewish Community at Antioch," 136. Eckhard Schnabel (*Paul the Missionary*, 71) suggests a figure between twenty thousand and thirty-five thousand.

The Hatay Archeology Museum is a treasure trove of Roman mosaics. Unfortunately, all (or virtually all) of them date from the second century AD and later. Some of the earlier mosaics appear to have been the ancient equivalent of welcome mats, bearing a number of symbols intended to ward off the evil eye and bearing the Greek legend *kai su*—in effect, "the same to you." These bear important witness to something that is rarely considered in the texts of the New Testament or in other literary sources: the intense superstition that gripped many members of the population and the accompanying fear of malign spiritual forces that could be harnessed by one's enemies.

4

PAPHOS

Paphos in the Ministry of Paul

The island of Cyprus has rich connections with the earliest history of the church. Barnabas, a generous and revered member of the Jerusalem church, and later a pillar of the Gentile mission alongside Paul, was a Levite from Cyprus (Acts 4:36). Jewish Christians from Cyprus were among the first to preach the gospel to Greeks as well as to Jews in Antioch-on-the-Orontes (11:19–21). The success of these Christians led Barnabas and Paul to make Antioch the first focus of their mission together. When the leaders of the Antioch Christian community commissioned Barnabas and Paul to undertake the so-called first missionary journey (13:1–3), their first stop was, perhaps not surprisingly, Barnabas's homeland of Cyprus.

Barnabas and Paul, accompanied by their young protégé, John Mark, began their preaching in Salamis, a major port city in northern Cyprus, and worked their way through the land to the southern port city of Nea ("New") Paphos, the capital of the Roman province of Cyprus (Acts 13:4–6). As Paul and his team preached the gospel in Paphos and presumably began to have success in reaching some of its inhabitants, they were summoned to appear before Sergius Paulus, the Roman proconsular governor of the island. According to Acts 13:7, Sergius Paulus's intentions were friendly and enlightened—he wanted to learn more about this message and was inclined to give it a fair and open hearing. The source of the hostility in the room came from an adviser to the governor named Elymas, also known as Bar-Jesus. Though Elymas was a Jew by ethnicity, the description of him as a magician suggests that he was at the very least lapsed, and quite possibly an apostate. His opposition to Barnabas and Paul came from his commitment not to traditional Judaism but to the baser drives of protecting his own turf in terms of influence with the governor. Elymas only succeeded in provoking Paul to call down a temporary blindness on the magician—a display of spiritual authority on Paul's part that appears to have convinced the proconsul of the power of this new faith. This is an especially important story in the Acts narrative since, like the episode of the conversion of the centurion Cornelius early in Acts 10, it shows that people well placed in the Roman government and military could be quite open and friendly toward the Christian movement.

The Archaeology of Paphos

New Paphos had been founded in the early Hellenistic period and served as the island's administrative center since the period of Ptolemaic rule over the island (early third century into the mid-first century BC). It sits about 12 miles west-northwest of Old Paphos, a much more ancient city with roots in the Archaic period. After the Romans incorporated Cyprus into their empire in 58 BC, they retained New Paphos as their administrative capital, no doubt due to its strategic importance as a commercial port city.[1] Dozens of recovered amphorae and other vessels bear witness to the active trade that passed through this port and thus incidentally to its potential for overseas communication throughout the empire.

Cyprus existed under the watchful eye of Aphrodite, whom the Cypriots claimed had been born on their island. A grand temple to Aphrodite stood in Old Paphos; several statues discovered in New Paphos bear witness to her presence there as well. New Paphos was also home to an Asclepion, a facility that served both as a shrine to Asclepius, the god of healing, and as a kind of hospital. Prayers, ritual prescriptions, and medicine were combined in the effort to provide remedies for a variety of ills. One of the more distinctive finds here involves thin clay vessels molded to fit particular parts of the body. These could be filled with hot water to provide a compress for the affected part. A cave sanctuary of Apollo also stood a short distance southeast of New Paphos.

Paphos received major facelifts in the second and third centuries AD, such that few remains, in the form in which they can be seen today, date securely back to the time of Paul and Barnabas's visit. One exception is a sizable theater that stands about a third of a mile east of the agora, though this structure

---

1. Fant and Reddish, *Guide to Biblical Sites*, 353.

The theater from the Hellenistic-Roman period.

was also expanded as the city grew during the Roman period.[2] As was typical during the Hellenistic period (that is, before the widespread use of poured concrete introduced during the Roman period), the theater was essentially carved into the side of Fabrica Hill, which thereby provided natural support for the stands that seated as many as eight thousand spectators.

Paphos is also home to a network of distinctive underground tombs from the Hellenistic period, entered through staircases carved into the rock.[3] These reflect the influence of Egyptian tomb architecture as practiced during the Ptolemaic period throughout the Ptolemaic empire. These so-called Tombs of the Kings were built to honor the memory and house the remains of the local elites of the Hellenistic and Roman periods rather than of royalty.

Paul's audience with Sergius Paulus would most likely have taken place in the proconsul's headquarters, a large complex (now known as "the House of Theseus") that would have included the living quarters for the governor, his family, and a sizable domestic staff.[4] This area has been extensively excavated.

2. Lavithis, *Paphos*, 30.
3. Lavithis, *Paphos*, 32.
4. The complex covers an area of 360 by 250 feet (Fant and Reddish, *Guide to Biblical Sites*, 354).

A colonnaded subterranean atrium, open to the sky, from one of the Tombs of the Kings. The burial chambers are located in carved chambers all around this central courtyard.

In its present state, the complex shows the results of significant remodeling from the second century, but the original layout is likely largely preserved. Paul would have entered through the main atrium, which was originally roofed save for an open space in the center, through which rainwater was collected and emptied into the central pool. The atrium opened into a large courtyard from which the various sectors of the complex could be accessed. The encounter with Sergius would have reasonably occurred in a public audience hall, though Acts gives no details about how public or private the interview was.

As Paul and his team left the governor's headquarters, they would not have seen or stepped over most of the beautiful mosaics for which the site is now famous. One particularly celebrated mosaic from the bathhouse in the southwest corner of the complex—the mosaic that gave the complex its name, House of Theseus—depicts the major players from the famous story of Theseus. The hero stands in the center, the monstrous Minotaur lies dying at his feet, and the princess Ariadne stands anxiously waiting—all of this set as the centerpiece in a mosaic labyrinth. Mosaics of this kind, however, probably represent the work of third-, fourth-, and even fifth-century AD artists.

The atrium of the so-called House of Theseus, the likely residence and administrative center for the Roman governor of Cyprus.

The principal audience chamber of the governor's mansion (or
possibly the waiting room for those seeking an audience). Note
the stone benches lining the walls.

A mosaic from the Hellenistic period depicting Scylla, one of the monstrous creatures known from Homer's *Odyssey* (Lavithis, *Paphos*, 20). Any mosaics in the governor's palace at the time of Paul's visit would likely have been of this simpler sort.

In the Acts narrative, it is during the mission in Paphos that Paul first begins to be named as such—that is, by his Roman cognomen rather than his less formal Hebrew name, Saul. It is significant that this change of moniker stands a decade or more removed from his conversion. It was, contrary to a very popular notion, not an indication of a radical shift in self-understanding and identity as a result of his conversion but rather an indication of missionary strategy. Before the Roman proconsul Sergius Paulus, "Saul" may have come to a new level of understanding regarding his call to become apostle to the Gentiles, choosing thenceforth to foreground his Roman name as most appropriate to that vocation. After their encounter with Sergius Paulus, Paul and his team set sail from Paphos, leaving its artificial harbor and crossing the waters of the Mediterranean to the cities of southern Türkiye, where they would begin planting colonies of the kingdom of God.

PART 2

CHURCH PLANTS

Paul is primarily remembered and celebrated in Acts for his work as the leader of a team of church planters active throughout the Roman provinces of Galatia, Macedonia, Achaia, and Asia. The careful reader of both Acts and the collection of Paul's letters will notice that Paul revisited, and sent others of his team to revisit, the majority of the congregations that he planted several times throughout the period of his ministry, continuing to nurture and guide these congregations even as he continued to hold each of them before God in prayer.

The archaeology and material culture of many of the sites covered in this section are particularly important because these were the environments of the believers to whom Paul addressed the majority of his surviving letters. Immersing ourselves in these contexts adds an important element to our own preparation for entering into these texts as they were heard by the audiences for whom the apostle composed them and for understanding the lived responses within these contexts that he sought to shape.

The framework of Paul's ministry in Acts admittedly does not make room for all that the apostle did over his decades of active ministry. Paul himself speaks of having conducted mission work (and if successful, church-planting work) in the province of Illyricum, which corresponds to the western coastal regions of the modern Balkan peninsula, prior to his journey to Jerusalem with the collection (Rom. 15:19). The Letter to Titus gives evidence of church-planting work on the island of Crete, with Titus being delegated by Paul to establish firm foundations for the assemblies there (Titus 1:5).[1] Nevertheless, as these phases of his ministry are not connected with particular cities in either area, they are not included in the following discussion.

---

1. The authorship of Titus (along with 1 and 2 Timothy) is a highly contested issue among biblical scholars (see deSilva, *Introduction to the New Testament*, 649–64, and the literature cited therein). Even if one decides that the Letter to Titus was written in Paul's name, rather than by Paul himself, it still bears witness to an early tradition concerning Pauline churches on the island of Crete.

5

PERGE AND
PISIDIAN ANTIOCH

Perge in the Ministry of Paul

Departing Cyprus, Paul, Barnabas, and John Mark sailed to the mainland, landing at Perge (also known as Perga) in the region of Pamphylia. Some have speculated that the coastline east of Antalya (ancient Attalia) has changed significantly over the past two millennia, such that Perge, which now sits several miles inland, was once a coastal city. This is not impossible, as centuries of silting significantly changed the landscape west of Ephesus, for example. However, it seems far more likely that access to Perge was, as Strabo attests, via a navigable river that flowed 3 miles east of the city (*Geogr.* 14.6.2), although this river is little more than a stream today. John Mark returned to Jerusalem from Perge rather than continuing inland into territories ever further from home (Acts 13:13), an act that caused him to fall out of favor with Paul for a long while and would have serious consequences for Paul's relationship with Barnabas as well (Acts 15:36–40; 2 Tim. 4:11).

The Archaeology of Perge

Perge is a well-excavated site, although much of what remains to be explored dates to the second century AD, when extensive renovations and building projects were undertaken, through the early Byzantine period. One can still see the remains of a fortified Hellenistic-period gate, which may mark the point

Remains of Perge's Hellenistic-period south gate.

The early Roman-period west gate in Perge.

at which Paul and his team entered the city as they walked from the eastern river port, as well as the west gate through which Paul and Barnabas—now without John Mark—would have begun their journey along the Augustan Way (in Latin, the *Via Sebaste*) toward the inland cities to the north.

Though dating from the second century, the main north-south street of Perge must have been a source of pride for the city, with its cascading pools of water running down the center of the street from the fountain house at its northernmost point almost to its southern terminus. The principal east-west street (the decumanus) was supplied with a lengthy series of water troughs inside the northern gate, no doubt a welcoming sight for weary travelers arriving from the Augustan Way. Both streets were flanked by colonnaded, covered sidewalks and recessed shops.

While she flourished in the second century rather than at the time of Paul's visit, a woman named Plancia Magna, the wife of a Roman senator and one of Perge's elite citizens, commands attention. She was a notable benefactor of the city, subsidizing a number of major public buildings. Dedicatory inscriptions honoring her and memorializing her generosity are among the most frequently encountered (and largest!) inscriptions on the site. One even names her "daughter of the city" after listing the priestly offices she held in the cults of Artemis and the Mother Goddess. As a woman of significant means, and one whose beneficence was rewarded with due recognition and honor, she shows us something of the influence and status that wealth and patronage afforded women as well as men during the early Roman period.

The cardo, looking south from the fountain house.

The decumanus, looking west toward the access to the west gate and the Via Sebaste.

Pisidian Antioch in the Ministry of Paul

Paul and Barnabas did not linger in Perge to evangelize the city, though they would upon their return journey before setting sail once again to return to Antioch-on-the-Orontes, this time from the seaport city of Attalia (Acts 14:25–26). Rather, they journeyed along the Via Sebaste, or Augustan Way, north into the region of Pisidia, to another Antioch, a city that would become an important landmark on the map of Paul's missionary work. Antioch was first a terminus of, and later a major junction of, the Via Sebaste. Augustus (in Greek, *Sebastos*) began construction of the Via Sebaste in 6 BC to facilitate troop movement to the eastern frontier. Why Paul and Barnabas were heading for Pisidian Antioch in particular, and so directly, is not explained in the Acts narrative. It may simply be that, after evangelizing Syria, Cilicia, and Cyprus, Paul and Barnabas thought it most logical to head on to the principal city of the next province to the west. Some have speculated, however, that Sergius Paulus, the Roman governor of Cyprus and a Christian convert through Paul's preaching and wonder working, might have had something to do with the ministry team's decision.

Inscriptions in Antioch bear witness to the fact that Sergius Paulus and his family had deep roots there, such that Paulus might have both requested that

An inscription found in Antioch bearing the family name Paullus and identifying a certain "L[ucius] Sergius Paullus, son of Paullus Ser[gius]," possibly the son of the proconsul of Cyprus known from Acts 13 as Sergius Paulus.

Paul and Barnabas visit his home territory *and* used his family connections to facilitate their entrance into and establishing of themselves in Pisidian Antioch, however brief their first visit turned out to be. Despite immediate hostility from members among the Jewish community, Paul and Barnabas appear to have planted the seeds of a congregation there before they were driven out of the city by the Jewish community's leaders in concert with the governing authorities. From Pisidian Antioch they journeyed east along the Via Sebaste to Iconium and Lystra, after which they made a short detour to Derbe. Paul and Barnabas visited Lystra, Iconium, and Antioch again on their way back from Derbe to Perge, "strengthening the disciples' souls, encouraging them to persevere in the faith, . . . appointing elders for them in every congregation" (Acts 14:21–23).

It seems most probable that Acts has Paul visiting Pisidian Antioch again a few years later when it speaks of Paul, Timothy, and Silas traveling through Phrygia and Galatia (Acts 16:6), for Paul undertook this journey explicitly to revisit and strengthen existing congregations: "Come," Paul says to Barnabas, "let us return and visit the believers in every city where we proclaimed the word of the Lord and see how they are doing" (15:36 NRSV). Though this became the point at which Paul and Barnabas parted ways, Paul took Silas on this planned journey, going "through Syria and Cilicia, strengthening the churches" (15:41 NRSV), and on specifically to Derbe and Lystra, where he

An inscription providing the complete name of the Roman colony of Lystra: Colonia Julia Felix Gemina Lystra. It records the colony's consecration of some object (an altar?) to "the Divine Augustus."

enlisted Timothy, and continued carrying word of the Apostolic Decree—the important resolution of the question of whether Gentiles needed to join themselves to the Jewish people through circumcision to benefit from Jesus's saving work. The most natural understanding of this trajectory would have Paul continue from Lystra to Iconium and Pisidian Antioch with his report of the decree—not taking a far detour to the north on a presumed evangelistic journey to the cities of North Galatia (Ancyra, Pessinus, and Tavium), especially without Luke giving any notice whatsoever of church-planting activity in these cities. Indeed, to speak of the journey begun in Acts 15:41 simply as Paul's "second missionary journey" is to misrepresent the first and longest leg of the journey. According to Acts, Paul's missionary work did not begin on this journey until he passed into Macedonia, where the church-planting work resumed. Paul would have visited Pisidian Antioch and its sister cities a fourth time, then, at the outset of his third missionary journey to Ephesus as he passed once again through Phrygia and Galatia with the goal of "strengthening all the disciples" (18:23 NRSV; cf. the same language in 14:22).

Although a matter of long-standing debate, many scholars believe that Paul's Letter to the Galatians was addressed to the congregation in Pisidian Antioch along with its sister churches in Iconium, Lystra, and Derbe, all of which fell within the Roman province of Galatia during the time of Paul's active ministry. We have clear documentation of evangelistic activity among these cities, and "Galatians" would be the term most appropriately and inclusively used by Paul to address people resident in all four cities, even in the context of calling them "*foolish* Galatians" (Gal. 3:1).[1] Pisidian Antioch, visited at least four times by the apostle and his team, emerges therefore as an important hub for the Pauline mission, even as it was an important hub for the imperial highway system and for the provincial imperial cult that jointly put the city squarely on the Roman map.

This is not to belittle the cities of Iconium, Lystra, or Derbe, or to minimize the importance of the Christian congregations planted there. From an archaeological point of view, however, these three cities have very little to offer in the way of helping us to imagine the setting, both physical and ideological, of Paul's ministry in Galatia. The tell of Derbe's acropolis remains undisturbed by archaeological activity to this day. The ancient site of Lystra, located on the Via Sebaste, the principal Roman road through the province, also remains unexcavated. One artifact bears witness to the city's location—an inscription, now housed in the archaeological museum of Konya. Beyond this, the remains of a Roman bridge, still visible within the renovated structure, are all that bear witness to a once-vibrant Roman colony.

The state of archaeology at Iconium is similar, but for an entirely different reason: Roman Iconium sits beneath the major modern city of Konya. While the archaeological museum there boasts a number of smaller finds—from

---

1. See the review of this debate and the argument in favor of locating the Letter to the Galatians among the congregations visited by Paul in Acts 13–14 in deSilva, *Letter to the Galatians*, 26–62, esp. 39–48.

ninety-one inscriptions from Roman Iconium to a marvelous third-century AD sarcophagus decorated with carvings of the twelve labors of Hercules—no excavations of any significance have been possible. Thus, Pisidian Antioch provides us with our best and fullest representation of the context of Paul's Galatian churches.

The Archaeology of Pisidian Antioch

Antioch was founded in the early third century BC, likely by Antiochus I Soter. It was one of many cities that would be named "Antioch" or "Seleucia" in honor of the rulers of the Seleucid Empire. Though technically within the region of Phrygia, the city sat close to the Pisidian border and came to be called "Pisidian" Antioch to distinguish it from the many other Antiochs in Asia Minor and Syria (thus Acts 13:14; Strabo, *Geogr.* 12.8.14).

Very little remains today of the Hellenistic-period city. The ruins of a temple dedicated to the Anatolian moon god Men, standing just a few miles outside the city, date back to the early Hellenistic period (though there is evidence that an earlier sanctuary existed there already in the Classical period). A small figure of Men, an altar about a yard high, and several votive steles celebrating some answered prayer have been found in Antioch and its vicinity. The worship of Men is thought to have been imported by the city's first settlers, some of whom came from the westernmost part of Türkiye, where Men was a prominent deity.

The theater in the heart of the city also originated in the Hellenistic period, though it was remodeled and expanded significantly in AD 311.[2] At its grandest, it extended *over* the road that originally ran alongside the theater (the Decumanus Maximus). Pedestrian

A representation of the moon god Men with the characteristic points of the crescent moon behind the figure's shoulders, found at Antioch.

2. An inscription provides the date. See Demirer, *Pisidian Antioch*, 59.

The partially excavated remains of the theater in Antioch. The second tier of seating has been significantly eroded or reappropriated. In the foreground are the traces of the stage building that would
once have risen as high as the top tiers of seating.

and wheeled traffic continued to pass through a wide tunnel created under the
top tier of seats.

Although Paul is remembered to have preached his first two sermons in
Antioch in a Jewish synagogue, there is no direct archaeological evidence of a
Jewish presence in the city, despite the overzealous claims of archaeologists to
have found such evidence below either the fourth-century Christian basilica in
the heart of the old city or the fourth-century Basilica of St. Paul built nearer
its northern edge. The literary evidence, however, is strong. Josephus records
that when the region of Phrygia was becoming unruly under Antiochus III
(ruler of the Seleucid Empire from 223 to 187 BC), the king resettled two thousand Jewish families from Babylonia to the "most important places" within
the regions of Phrygia and Lydia to stabilize the area (*Ant.* 12.146–53, trans.
Marcus). These settlers were granted land for houses and crops, distributions
of food until their crops became productive, and exemption from taxes for
ten years, ensuring their goodwill toward the crown. Antioch would surely
have been one of these "important places."

The region was incorporated into the Roman province of Galatia upon
the death of Amyntas, one of Rome's client kings, at the hands of hostile
local tribes in 25 BC. Shortly thereafter, the emperor Augustus elevated the
city's status to that of a Roman colony—the Colonia Caesarea Antiochia—
and injected new life into the city by settling upward of three thousand

A portion of the two-story aqueduct that brought water from the hills north of the city.

veterans and their families there. These families would have felt a strong bond of personal loyalty to the *pater patriae* (the "father of the fatherland," as Augustus and his successors were named throughout the empire) as their own families' patron.

The city's water supply was increased to accommodate the growing population. A new aqueduct, a two-story arched structure, was constructed to bring in water from the hills north of the city. The aqueduct brought water to the *castellum aquae* (the principal reservoir) and a nymphaeum, a large ornate pool (about 88 by 10 feet, with a depth of 5 feet) from which residents could draw water, both on the north side of the city.[3] A modest but adequate bath complex was added west of the nymphaeum later in the first century AD.

Stone water conduits and clay pipes distributed water throughout the city to bathhouses, other fountains, and public latrines, both flushing the waste and providing water for personal hygiene. One of the easily overlooked achievements of the Roman Empire is its emphasis on supplying running water throughout its cities. After the Byzantine period, Europeans, at least,

3. Demirer, *Pisidian Antioch*, 90.

The nymphaeum at the north end of Antioch (top). Such water pools were often magnificent structures in their prime. The nymphaeum at Antioch might once have resembled the one at Aspendos,
a city not far from Perge (bottom). Statues of gods and nymphs (hence the name "nymphaeum"),
particularly associated with water, would have once stood in the niches.

would not again enjoy this level of sanitation, personal hygiene, and readily
available clean water until after the Renaissance.

The city's internal roads were also improved. In the typical Roman fashion,
there was a major north-south road called the Cardo Maximus and a major
east-west road called the Decumanus Maximus.

The cardo began at the nymphaeum, ran south past shops and the major
public buildings and the plaza of the city center, and continued south until
it intersected with the decumanus. The full extent of the cardo south of the
decumanus awaits further excavation.

The entrance to the northern bath complex.

The cardo, looking south from the nymphaeum.

The decumanus, looking east toward the cardo.

Shops or offices alongside the decumanus.

"To Jupiter Best and Greatest, Augustus, and the genius [the protective spirit] of the colony."

A life-size statue of Jupiter, identifiable by the eagle, his avatar, depicted at his waist (Yalvaç Museum).

The remains of the foundations of the Augusteum, most of the marble and well-cut ashlars having been taken and repurposed long ago. Note the remains of a once two-story semicircular portico behind it and the square holes in the carefully cut rock wall into which beams were once inserted to help support the second story.

Franck Devedjian / CC BY-SA 4.0 / Wikimedia Commons

A digital reconstruction of the Augusteum in the early Roman period.

The decumanus ran west from the cardo past the theater, latrine, and another host of shops. Its eastern wing, beyond the cardo, also awaits further excavation. A stretch of three or four shops or offices along the decumanus are particularly well preserved, probably because they were once sheltered by the renovated and extended theater.

Very few public buildings survive or have been uncovered on the site. The city no doubt had the usual assortment of temples. An inscription bearing a dedication "to Jupiter Best and Greatest" as well as a cult statue of Jupiter were discovered on site, suggesting the presence of a temple to the chief deity of the Roman pantheon, as would be appropriate and typical for a Roman colony. By far the most impressive structure on the site today, as no doubt in Paul's lifetime, is the Augusteum, a monumental temple built to honor Augustus as a god, likely completed by the turn of the era. The temple had a footprint of about 85 by 50 feet, with an estimated original height between 45 and 55 feet. The sacred space was rendered far more impressive by the construction of a two-story semicircular portico behind the temple, space for which was carved out of the rock ledge now visible. Straight porticoes extended from the tips of the semicircle past the temple, creating an overall space of about 10,000 square yards for the temple and its sacred precincts.

A colossal cult image of Augustus would have sat within the temple, visible through a pair of large doors in the front. In all likelihood, the temple would have been dedicated also to the goddess Roma, the deified personification of the city of Rome itself, whose cult image would also have been housed within. It was Augustus's practice to insist that temples be built not to him alone but only in tandem with the goddess in whom the Senate and the Roman people could see a reflection of themselves.

Remnants of the ornate carvings that once adorned the porticoes, featuring the common sacrificial motif of garlands and the skulls of bulls, litter the surrounding area. These decorations are reminiscent of the sacrifices that would have been performed here to honor Augustus on the twenty-third of every month, in celebration of his birthday on September 23, expressing loyalty and gratitude to the emperor for his god-size gifts and for his particular benefactions to this colony, as well as to petition the other gods, like Jupiter Best and Greatest, for the emperor's continued well-being during his lifetime. The worship of Augustus continued long after his death and his official recognition as a god by the Senate, after which it was customary to refer to him as "the Divine Augustus" in all public inscriptions.

The city fathers and rich donors further aggrandized this monument by constructing a triple-arched gateway, called a propylon, to the sacred area, approached by a staircase of twelve steps. Nothing remains of this building today except for its footprint. The propylon was decorated with statues of members of the imperial family. Two surviving carved reliefs show captives bound and

The scant remains of the propylon (top). The propylon was originally a magnificent three-arched gateway similar to others found throughout the empire, like the one from the port city of Antalya (bottom), erected during the reign of Hadrian.

Relief of a subjugated captive from the propylon.

kneeling before a male figure, perhaps Augustus himself. The reliefs are likely to have commemorated the successful punitive expedition of Publius Sulpicius Quirinius (known from Luke 2:2) against the tribe of the Homanadenses, who were responsible for the death of Amyntas, the client king of the region, in 25 BC. Such "art" communicated a clear message to the indigenous inhabitants around Antioch: one way or another, they would submit to Roman rule. The propylon once bore the dedicatory inscription "To the emperor Augustus, son of the deified Caesar, Pontifex Maximus, consul for the thirteenth time, tribune of the plebs for the twenty-second time, acclaimed imperator for the fourteenth time, Father of the Fatherland," dating the edifice to 2–1 BC.[4]

During the reign of Tiberius, a rich citizen named Titus Baebius Asiaticus paved a large open area in front of the propylon. An inscription reveals that it was named Tiberius Square (*Tiberia Platea*) in honor of Augustus's successor.[5] Once surrounded by shops, bars, and restaurants, this area functioned as a place for recreation and commerce. Some of the few remaining paving slabs still bear the markings of the game boards that were chiseled into them in antiquity. Citizens would gather to enjoy some of the benefits of the imperial peace here in the shadow of the great Augusteum complex.

One of the most important inscriptions from the Augustan period is the *Res gestae divi Augusti* (the things accomplished by the Divine Augustus). The emperor composed this text himself in the months prior to his death, intending it to be the epitaph on his life's achievements. He ordered that this lengthy document be engraved on bronze plates and placed in front of his mausoleum on the Field of Mars in Rome; it was essentially an advertisement

4. Latin text given in Demirer, *Pisidian Antioch*, 78.
5. The inscription itself preserves an edict from AD 89–92 in which the governor, Lucius Antistius Rusticus, fixed the price of grain in the wake of a bad crop year to avoid price gouging. See Robinson, "New Latin Economic Edict."

About two hundred pieces of the *Res gestae* inscription in Latin, apparently demolished in antiquity, were found in the area of Tiberius Square. Many of these pieces are now assembled, like a jigsaw puzzle missing many pieces, in the archaeological museum in Yalvaç, the modern town that adjoins the archaeological site.

of his benefactions and accomplishments that stretched the length of a city block. The inscription speaks of his deliverance of the Roman world from civil war (that is, the war he himself waged against Marc Antony and Cleopatra VII, effectively brought to an end with Octavian's victory in the naval battle at Actium in 31 BC), his successful neutralizing of threats to the borders, his lavish benefactions on the Roman people, the staggering number of public buildings erected "at his own expense" (that is, no doubt largely from his share in the spoils of war), his diligence in rewarding veterans, and the many public honors awarded to him on account of his virtue. A copy of the lengthy inscription in both Latin and Greek was found inscribed in the ancient Temple of Rome and Augustus in Ancyra (modern Ankara), in Apollonia in Lysia, and here in Pisidian Antioch on the propylon in front of the Augusteum.

Two sentences from the *Res gestae* are particularly appropriate as we consider Antioch. Augustus recalls how "citizens everywhere, privately as individuals and collectively as municipalities, sacrificed unremittingly at all the shrines on behalf of my health" (2.18–20).[6] The Augusteum in Pisidian Antioch was one such temple where such sacrifices were offered to the emperor as to a god, "matching the greatness of his virtue and repaying his benefactions towards them," as Nicolaus of Damascus, a personal acquaintance of Augustus, explains regarding the logic of the imperial cult (*Life of Augustus* 1).[7] In another place, Augustus recalls, "In Africa, Sicily, Macedonia, the two Spanish provinces, Achaia, Asia, Syria, Narbonian Gaul, and Pisidia, I settled colonies of soldiers" (5.35–36).[8] Pisidian Antioch was one of these veteran colonies, whose inhabitants felt a personal debt of gratitude to the emperor who had provided them and their descendants with precisely the economic footing for which they had endured twenty years' service in the legions of Rome.

Pisidian Antioch and Paul's Gospel

Paul's letter to the Christians here and throughout the cities in South Galatia does not seem to intersect as much with the material culture of Pisidian Antioch as does, for example, 1 Corinthians with Corinth. In part, this is probably because the challenges Paul must address in Galatians have erupted upon the congregations in this province from outside the province—Jewish Christian teachers who were following Paul's steps in order to "correct" his

---

6. Translation from Danker, *Benefactor*, 261.
7. Translation from Price, *Rituals and Power*, 1.
8. Translation from Danker, *Benefactor*, 267.

errors vis-à-vis the ongoing role of the Torah in defining both the people of God and alignment with God's righteousness.[9] In part, however, this is also due to the admittedly scant state of the excavations of Pisidian Antioch when set alongside the work that has been done to bring ancient Corinth or Ephesus to light.

Nevertheless, the lived spaces of Pisidian Antioch that have been unearthed, being prominently centered on the expansive cult site of the Augusteum, suggest that Paul's audience—both his converts and their unsupportive neighbors—would have heard significantly political overtones in his initial and ongoing proclamation of a "son of a god" (see, e.g., Acts 13:33; Gal. 2:20; 4:4) who came as a "savior" (Acts 13:23; cf. 13:26) to bring deliverance to the whole world, whose coming was "good news" ("gospel") for all people.

The term "gospel" (*euangelion*), no doubt as common in Paul's preaching (see the use of the verb form in Acts 13:32 and 14:7 and the noun form in 20:24) as it was in his letters—seven times in the letter he would later send to the Christians in Antioch (Gal. 1:6, 7, 11; 2:2, 5, 7, 14)—appears in imperial as well as Christian contexts, though in plural forms rather than the singular typical in Christian discourse. An inscription from Priene in the Roman province of Asia, dated to about 9 BC, looks back to Augustus's birth as "the beginning of good news [*euangelion*]" for the whole world. Josephus applies the term to Vespasian's accession to imperial power at the end of the civil wars of AD 68–69 (*J.W.* 4.656). A gymnasiarch in Pergamum also uses the term when honoring Augustus (*IGR* 4.317).

Augustus was lauded as "son of the deified [Julius]" (*divi filius*) on the legends of coins and in public inscriptions, as were his own successors in relationship to him ("son of the deified Augustus," *divi Augusti filius*) after his death and formal divinization by the Senate. While Latin distinguishes between a "god" (*deus*) and a "deified being" (*divus*), Greek does not. Augustus and many of his successors were called "son of a god" (*huios theou*) in Greek, using the phrase that would also be applied verbatim to Jesus in the New Testament and, no doubt, in the early preaching of Christian missionaries.

Augustus was also hailed as a "savior" (*sōtēr*) in inscriptions and eulogistic hymns, a term that became, of course, another common way to speak of Jesus in early Christian circles. And what Paul calls "this present evil age" (Gal. 1:4), from which deliverance is desperately needed, the majority in Pisidian

---

9. On the pastoral situation that evoked the Letter to the Galatians and the likely elements of the rival teachers' promotion of taking on the yoke of the Torah (the law of Moses) as the path to completing the journey toward alignment with the righteousness that God requires and for which Jesus has opened the way, see deSilva, *Letter to the Galatians*, 7–26.

Antioch would have celebrated as the golden age of the Augustan Peace. When Paul identifies that "Savior" (Acts 13:23), that agent of deliverance, as Jesus, "the Son of God" (Gal. 2:20; cf. 4:4), he applies titles commonly ascribed to the emperor in Rome to a Judean provincial who had been shamefully executed for sedition. His message would have been heard in Antioch as a challenge to imperial ideology on all fronts, as would the witness of Christians increasingly during the first three centuries of the church throughout the empire.

ROMAN PHILIPPI

Philippi in the Ministry of Paul

After passing through the cities of Syria, Cilicia, and South Galatia strengthening the congregations that he had already planted, Paul and his team ventured by ship from Alexandria Troas on the western coast of the Roman province of Asia to the Roman province of Macedonia. According to Acts, they traveled via the island of Samothrace and made landfall at the harbor of Neapolis, the modern city of Kavala, which still boasts a small but active harbor. From here they followed the Via Egnatia, which passed from the east through Neapolis, westward to Philippi, a 10-mile journey. Paul's movements in Macedonia provide a snapshot of how important the Roman road system was to Paul's missionary work, as he and his team would continue to follow the Via Egnatia through Amphipolis and Apollonia to Thessalonica, the next site of active mission work, and then on to Beroea.

The Via Egnatia was laid in the period of the Roman Republic. It was begun under the supervision of Gnaeus Egnatius, the proconsular governor of Macedonia in the mid-second century BC, from whom it took its name. The Via Egnatia would come to stretch all the way from the Adriatic Sea, the sea separating Italy from Greece, to modern Istanbul. Chiefly constructed for the movement of troops and their supplies, the road also became a major artery for trade and civilian movement. Thus after the long climb from the port of Neapolis, the Via Egnatia brought Paul to the eastern gate of Philippi and through the fortifications that had been constructed by Philip II of Macedon, father of Alexander the Great.

According to the narrative in Acts, Paul and Silas began their work among the small Jewish community in Philippi, with Lydia, a propertied convert,

The modern harbor in Kavala, the site of ancient Neapolis.

Philipp Pilhofer / CC BY-SA 3.0

A section of the Via Egnatia between Kavala (Neapolis) and Philippi, no doubt traveled by Paul on his way from the former to the latter.

opening up her home to the apostolic team and, no doubt, hosting assemblies of converts. Paul and Silas ran afoul of a pair of local slave owners by casting out the spirit that allowed the slave to prophesy, destroying her profitability. The slave owners brought Paul and Silas to the attention of the magistrates and appealed to Gentile anti-Jewish sentiments to advance their case against

The Neapolis (eastern) Gate of Philippi, seen from outside (top) and inside (bottom) the city.

The archaeological site of Philippi.

them: "These men are disturbing our city; they are Jews and are advocating customs that are not lawful for us as Romans to adopt or observe" (Acts 16:20–21 NRSV). The pair were beaten and imprisoned overnight, but an earthquake freed them from their bonds and led to the conversion of another household—that of the jailor. The following day, Paul—who, as a Roman citizen, was legally protected against such treatment as he received—wrested the ancient equivalent of an apology from the magistrates, who escorted Paul and Silas out of the city, probably by its west gate, setting them on the road toward Thessalonica. This would have restored their honor in the public eye (note especially 16:37), something perhaps more important for the converts and their ongoing witness in the city than for Paul himself.

Paul would have several occasions to return to visit his congregation in Philippi, which became a community especially close to his heart, over the course of his ministry. Both 1 Corinthians 16:5 and 2 Corinthians 1:16 refer to another visit to the Macedonian churches. Acts 20:1–6 speaks of Paul's spending a Passover in Philippi just prior to his return to Jerusalem in AD 58, perhaps the same visit to which Paul refers in 2 Corinthians 8 and 9 regarding the completion of his collection project for the church in Judea, in which the

Macedonian assemblies participated in exemplary fashion. The Philippian Christians would also maintain contact with Paul at their own initiative, sending gifts with emissaries like Epaphroditus to support his work elsewhere and to sustain him during a rather trying imprisonment. It was, in part, to thank them for this last gift that Paul wrote his letter to the Philippians.

The Archaeology of Philippi

The archaeological site of Philippi is one of the more impressive biblical sites in Greece, far surpassing Thessalonica and Beroea, both of which have the disadvantage, archaeologically speaking, of continuous occupation—and significant urban growth—to the present day. Even so, recent estimates suggest that only 15 percent of the ancient city has been excavated. We also face a greater challenge—here more pronounced than at either Corinth or Ephesus—when it comes to recovering the definitive shape and architecture of the Philippi of the Julio-Claudian period, when Paul would have visited the city, because of the extensive remodeling of the city under the Antonine emperors (especially under Marcus Aurelius) and, of course, the city's post-Constantinian life as a burgeoning center of Christian community and worship. Nevertheless, the approximations of Philippi in the time of Paul that are possible on the basis of the excavated realities are far closer than the approximations that we would inevitably make on the basis of uninformed imagination.

Philippi already had a history more than four hundred years old by the time Paul passed through its eastern gate. It began as a small agricultural settlement called Krenides (Appian, *Bell. civ.* 4.105) that, faced with Thracian invasions in

Portions of the fortification walls built by Philip II.

The theater (top) and the retaining wall supporting a portion of its tiers of seating (bottom).

the mid-fourth century BC, called on Philip II of Macedon for his help defending against this threat. Philip, recognizing the settlement's potential strategic value for his own regional aspirations, took control of the city for himself and supplied it with a vast fortification wall that was 7 to 8 feet thick with a perimeter of over 2 miles. Defensive towers at regular intervals completed the

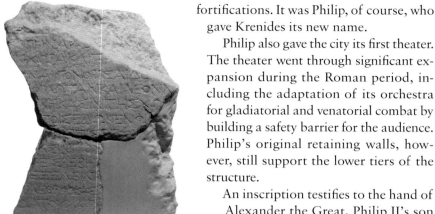

fortifications. It was Philip, of course, who gave Krenides its new name.

Philip also gave the city its first theater. The theater went through significant expansion during the Roman period, including the adaptation of its orchestra for gladiatorial and venatorial combat by building a safety barrier for the audience. Philip's original retaining walls, however, still support the lower tiers of the structure.

An inscription testifies to the hand of Alexander the Great, Philip II's son and successor, in establishing the boundaries of the city's agricultural territory, the hinterlands over which it would have jurisdiction. The area of a city's hinterlands was often decided on the basis of the amount of arable farmland that would be required to feed the inhabitants of that city. The productivity of farming villages located within those hinterlands

Fragments of an inscription recording the decree of Alexander the Great concerning the extent of Philippi's territory.

would be directed toward sustaining the city's population.

In 168 BC, the forces of the Roman Republic defeated Philip V's son Perseus and brought an end to that great dynasty. Philippi, along with all of Macedonia, came under Roman rule and was organized into a Roman province by 146 BC. In 42 BC, the climactic battle between the armies of Julius Caesar's assassins (Brutus and Cassius) and the armies of Caesar's avengers (his right-hand man, Marc Antony, and his adopted heir, Octavian) was fought on the plains just south of Philippi. After their victory, Antony and Octavian rewarded their veterans with grants of farmland around Philippi, where they were settled. After the alliance between Antony and Octavian dissolved into another civil war that effectively ended in 31 BC with Antony's defeat in a naval battle near Actium, Octavian, now the emperor and soon to be named "Augustus," graciously settled many of his opponent's veterans—the losers in the civil war—in Philippi, since they had lost their right to possess land in Italy.

Octavian formally re-founded Philippi as a Roman colony, naming it the Colonia Iulia Augusta Philippensis after his wife, Livia (also known as Julia). The inhabitants thus also enjoyed the privilege of Roman citizenship. The thousands of veteran families who were granted the land and the se-

During the reign of Claudius, Philippi kept the memory of Augustus's victory and his benefactions toward veterans alive with coins bearing an image of the deified winged figure of Victory and the legend "Vic[tory of] Aug[ustus]" on one side; military standards celebrating the establishment of a cohort of veteran praetorians at Philippi decorated the other side.

cure economic footing it brought thus owed Octavian a deep and personal debt, which would be shown in their fierce loyalty to his line and to Rome.

The enfranchisement of so many new families in Philippi, however, would have meant the *dis*enfranchisement of a good many as well, people who were dispossessed of their lands to make them available as grants to the veterans and who found themselves on the outside of the government of a city in which they had formerly been fully enfranchised citizens. Unable to simply pick up and leave, many would have remained on dramatically reduced plots of land and worked as tenant farmers or in support industries for the colony.[1] Politically, they were now aliens with right of abode in a city that was no longer their own.

The Via Egnatia passed through the city of Philippi and thus also served as its principal east-west corridor. As Paul continued to walk along the Via Egnatia, then, he would have passed through several residential areas. Though the houses themselves continued to be reused, altered, and even rebuilt throughout the Roman and Byzantine periods, their first-century layout would not have been much different.

Paul would also have passed a Roman bathhouse that, though modified throughout the period of the city's habitation, had stood alongside the Via Egnatia since the time of Augustus.[2] It consisted of apodyteria (changing rooms),

---

1. Brélaz, "First-Century Philippi," 162. It seems likely that those who originally lived in Philippi were compensated for their land. Laura Salah Nasrallah (*Archaeology and the Letters of Paul*, 118–19) points to a paragraph in the *Res gestae* (16) where Augustus speaks of expending large sums on the acquisition of property both in Italy and abroad. Even so, invoking eminent domain, even with compensation, is not generally a welcome phenomenon.

2. Koukouli-Chrysantaki and Bakirtzis, *Philippi*, 57.

Segments of the Via Egnatia as it runs alongside the forum of Philippi.

A residential area east of the forum. Visible to the right is one of Philippi's north-south streets, showing clearly the Roman drainage system in place under the roads.

a latrine, and the facilities for the typical progression from the caldarium (or sauna) to the tepidarium (a warm pool) to the frigidarium (the cold plunge), which braced the bather to return to the day's activities. The caldarium was a small marvel of ancient engineering. Clay tiles in stacks supported a secondary floor while a furnace blew hot air into the spaces under it and often also through clay pipes within the walls. This allowed the sauna to achieve its desired temperature. Caldaria were often equipped with large basins, the contents of which could be ladled out onto the floor to create steam.

The Via Egnatia would then have brought Paul to the administrative forum of the city. Some of the best-preserved sections of the entire road are to be found here, running both to the east and to the west of the forum. The forum as it currently stands presents the remains of a major late second-century renovation project under the emperor Marcus Aurelius. The earlier forum, however, was likely laid out in a similar fashion and likely contained buildings that, while less grandiose, served many of the same functions as those dating from Marcus's facelift.[3] The forum had columned porticoes on the three sides not running alongside the Via Egnatia and administrative offices and temples

3. Koukouli-Chrysantaki, "Colonia Iulia Augusta Philippensis," 15; Nasrallah, *Archaeology and the Letters of Paul*, 114.

A first-century AD bathhouse in Philippi.

The second-century forum of Philippi, seen from the mountain shrines above.

lining the two shorter sides. Some of these spaces have been identified as the city archives, a public library, and the city's council chamber.

The forum's broad open space sat five steps lower than the porticoes and was well equipped with a drainage system running around the perimeter to keep rainwater from collecting. According to the report in Acts 16:19–22, it was to the previous version of this civic forum (misleadingly rendered as "marketplace" in some English translations, as the Greek *agora* can be used to name either a civic or a commercial forum) that Paul was brought before the city magistrates and subjected to a particularly Roman punishment—being beaten with rods. Lictors, who served as bodyguards and enforcers for Roman magistrates, carried bundles of such rods, or thin dowels, as a symbol of their authority.

South of the administrative forum and parallel to the Via Egnatia ran another major east-west street that traversed the commercial and residential districts. Though the road was repaved in the Roman period, hence the flagstones now visible, it had been part of the original Hippodamian (or grid) plan of the Hellenistic city. A series of twenty shops once lined the street to the north, sitting just below the forum. The area south of this street was given largely to commercial activity as well. It is clearly identified as a macellum—essentially a meat market—in a dedicatory inscription to the goddess Fortuna (the deified personification of destiny or fortune) and the genius, or protective spirit, of the marketplace.

Again, the commercial forum that we can see today is a second-century reconfiguration of the market space. The Hellenistic and early Roman city, however, would also have required and made provision for a commercial agora, and major architectural updates to a key space did not frequently involve significant relocation of that space. It is thus reasonable to imagine the commercial agora adjoining the administrative forum in Paul's time as it did a century later.

The forum from the south corner. Note the well-preserved flagstones of the forum pavement, the provisions for drainage around the perimeter, and the steps ascending to the remains of one of the three porticoes.

A row of shops below the long southern side of the civic forum.

The shape of the Roman commercial agora is obscured by the remains of a grand fifth-century Christian basilica that was constructed over most of this space. Some pre-Constantinian facilities were left untouched, however, such as a latrine that was once connected to a second-century gymnasium and, probably, bath complex. This typical latrine once offered forty-two seats for the comfort of Philippi's residents. Waste was continuously flushed out beneath the seats while water flowing in the channel in front of the seats allowed for personal hygiene with the help of sponges on sticks kept on the premises.

A votive inscription identifying the macellum.

On the north side of the administrative forum, on the other side of the Via Egnatia, Paul would have found the main religious district, though some temples, such as shrines related to the imperial cult, were to be found within the forum itself. The temple in the northwest corner of the forum served as an imperial cult temple in the second century, and it seems reasonable to believe that this temple had existed on that spot in some form since the early first century, perhaps even since the city's refounding under Augustus. Inscriptions bear witness to priests—and therefore cults—of Julius Caesar, Augustus, and Livia by the time of Paul's visit, as well as to a cult of Claudius by the midcentury, none of which is surprising given the city's debt of gratitude to the imperial family.[4] Another temple sat in the northeast corner of the forum, at least by the Antonine period, though the deity to which it was dedicated is unclear.

A monumental staircase led to a small temple built in the Hellenistic period, possibly a *hērōon*, or hero shrine, dedicated to Philip II as the divinized founder of the city.[5] It was here that the inscription recording Alexander the Great's decision about the city's hinterlands was discovered.[6]

4. Harrison, "Excavating the Urban and Country Life," 25–26.
5. Koukouli-Chrysantaki, "Colonia Iulia Augusta Philippensis," 19.
6. Koukouli-Chrysantaki and Bakirtzis, *Philippi*, 33.

Three figures—a statue of Athena and two flanking statues of the goddess Victory—that are believed to have decorated the peak and front corners of the roof of the temple in the northeast corner of the forum.

It is likely that a temple to the Capitoline triad of Jupiter, Juno, and Minerva sat prominently on the terrace below the acropolis and overlooking the forum, an ever-present symbol of the watchful oversight and protection not merely of the gods but of the quintessentially *Roman* gods.[7] These were the deities worshiped in the Temple of Jupiter on the Capitoline Hill of Rome, overlooking the civic forum there as well. A shrine to Livia Augusta, the deified wife of Augustus, also sat upon this terrace, perhaps as early as the reign of Claudius (under whose auspices she was finally deified).

Almost nothing remains of these structures as Philippi continued not only to be occupied but to become a major center of Christianity during the Byzantine period. Thus the ancient Roman sacred area is dominated now by the remains of a sixth-century Christian basilica.

The remains of a series of shrines, partially carved into the rocky side of the lower acropolis, bear further witness to the once-varied religious life of the city. One such sanctuary was clearly devoted to the goddess Artemis, as can be seen from a trio of worn reliefs carved into the rock wall. Artemis was portrayed here as a huntress bringing down a deer. A second sanctuary was dedicated to the worship of Silvanus, a Roman forest god. The remaining portion preserves lists of the names of devotees of Silvanus and details of their donations to the construction and maintenance of the shrine.

7. Brélaz, "First-Century Philippi," 156–57, 174; also Oakes, "Imperial Authorities in Paul's Letter," 233.

A third sanctuary was devoted to a group of deities whose cult images once stood within three carved niches, but no traces of these have remained such as would identify the shrine. These so-called rock sanctuaries are dated to the second century. The worship of Silvanus, however, an ancient *Italian* woodland god, would likely have been imported quite early in the Roman colony's history.[8]

A nearby shrine was dedicated to the popular Mother Goddess, identified with Cybele. A large compound of shrines further up the side of the acropolis was dedicated to the Egyptian deities Isis, Osiris, and Harpocrates. Remains of statues of the goddess Tyche, or Fortuna, and dedicatory inscrip-

A second-century votive inscription located at the Neapolis gate invoking the protection of Isis Regina, or Queen Isis, over the colony as a whole. The inscription incidentally provides the full name of the Roman colony (fourth line from the top).

tions to "Apollo, Protector of Villages," Artemis, and other deities bear witness to the wider range of deities once honored here.

A sanctuary of Dionysus is believed to have been located near the theater, as the performance of tragedies and satyr plays in the theaters of Greek cities had been closely linked to the worship of Dionysus since the Classical period.[9] This is reinforced by the decorative motifs on the pillars supporting the portico of a small forum right in front of the theater—on each, a maenad, a frenzied female worshiper of Dionysus, is featured—as well as by a votive dedication of the portico to the deities "Liber and Libera," alternative names for Dionysus and either Ariadne, his bride, or Proserpina, the reluctant bride of Hades who is also connected to the agricultural cycle.

In many cases, it is difficult to establish that a particular cult or temple existed during the mid-first century. In some cases, as in the cults of major deities like Apollo and Artemis, where the evidence predates and postdates the first century, it is fair to assume continuity of worship in some form throughout the whole period. In other cases, as in the cults of the Egyptian gods, it is more

8. Koukouli-Chrysantaki and Bakirtzis, *Philippi*, 26; Brélaz, "First-Century Philippi," 173.
9. Koukouli-Chrysantaki, "Colonia Iulia Augusta Philippensis," 18.

Excavated side of a forum that once stood in front of the theater. Maenads and other Dionysian motifs decorate the facade.

difficult to demonstrate their presence in Paul's Philippi. What is abundantly clear, however, is that Philippi was a city in which the cults of the traditional Roman gods, alongside the cult of the emperors, were as thickly woven into the social fabric as in the other cities of the eastern Roman Empire.

In Paul's letter to the Christians in Philippi, we hear indications that the believers have endured and continue to endure unwelcome social pressure—what we would call persecution—as he urges them to be "in nothing intimidated by those who oppose you, . . . because it has been granted to you on Christ's behalf not only to put your trust in him but also to suffer for him, enduring the same contest as you witnessed befalling us and now hear has befallen me" (Phil. 1:28–30). We would probably be correct to attribute this pressure to the Christians' defection from participating in the cults that honored the gods their neighbors believed to ensure the well-being and prosperity of the city and its inhabitants. What Paul would celebrate in the lives of their Thessalonian sisters and brothers—"how you turned to God from idols, to serve a living and genuine God" (1 Thess. 1:9)—would have been censured by the very pious neighbors of the Christ-followers, whether in Thessalonica, Philippi, Corinth, or Ephesus.

A number of the gods and goddesses worshiped in Philippi were attached particularly to the boundary of life and death—and the successful crossing of this boundary. Very often, these would be the deities at the center of mystery cults, in whose power initiates hoped to share and the assurance of whose favor and protection they sought to obtain as a means of allaying their own fears and concerns for a good afterlife. Isis, for example, gathered and revivified the parts of her dismembered husband, Osiris. Cybele, though mourning three days for her lover, Attis, restored him to life. The infant Dionysus was said to have been dismembered and eaten by the Titans at Hera's instigation but was reborn.

The gospel that Paul brought spoke quite directly to the concerns of many first-century people, offering a death-and-resurrection mystery of a decidedly different sort. It was not one of distant, ancient myth but one of recent history, and one that combined both mystical and ethical elements in the initiate's path to resurrection: conformity with the mind that Christ Jesus manifested in his self-giving death in obedience to God (Phil. 2:5–11). And if "sharing in his sufferings" becomes a path to, and the primary assurance of, sharing in Christ's resurrection—if "to die is gain"—then the pangs of social pressure to conform (whether from family, associates, or official representatives of the city) lose their coercive power (Phil. 1:21; 3:10–11).

Acts relates that when a Sabbath came, Paul and his team would go outside the city gates to look for the "place of prayer" beside the river where the small Jewish community—here, it would seem, composed entirely of women—gathered (16:13, 16). Here they met Lydia of Thyatira, a seller of purple-dyed fabric. The presence of this merchant from Roman Asia in Roman Macedonia is another witness to the mobility that imperial commerce both encouraged and necessitated, incidentally corroborated by other inscriptions speaking of *purpurari*, purple-dyers or dealers in purple cloth, in later Roman Philippi—including one "Antiochus, son of Lucas, from Thyatira."[10] While streams are readily accessible outside both the east and the west gates of the city, tradition, at least, favors the view that Paul encountered his first converts

---

10. Harrison, "Excavating the Urban and Country Life," 36–37.

Images of Isis (left; from the National Archaeological Museum of Naples), Cybele (top right; from the Ephesus Archaeological Museum), and Dionysus (bottom right; from the Kunsthistorisches Museum Wien in Vienna), three deities that were frequently at the center of mystery cults in antiquity.

in Philippi beside the stream lying a mere third of a mile outside the western gate of the city.

Acts 16:13 is, in fact, our only evidence—literary or otherwise— for anything like a Jewish community in Philippi during the first century. Philo speaks of settlements of Jews in Macedonia in general but does not specify Philippi as the locus of one. The reserve of Acts in this regard, speaking only of a "place of prayer," a *proseuchē*, which may refer to a designated building or merely a designated space, is noteworthy. The earli-

The Nikostratos inscription.

est evidence for an actual synagogue in Philippi comes from a third-century AD inscription specifying fines to be paid to the synagogue if a particular grave—that of one Nikostratos—was co-opted for the burial of a second corpse.[11] Indeed, there is little evidence for the Jewish community of that period beyond a second grave stele, marking the resting place of one Simon of Smyrna. Acts quite appropriately does not speak of Jewish opposition to Paul and Silas in Philippi. If the author were inclined to invent elements of his story out of whole cloth, it would have been natural to follow the pattern that was established in the cities of South Galatia (namely, Pisidian Antioch, Iconium, and Lystra) and would appear again in Corinth.

One feature of the public face of Philippi that requires examination at this point is the phenomenon of the honorific inscription recording the offices held by, and honors awarded to, elite and semi-elite citizens of the colony. The bulk of these reflect military careers, which should not be at all surprising given the origins of the Roman colony and the propensity within the ancient world for sons and grandsons to continue in the same profession as their forebears. Nevertheless, these inscriptions clearly reflect the tradition of the *cursus honorum*—the sequence of offices, and thus the catalogue of accrued honor, whether commemorated in the civilian form of a string of civic offices or in the military form of military offices, generally in increasing rank.

11. See the extensive discussion in Koukouli-Chrysantaki, "Colonia Iulia Augusta Philippensis," 28–35.

Honorary inscriptions of C. Mucius and P. Mucius.

Outside of Philippi along the Via Egnatia stands a 12-foot-high monolithic monument bearing the inscription "Caius Vibius Quartus, son of Caius, of the tribe Cornelia, soldier of the V legion Macedonia, decurion of the Ala Scubulorum, prefect of the Cohort III Cyrenaica, tribune of the II legion Augusta."[12] What Quartus wants remembered of him is his paternal line, his Roman tribe, and his rise through the ranks from soldier to decurion to prefect to military tribune—a respectable run indeed.

Two chest-high inscriptions honoring a pair of brothers who were military veterans still stand in Philippi's civic forum. These were erected in accordance with the testament of each brother by the surviving son of one of the pair. What we learn about the brothers is the offices they held: Caius Mucius was the commander of a company of javelin throwers and the prefect of a cohort in the Sixth Legion Ferrata. Publius Mucius, of the Voltinia tribe, was a veteran of the same legion and held the highest civic office of duovir in Philippi. The latter is an especially noteworthy distinction. Only a hundred or so people would serve as a duovir of Philippi in a lifetime.

Also in the forum stands an honorific inscription: "To Lucius Tatinius Cnosus, son of Lucius, of the tribe Voltina, soldier of the fourth praetorian cohort, *singularis* and *beneficiarius* of the tribune, lieutenant, *beneficiarius* of the praetorian prefect, *evocatus* of the emperor, decorated with necklaces and with the golden crown by the emperor Domitian Caesar Augustus, centurion of the fourth cohort of the watchmen, centurion of the *statores*, centurion of the eleventh urban cohort, the veterans who served under his orders in the watchmen having received their honorable leave."[13] This is an even more impressive cursus honorum in both active military and postdischarge veteran service.

But perhaps the most impressive performance is captured in the honorific monument that Tiberius Claudius Maximus erected to commemorate his own cursus honorum:

> Tiberius Claudius Maximus, a veteran, erected this in his lifetime; knight in Legion VII Claudia Pia Fidelis; made quaestor of knights, *singularis* of the legate of the same legion, *vexillarius* of knights; decorated for valor in the Dacian War by Emperor Domitian; named *duplicarius* in the Second Ala Pannoniorum by the Divine Trajan; named scout during the Dacian War by the same; decorated twice for valor in the Dacian and Parthian Wars; named decurion in the same ala by the same for capturing Decebalus and bringing his head to him at

---

12. Translation from Harrison, "From Rome to the Colony of Philippi," 336–37.
13. Translation slightly adapted from Harrison, "From Rome to the Colony of Philippi," 339.

An inscription honoring L. Tatinius Cnosus.

Ranistorum; granted honorable leave by Terentius Scaurianus, consul of the new province of Mesopotamia.[14]

The passion for achieving honor and seeing one's honor publicized and memorialized is certainly not distinctive to Philippi. This is, rather, a characteristic deeply rooted among most of the cultures united within the Roman Empire. Paul uses this cultural convention rather distinctively and startlingly in Philippians. One of these occurrences is Paul's own construction of a cursus honorum appropriate to his location in Jewish culture: "Circumcised on the eighth day, of the race of Israel, of the tribe of Benjamin, a Hebrew born from Hebrews; concerning the law, a Pharisee; concerning commitment, a persecutor of the church; concerning righteousness defined by the law, blameless" (Phil. 3:5–6). The content is culture specific, but the form would unquestionably be heard as a kind of cursus honorum, the significance of which

14. Translation adapted from Harrison, "From Rome to the Colony of Philippi," 340.

comes only in the following verse as Paul discards—and considers "trash" or "sewage"—these accrued honors in favor of the immensely greater value he has discovered in Christ.

The second and more impressive example is Paul's construction of a cursus honorum for Jesus—which one notable scholar has called a "cursus pudorum," a sequence of degradations.[15] How different from the upward-climbing paths to the acquisition of honor, all laid out by and serving the structures of the Roman political and military order, memorialized on stone monuments around the forum and beyond, is the cursus that Jesus pursued: "Who, being in the form of God, did not consider equal status with God as something to cling to, but

A small altar dedicated "to a subterranean god."

emptied himself, taking the form of a slave, coming into being in the likeness of humans; and, being found in human likeness, he abased himself, being obedient to the point of death—even death on a cross" (Phil. 2:6–8). Of course, it is the end of this sequence that transforms voluntary self-abasement for the sake of obedience to God into the supreme cursus honorum, vindicating the path by means of the end: "Therefore God super-exalted him and graced him with the name that stands above every name, in order that, in the name of Jesus, every knee might bend—of heavenly beings and terrestrial beings and subterranean beings—and every tongue confess that Jesus Christ is Lord to the glory of God the Father" (Phil. 2:9–11).

Christ's revolutionary path to the highest honors challenges the logic of the typical Roman cursus honorum. It is not by filling the offices and climbing the ranks of local, military, or imperial hierarchies that one attains the greatest honor. It is by responding obediently to God's call to empty oneself for the sake of others and advancing God's good purposes for them.

The lordship of Jesus over all beings "heavenly," "terrestrial," and "subterranean," while of course being truly all-inclusive, would likely also call to mind typical expressions for the whole range of pagan gods, some of whom were conceptually located in heaven, some on the face of the earth, and some

15. Hellerman, *Reconstructing Honor in Roman Philippi.*

A fifth-century Christian basilica. The standard floor plan of the basilica—the main central aisle leading to a rounded apse flanked by two smaller side aisles—can be plainly seen.

in the underworld.[16] Christ's exaltation, of course, also places him above all spirit beings, human authorities (like the entirety of the Roman imperial administration), and human subjects. It is quite likely that Christ's resurrection and exaltation to the right hand of God would have been heard over against, and as something superior to, the death and "apotheosis by vote" that a number of Roman emperors had enjoyed to this point. Being physically raised from the dead to an indestructible life has a power and authenticity to it that casts a long shadow on the Roman counterfeit (which, incidentally, would come to involve staged subterfuge, like the releasing of a live eagle from beside the funeral pyre as evidence of the emperor's ascent as a god to the starry realm).

Before we leave this Roman colony, it is worth attending to more of Paul's political language in Philippians. First, Paul tells the Philippian Christians, "Conduct yourselves in a manner worthy of the gospel of Christ" (1:27). The verb rendered "conduct yourselves"—*politeuesthe*—has clear civic overtones. He implicitly suggests that the *ekklēsia* is a kind of civic body, a political entity whose conduct must align with a particular set of civic values determined by the larger kingdom of which they are a colony. In chapter 3, we encounter another such example of political language, this time offered by Paul as a rationale for living in conformity with Christ's death and pressing ever forward in response to God's call: "For our commonwealth is in the

16. For extensive documentation concerning the use of some such tripartite phrase to capture the whole range of deities in ancient literature and inscriptions, see Long and Giffin, "'Every Knee Bowed,'" 255–63.

heavens, from which we also await a deliverer, the Lord Jesus Christ, who will transform the body of our degradation into that which conforms to his glorious body, according to the power that enables him also to subject all things to himself" (3:20–21). Paul is preaching and writing in Greek to converts (most of whose recorded names reflect Greek identity),[17] and the promise of enfranchisement in a heavenly commonwealth might have been particularly attractive for the Greek noncitizens of a Roman colony—though his call to all would have been to recognize that their first and highest political loyalties must now always be to the kingdom of God's Son. The history of the growth of Christianity in this city, to which the late Roman and Byzantine basilicas attest, shows that Paul had indeed planted a very secure colony of the kingdom of God here in the heart of a colony of the Roman Empire.

17. Euodia (Phil. 4:2), Syntyche (4:2), and Epaphroditus (2:25) are Greek names; Clement (4:3) is of Latin origin.

7

THESSALONICA

Thessalonica and the Ministry of Paul

Having been asked to leave Philippi after their run-in with the authorities there, Paul and Silas set out to follow the Via Egnatia further west and deeper into Macedonia. They traveled through the port city of Amphipolis and the smaller village of Apollonia before arriving at Thessalonica, a journey of about 100 miles.

Acts 17:1–10 gives the impression that Paul spent a very short time in Thessalonica—perhaps preaching for only a few weeks ("three Sabbath days"), and that primarily in the synagogue among Jews and Gentile adherents, before his audience's hostility led to trouble with the authorities and a hasty departure. In light of Paul's own testimony, however, he must have stayed in the city long enough to establish himself in his trade, as he writes, "You remember our labor and toil, brothers and sisters; we worked night and day, so that we might not burden any of you while we proclaimed to you the gospel of God" (1 Thess. 2:9 NRSV). He was also there long enough to have received support more than once from his friends in Philippi: "No church entered into partnership with me in giving and receiving, except you only. Even in Thessalonica you sent me help for my needs once and again" (Phil. 4:15–16 ESV). And while Luke really only tells us of initial efforts to preach Jesus in a local synagogue in Thessalonica, Paul writes back to the congregation, saying, "You turned to God from idols" (1 Thess. 1:9), implying a significant outreach to Gentiles as well. Nevertheless, the testimony of both Luke and Paul agree that he was forced to flee the city against his wishes and continue his mission elsewhere, leaving behind the converts about whom he cared deeply and whose grounding in the faith he sought to secure by any means left open to him, which included sending Timothy back to the city to encourage them and sending with his emissaries the two letters that have continued to nourish the church in every age (cf. 1 Thess. 2:17–3:3).[1] Paul would again visit his converts (and *their* converts) in Thessalonica at the same time he visited Philippi (1 Cor. 16:5; 2 Cor. 1:16), and representatives of both congregations would travel with him to Corinth as Paul and his team gathered the collection for the poor among the Christ-followers in Judea (2 Cor. 8:1–5; 9:1–5).

The 260th milestone of the Via Egnatia. The name of Egnatius and his position as proconsul are clearly represented in the second and third Latin lines. This information is repeated in Greek below.

The Archaeology of Thessalonica

Discovering ancient Thessalonica is significantly hindered by the fact that it is buried beneath a thriving, sprawling modern metropolis—now the second largest and busiest city in Greece! Spaces available for excavation are highly limited. As a result, we do not have the benefit of evidence of first-century synagogues or a Jewish presence in the city. We see very little in the way of commercial or industrial spaces, such as might have given us some idea of the circumstances under which Paul carried out his trade so as not to burden his converts (1 Thess. 2:9–10; 2 Thess. 3:6–9). We have no significant residential areas that might yield examples of the kinds of houses that would host Christian gatherings. Traces of its past, however, peer through the modern city and its inscriptional record, allowing us some windows into the setting of Paul's second church plant in Macedonia.

Thessalonica was founded in 316 BC by Cassander, first a general of Alexander the Great and then one of his successors. The location provided a

---

1. While the authorship of 1 Thessalonians is hardly ever contested, the same cannot be said of 2 Thessalonians. See the arguments both against and in favor of the authenticity of the latter text in deSilva, *Introduction to the New Testament*, 472, 474–75.

An administrative complex and residence from the Hellenistic period.

natural harbor on the Aegean and would become a strategic center for both trade and naval defense. Cassander named the city after his wife, Thessaloni-keia, who was the daughter of Philip II and a half sister of Alexander the Great—and Cassander's link to a royal claim.

Some of the foundations of Cassander's walls and defensive towers, which enclosed only about 150 acres of the settlement,[2] can be seen in one of the many narrow windows into the city's ancient past that the modern city affords. The demolition of an apartment building in Kyprion Agoniston Square allowed for the discovery of another remnant from the city's pre-Roman

2. Veleni, *Macedonia—Thessaloniki*, 61.

past: a sprawling house and administrative complex that may have served as a royal residence for Cassander's successors (see photos on p. 80).[3] The block also has remains of a lavish peristyle house from the first century AD. Its presence makes it all the more tempting to speculate that the complex served as the headquarters for the Roman proconsular governor of the province of Macedonia. So much of ancient Thessalonica lies buried under modern Thessaloniki, however, that it would seem to smack too much of luck for the one apartment complex demolition to yield so important a discovery.

Just 800 feet southeast of this complex sit the remains of the Roman forum, its present structures reflecting the second-century AD renovations of the space. Excavations beneath the forum uncovered a bath complex from the Hellenistic period. The complex featured a hot and a cold pool as well as a sauna or sweating room.[4] The individual clay tubs in the sauna chamber are a distinctive feature of pre-Roman bathhouses. The bathhouse might indicate the location of the Hellenistic-period gymnasium, a large facility that served the goals of education and physical training as well as recreation, though further excavation is once again prevented by the needs of the living city.

Another structure, now mostly lost, sat in the area south of the bathhouse and suggests that this was once the location of a large public area, which would align well with its identification as a gymnasium complex.[5] The structure was once part of a rather grand portico (see photos on p. 83).

Inscriptions from nearby Kalindoia, a city within the prefecture of Thessalonica, bear witness to a vibrant gymnasium there and to the appreciation of the male youths, known as "ephebes," who enjoyed their training as citizens-to-be therein. These first-century inscriptions particularly honor the gymnasiarchs, local benefactors of the institution who became thereby the facility's directors, listing the names of scores of ephebes expressing their gratitude for these patrons' personal subsidizing of the expenses of the institution and of the ephebes' training and learning.

The Roman Republic was already building its "empire" throughout the second century BC. In 146 BC, Macedonia was formally incorporated into that empire as a province. Because of its size and location, Thessalonica then became the capital of the new province. It was at this time that Gnaeus Egnatius, the senator who became the first regular proconsular governor of Macedonia, began the construction of the highway through Macedonia that

---

3. Veleni, *Macedonia—Thessaloniki*, 69.
4. Veleni, *Macedonia—Thessaloniki*, 72.
5. Veleni, *Macedonia—Thessaloniki*, 74.

Several rooms of a bathhouse from the Hellenistic period, found below the level of the Roman forum.

A line drawing from 1794 showing the Hellenistic structure still standing amid the residential areas that grew around and engulfed it.

Reliefs that once adorned a decorative tier above a portico in the Hellenistic-period gymnasium complex south of the bathhouse. Pictured left to right are Ganymede, one of the Dioscuri (either Castor or Pollux), Aura, and Victory.

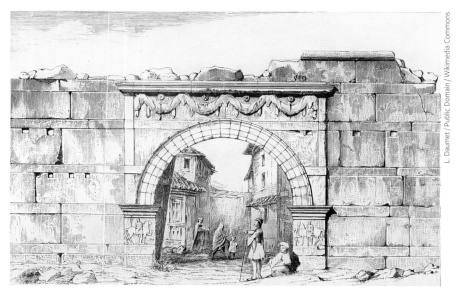

A drawing by Honoré Daumet (1864) of the Golden Gate in Thessalonica, built in honor of Octavian and Antony's victory over Caesar's assassins.

would bear his name.[6] A century later, in the midst of the civil wars that followed the assassination of Julius Caesar in 44 BC, Thessalonica sided with Marc Antony and Octavian, refusing to lend support to or even admit Caesar's assassins, Brutus and Cassius, into their city. After the victory of the Caesarean party, the city built a triumphal arch to honor Antony and Octavian, Caesar's avengers, though this was dismantled in 1911 as part of a civic improvement project and thereafter lost.[7]

For its loyalty, Thessalonica was made a free city and exempted from paying taxes. When Octavian and Antony became rivals themselves in another civil war, Thessalonica favored Antony, though quickly vowed its support and loyalty to the victor after Antony's defeat in 31 BC. Under Roman rule, Thessalonica flourished as a hub of business and trade between the east and the west.

The cities of Macedonia had a system of dating inscriptions that was unique in the Roman world and reflective of their particular history. During the period of Macedonian kings, documents and inscriptions would simply be dated by the regnal year of the king followed by the month and day within

6. The Via Egnatia was constructed over the span of 146–120 BC (Veleni, *Macedonia—Thessaloniki*, 45).
7. Veleni, *Macedonia—Thessaloniki*, 58.

The inscription on this base of a statue honoring the emperor Claudius exemplifies the dual dating system used in Macedonia. It is dated to "Year 76" of the Actium period and "Year 192" of the provincial period, both yielding a date of AD 44.

that year. But with the formation of the province in 146 BC, a new dating system was introduced. And when Octavian defeated Antony at Actium in 31 BC—thus ushering in what would be celebrated as the new era, even the golden age, of peace—a new starting point for keeping track of time was established. Inscriptions from the Principate, or the period of the Roman emperors, therefore bear two dates—one reckoning from 146 BC, the other from 31 BC, both kept in the minds of the populace as key era-defining events.

Paul remembers how his converts in Thessalonica "turned to God from idols, to serve a living and true God" (1 Thess. 1:9 NRSV), and there were indeed many idols from which to turn. Inscriptions demonstrate that cults of Rome and Roman benefactors were in place already during the Republican period.[8] Thessalonica was quick to erect a temple to the divinized Julius in or near 27 BC. In their devotion to the imperial house, the Thessalonians had moved a fifth-century temple originally dedicated to Aphrodite (Venus) from a more remote site in their territory, installing it a short distance to the west

8. Burnett, "Imperial Divine Honors," 70.

Architectural and statuary features of the temple of the imperial cult recovered and displayed in the Archaeological Museum of Thessaloniki.

of the administrative center. Since Julius Caesar had traced his own mythical ancestry to the goddess Venus, the Thessalonians probably thought this relocation and rededication to be particularly appropriate.[9]

Some archaeologists affirm that the older temple was moved because it sits on newer foundations from the Roman period and because the temple's stones have small letters written in the style known from the Roman period in its corners. These letters were the architects' guides to proper reassembly in the new location. Others dispute the "relocation" hypothesis and suggest that the appearance of the older blocks in the structure is a simple case of recycling.[10] In either case, an imperial temple came to stand in downtown Thessalonica by the Augustan age.

9. Veleni, *Macedonia—Thessaloniki*, 85.
10. See discussion in Burnett, "Imperial Divine Honors," 75–76.

The temple had massive Ionic columns standing 7 yards tall atop a five-stepped podium. It featured cult images of Julius as well as the goddess Roma, the deified personification of the city at the heart of the empire. Cultic honors for Augustus himself followed, as well as for other members of the imperial household who had been elevated to divinity.[11] The iconography of the breastplate carved on one of the cult images of an emperor features the fairly common motif of two winged images of Victory preparing a Roman trophy, essentially a Roman military helmet, breastplate, and some number of shields and weapons arranged on a cross-frame. Two captives sit bound at its foot. The cult of Roma and her emperors has been aptly described as "the apotheosis of power."[12]

Statues of emperors adorned the public spaces of the Roman city as well, as the discovery of inscribed statue bases attests.

Torso of a cult image from the imperial temple, most likely a representation of the goddess Roma.

Inscriptions naming an agonothete, a patron who provided for imperial games, in connection with priests of the emperors bear witness to the athletic contests held in honor of the emperors on a regular basis. All of this points to a strong commitment on the city's part to Rome and its rulers.

Thessalonica was home to temples of the traditional Greek and Roman gods but also nurtured many foreign imports. Prominent among these was the cult of the Egyptian gods Isis, Osiris (under the Ptolemaic name for this god, Serapis), and Horus (under the name Harpocrates). This was organized as a mystery cult and thus offered a more individual and intimate connection with deities than the public cults of the emperors or traditional gods. The cult was well established in Thessalonica by the third century BC, as witnessed by an early cult image of Isis, a votive stele from that period depicting the donor's parents as priests of Osiris, and inscriptions referring to a temple of Serapis.[13]

---

11. A group of inscriptions speak, for example, of the office of "the priest and president of the imperial games for Emperor Caesar Augustus" or "for Emperor Augustus, son of a god" (Burnett, "Imperial Divine Honors," 73, 79).

12. Cochrane, *Christianity and Classical Culture*, 74.

13. Harrison, "Epigraphic Profile of Thessalonica," 4, 19.

A particularly large inscription housed in the Archaeo-logical Museum of Thessaloniki bears a dedication by one Manius Quartus to "Serapis, Isis, Anubis, and the gods sharing the temple," attesting both to the continued existence of such a temple and to the range of Egyptian deities worshiped there in the late second or early first century BC. Another inscription from the turn of the era bears witness to a large donation made by Posilla Avia, a woman from a wealthy Roman merchant family, for the purpose of repairing the temple and constructing a new vestibule.

Among the artifacts from Thessalonica re-lated to this cult is a small piece of a larger in-scription recording a hymn to Isis in the form of a first-person revelation by the goddess to her devotees. In this text, Isis claims to have been active in everything from the creation of the cos-mos (separating the earth from heaven and setting the course of sun, moon, and stars) to the right ordering of human life (creating agriculture, instilling love between the sexes and affection in the hearts of parents for offspring, instruct-ing people in worship and justice). Another

A statue, perhaps a cult image, of Augustus from Thessalonica, carved in a manner reminiscent of statues of deities, particularly Zeus (who is similarly often depicted half-naked, standing, and holding a scepter).

The heads of cult images of the Egyptian deities Serapis and Isis and a complete statue of their divine son, Harpocrates. The cult of this trio became particularly popular in Egypt during the Ptolemaic period.

The head from a third-century BC statue of Isis and a votive relief of two devotees pouring a libation sacrifice before Serapis.

inscription records a poem by a certain Damaios recounting the myth of the murder and dismemberment of Osiris (aka Serapis) by his evil brother, Set, and of Isis's search for, recovery of, and revivification of her divine husband, who became the chief god of the afterlife. The nature of the cult myth suggests that the worship of Serapis/Osiris, Isis, and Harpocrates was especially concerned with securing a blessed existence beyond death. A particularly interesting group of finds in the Serapeion, or shrine to Serapis and Isis, are votive steles with one or two ears carved in relief and dedicated to one or the other of these deities. These votive reliefs suggest a conviction that Isis and Serapis had heard and answered the prayers of their petitioners, quite contrary to the typical claim in Hellenistic Jewish anti-idolatry polemic: "Their idols have ears, but they cannot hear" (cf. Pss. 115:6; 135:17). Inscriptions also attest to the worship of Dionysus, particularly in the form of Dionysiac mysteries that promise a joyous afterlife through union with the god

A carved relief of an ear dedicated to Isis sometime during the first century BC by one Marcus Agelleios.

A Dionysiac scene. A procession of maenads, instrumentalists, a satyr, and torchbearer precedes Dionysus and his bride, Ariadne, riding in a chariot drawn by a pair of panthers.

and appear to have celebrated freedom from the fear of death with freedom from sexual restraint and moderation generally.

Worship of Demeter and her daughter Persephone—two goddesses tied to the annual cycle of agriculture—is also attested at Thessalonica, with a sanctuary from the turn of the era having been discovered in the upper city. Persephone's beauty aroused the desire of several of the gods, but it was Hades who took the initiative, seized Persephone, and carried her off to the underworld. Her mother, Demeter, the goddess of the earth's fertility, mourned and caused vegetation everywhere to wither and die. To prevent a universal famine, Zeus ordered Hades to release the girl, but Hades tricked Persephone into eating several seeds from a pomegranate in his realm, which bound her to it and to him. As a result, Persephone would spend eight months above ground, during which time Demeter would rejoice and the earth flourish, and four months in the underworld with her husband, during which time Demeter would mourn and the earth suffer winter. Adult women celebrated special rites and offered sacrifices every spring to Demeter in connection with the return of Persephone, Demeter's joy, and earth's fertility.

A particularly local cult involved the worship of Kabeiros. Kabeiros was an ancient king who was murdered by his brothers but who was believed to live on in the divine realm and was expected to return to bring glory to Macedonia and his devotees. The basic contours of a ruler who died, lived on in the unseen realm, and would return in glory and power could not help but resonate, in some minds at least, with Paul's proclamation of an executed, risen, returning Lord. There is as yet, however, no hard evidence that a cult of Kabeiros existed in Thessalonica prior to the second century AD.[14]

14. Harrison, "Epigraphic Profile of Thessalonica," 23–24.

A carved relief showing Hades, the god of the underworld, carrying off a reluctant Persephone in his chariot drawn by four horses.

The forum seen from the southeast corner, looking above the remains of the administrative buildings there.

Not every deity in Thessalonica had a name. In the first century AD, Caius Julius Orios erected a column in thanksgiving to "the most high god, the great savior" for intervening to save Orios from some danger by warning him in a dream. This is probably not to be taken as a sign of belief in the God of Israel, also called "God Most High" in many texts, but rather as the way a philosophically minded Roman thought of deity—beyond the many faces of the traditional gods.

An inscription that was once incorporated into a triumphal gate in Thessalonica (the Golden Gate) celebrating Marc Antony and Octavian's victory at Philippi. The first word in the inscription refers to "serving as politarchs."

The archaeological centerpiece in modern Thessaloniki is the ancient Roman forum. Like the forum in Philippi, the Roman forum of Thessalonica was significantly reworked in the second century, such that its first-century shape—indeed, even its first-century location—is a matter of some conjecture. At some point early in the Roman period, the administrative center moved from the old Hellenistic palace to this new location. The three-acre forum that we can now see on this site represents a second-century project. The original forum was reputed to be surrounded by a bathhouse and gymnasium, a Serapis temple, and the administrative offices of the proconsul.[15] The presence of a bath, and likely a gymnasium, to the southwest of the later forum suggests that the first-century forum did not lie far from its successor. In any event, it was to the first-century precursor of the currently excavated forum that the hostile crowds brought some of Paul's principal converts to accuse them, and more particularly their teacher, before the authorities: "These people who have been turning the world upside down have come here also, and Jason has entertained them as guests. They are all acting contrary to the decrees of the emperor, saying that there is another king named Jesus" (Acts 17:6–7 NRSV).

15. Harrison, "Epigraphic Profile of Thessalonica," 2.

In a testimony to Luke's attention to historical detail, an inscription on a block once embedded in the Golden Gate, the monumental gate erected to celebrate Marc Antony and Octavian Caesar's triumph over Julius Caesar's assassins and their army, speaks of city magistrates "serving as politarchs," an uncommon designation for a city's leading citizen or citizens (see photo on p. 92). The term appears also near the bottom of the inscription on the base of an honorific statue of Claudius from AD 44 (see photo on p. 85).[16] This is the same term that Luke uses to designate the authorities in the forum in Acts 17:6.

The most notable remains in the upper forum are those of the reconstructed odeon, a small theater originally constructed for poetical and musical recitations and possibly also to serve as the city's council chamber. The odeon may date back only to the renovations of the forum in the second century AD. In the late second or early third century, the odeon was converted into a miniature arena for gladiatorial and venatorial combats, the latter of which pitted human beings against beasts. Administrative buildings flank the odeon, all of them predating it. Discoveries of furnaces and clay molds for the production of bronze blanks—that is, the smooth disks that would be struck into actual coins—reveal that one of these buildings served as the city's mint, the facility where official coinage was cast.

The remains of the administrative buildings on the northern half of the east side of the forum.

16. Indeed, the term appears in at least twenty-seven inscriptions from the city. See Horsley, "Appendix."

The pavement, steps, and remains of perpendicular porticoes from the southeast corner of the forum. Note also the provision for drainage around the perimeter.

The road, row of shops, and cryptoporticus running parallel to (and, in the case of the last, partially under) the south, long side of the forum.

One aisle of the cryptoporticus.

The forum itself was surrounded by columned porticoes on three sides, open to the north, with great flagstones serving as the pavement of the central open area. A road ran south of, and below, the forum through what appears to be the beginning of a commercial district. Shops once lined the street. An underground double portico may have served as a kind of shopping arcade prior to the second-century remodeling of the administrative forum (after which it became more of a storage facility).

THESSALONICA AFTER PAUL

Roman Thessalonica underwent a major overhaul during the reign of Galerius in the last years of the third century and early years of the fourth. The emperor Diocletian, finding the oversight of the empire overwhelming, divided the task between himself and a colleague. Both held the title of Augustus, one ruling the west and the other the east. Diocletian also appointed two supporting administrators and eventual successors, giving them the title of Caesar.

Galerius, a seasoned and high-ranking soldier, was made one of these Caesars in 293. He married Diocletian's daughter in 297 and became the eastern
Augustus in 306 upon Diocletian's retirement. Thessalonica became his capital.
The center of the old city is dominated by his works, chiefly by a vast palace and
bath complex that also served as his administrative center. A triumphal arch—
the entryway into Galerius's administrative center—celebrates a major victory
that he won over the Sassanid forces in Persia, reestablishing the strength of the
eastern front of the empire. A carved relief in one of the blocks in the Galerius
Arch shows the four imperial colleagues—Diocletian, Maximian, Constantius,
and Galerius—offering sacrifice together, gathered around the flame on a small
altar while a bull waits off to the right to be slaughtered. Diocletian and Maximian are both known for their relentless persecutions of Christians throughout
the empire. Close by the arch itself is a massive mausoleum Galerius intended
for himself that was, however, never completed.

The palace complex was also linked to a theater and stadium that may represent renovations of older facilities present during Paul's visit. We know from
inscriptions that the city hosted Olympic-style games every four years throughout
the Roman period, though archaeologists cannot confirm the location of the athletic facilities that would have provided the venue for such games prior to Galerius.

The Implications of Paul's Gospel for the Thessalonians

Paul's converts were subjected to significant social pressure in connection
with their new allegiances and convictions. Paul acknowledges this to have
been the case from the outset when he writes, "You became imitators of us
and of the Lord, receiving the word in much affliction with the joy of the
Holy Spirit" (1 Thess. 1:6). He returns to this reality again later in the letter:
"For you yourselves became imitators, brothers and sisters, of the assemblies
of God that are in Judea in Christ Jesus, because you yourselves endured
the same things from your own compatriots as they themselves did from
the Jews" (2:14). Indeed, this was the reason Paul had sent Timothy back to
them, to make sure that none of them would be shaken in their newfound
faith because of the backlash.

Their neighbors' hostility was most likely prompted by the converts' new
and *exclusive* religious allegiance: "You turned to God from idols, to serve a
living and genuine God and to await his Son from the heavens, whom he raised
from the dead—Jesus, the one rescuing us from the coming wrath" (1 Thess.
1:9–10). Unlike devotees of Demeter or Isis or Dionysus, Christ-followers did

not add the worship of the God of Israel to a pantheon of honored divinities. They renounced the worship, and even the reality, of any god beside the One. This would have been regarded by their pious neighbors as a grave and inexplicable affront to the gods—both the traditional gods and the newer imperial deities—and a threat to the stability and flourishing of the city, which depended on the favor of these gods.[17] And given the inextricable weave of civic, social, and religious life in the Greek or Roman city, exclusive allegiance to one God would have meant withdrawal from a great many settings and, with this withdrawal, the appearance of violating the social bonds that unified the city.

The gospel Paul proclaimed was also far from subtle in its subversion of the public gospel of peace and order eternally secured from the gods through the mediation of the god Augustus and his successors and their representatives. Paul recalls that while he was present with his converts in Thessalonica, he and his team were "encouraging and urging and testifying to [them] in order that [they] might walk in a manner worthy of the God who is calling [them] into his own kingdom and glory" (1 Thess. 2:12). Even though this other kingdom was not of this world, it still raised questions about loyalty to the present kingdom of which the city of Thessalonica was a part. But God's kingdom would not, Paul proclaimed, remain innocuously on some other plane of existence: "The Lord himself will descend from heaven with a command, with the voice of an archangel, and the dead in Christ will rise first. Then we who are still living, who remain, will be caught up at the same time with them in the clouds for the purpose of greeting the Lord in the air. And thus we will always be with the Lord" (4:16–17).

Throughout the early Christian movement, Jesus was called "Lord" in a manner that directly or indirectly expressed allegiance to a different *kyrios* (lord) than the Roman emperor. The return of Jesus and the believers' going up into the air to greet him is depicted in a manner reminiscent of the greeting, the *apantēsis*, that emperors received from the inhabitants of cities and regions as the emperors toured the provinces. And this Lord Jesus would be reentering the realm of earth and sea, over which the emperors were presently called "lords." Perhaps the part of the "good news" concerning forgiveness and reconciliation with God was innocent enough to the Thessalonian Christians' neighbors, but the rest of the good news concerning the decisive establishment of Jesus's kingdom on earth? That was not.

"About the times and the seasons, brothers and sisters, you have no need for me to write to you, for you yourselves know accurately that the day of the Lord comes as a thief in the night. When people say 'peace' and 'security,'

17. So also Burnett, "Imperial Divine Honors," 65, 84–86.

Bronze coins from the reign of Vespasian featuring "Pax Augusti"
(the peace of Augustus) on the reverse and from the reign of
Nero featuring "Securitas Augusti" (the security of Augustus)
on the reverse.

then sudden destruction overtakes them like labor pain overtakes the pregnant woman, and they will surely not escape. But you, brothers and sisters, are not in the dark such that the day will overtake you like a thief" (1 Thess. 5:1–4). "Peace" and "security" were common catchwords for the benefits of Roman imperial rule. The terms, along with their divinized personifications, were stamped onto the reverses of many coin issues. Augustus, particularly, foregrounded "peace" in his propaganda through multiple media, not least of which was the Altar of the Augustan Peace, which was erected on the Field of Mars in Rome and publicized throughout the empire on coinage. Whether or not "peace and security," taken together, was already a Roman slogan in the first century, the two terms were separately important as catchwords of Roman imperial propaganda, and the political resonances of Paul's letter at this point would have been unmistakable.[18]

Paul's "good news" involved a significant and subversive change of perception: all this talk of peace and security was a deception. Paul called the community to be always on the lookout for the day that would erupt into the status quo of the Roman peace and overturn the order of the powers that be, ushering in the eternal kingdom of God and God's anointed one—to replace the rule of Rome and its emperors that was everywhere celebrated as eternal. Deliverance—salvation—had not come to the world through Augustus and the peace he had established and that his successors maintained through the irresistible might of their legions. Deliverance—salvation—was a future reality for which the people in Thessalonica must still hope, and it would come through the Lord Jesus, with whom they would all do well to align themselves!

---

18. See the arguments and counterarguments in Weima, "'Peace and Security'"; J. White, "'Peace and Security' (1 Thess 5.3): Is It Really a Roman Slogan?"; J. White, "'Peace' and 'Security' (1 Thess 5.3): Roman Ideology"; Cadwallader, "Return to 'Peace and Security.'"

We might therefore regard with greater sympathy the response of the Jews of Thessalonica to whatever portion of this teaching Paul had brought to their city—and their synagogue—in his founding visit.[19] Calling for loyalty to a troublemaker crucified by the Roman authorities in Judea and speaking of this "anointed one," this *Lord*, returning to inaugurate his kingdom on earth was clearly subversive. The Roman order was celebrated throughout the empire as eternal; prayers and sacrifices were made on behalf of its continuing forever in an unending cycle of peace. Foretelling the end of this order, an order that would yield its place of supremacy to the kingdom of a returning provincial criminal, was also subversive. And the Jewish community in Thessalonica knew that the Jewish community in Rome, whether in whole or in part, had been expelled from Rome. According to the Roman historian Suetonius, this expulsion was due to some civil disturbances instigated by someone named "Chrestus"—commonly understood to represent Suetonius's misunderstanding of the nature of the inner-Jewish unrest concerning the proclamation of "Christus" by some of their number (Suetonius, *Claud.* 25.4). The Jews in Thessalonica would have had good reason, therefore, to nip this thing in the bud in their own city and to prove themselves a group loyal to their emperor by being quick to inform the civil authorities of those who made *any* subversive rumblings, even against people once attached to their synagogue.

19. On the historicity of the Acts account of this conflict, see Still, *Conflict at Thessalonica*, 61–82. The Acts account does not, however, tell the whole story, as it says nothing about the hostility the converts met from their *Gentile* neighbors after Paul's departure.

8

BEROEA

Beroea in the Ministry of Paul

According to Acts, Paul came to Beroea having fled from a riot in Thessalonica, which was stirred up by opponents within the Jewish community there. He and Silas did not continue to follow the Via Egnatia, which they had taken from Neapolis to Philippi to Thessalonica. They also chose not to follow the main road leading south along the Aegean coastline, perhaps hoping to make it more difficult for their opponents to follow them. Luke remembers the Jewish community in Beroea being much more receptive to Paul, Silas, and their message. Indeed, he commends them for both their openness and their commitment to examining the Scriptures to test Paul's claims about Jesus. A solid core for a Beroean congregation was formed in the short time Paul spent in the city before opponents from Thessalonica tracked him down and stirred up trouble once again (Acts 17:10–14).

The Archaeology of Hellenistic-Roman Beroea

Because the city of Beroea has been continuously inhabited, only the scantiest archaeological traces of Roman Beroea remain visible throughout the modern city of Veroia.

When Rome assumed control of Macedonia in 168 BC, it divided Macedonia into four administrative districts. Beroea was made the capital of its district until Macedonia was reorganized into a province with a single capital, Thessalonica, in 146 BC. The city maintained its Greek political institutions

Remains of Hellenistic-period fortifications: the base of one of the many towers that guarded the city's approaches (top) and a portion of the city's northern wall (bottom).

under Roman rule, with a city council whose rulings were ratified by the citizen body, though their purview had become far narrower after Rome annexed the territory. Segments of two Roman roads laid in the second century AD can be seen along the modern Mitropoleos and Venizelou Streets. These nearly perpendicular streets were probably the principal cardo and decumanus through Roman Beroea, though they are off from a true north-south axis by forty-five degrees. It seems likely that these roads represent repairs of earlier roads that were in use during the Hellenistic period.[1]

1. Brocas-Deflassieux, *Béroia*, 48.

Remnants of Roman roads incorporated into modern Veroia's Mitropoleos Street.

Inscriptions from the first century BC contain the names of several *agoranomoi*, bearing witness to the existence of an agora in the city—though this would have been a given.[2] The discovery of the foundations of a large complex under the Church of St. Anthony (as well as an unusual number of bronze coins from the Hellenistic period) has led to the tentative location of the agora in that vicinity.[3] It is not yet known whether the city had separate administrative and commercial forums. The city surely had a theater,[4] but its remains have not been located. A partial footprint of a smaller odeon from the Roman period, however, was found beneath some houses in the south-central area of the ancient city.

Inscriptions and artifacts found throughout the city permit some reconstruction of what Beroea was like in the first century AD, especially in regard to its religious life, even though both archaeological and inscriptional evidence for the early Roman period are slight. One inscription from the second half of the first century attests to the cult of the emperors in the city. It makes mention of a certain Tiberius Claudius Peierius, who was a high priest of the emperor cult for life, as well as a gymnasiarch and agonothete.[5] As a gymnasiarch, he would have been responsible for ordering the educational

2. Tataki, *Ancient Beroea*, 448.
3. Brocas-Deflassieux, *Béroia*, 62.
4. Brocas-Deflassieux, *Béroia*, 100, 102.
5. Tataki, *Ancient Beroea*, 199.

An inscription honoring Tiberius Claudius Peierius.

and athletic life of the young citizens in training as well as for contributing substantial funds to the gymnasium's operating expenses. As an agonothete, he would have officiated over and largely subsidized the athletic games held in honor of the emperor on some important festival occasions. The inscription also mentions the Macedonian Koinon (the "assembly of Macedonians"), the body entrusted with, among other things, the promotion and execution of the imperial cult in the province, which had its seat in Beroea. Indeed, by the end of the first century AD, Beroea had been awarded the honor of building a provincial temple of the imperial cult to one of the Flavian emperors, which was likely constructed near the northwestern gate of the city.[6] A second contemporary inscription names a Tiberius Claudius Ptolemaius as a "high priest and agonothete" of the imperial cult as well as two other citizens who were also members of the Macedonian Koinon.[7] The emperor Claudius had been honored with a monument, though its precise nature—and whether or not there had been any cultic activity associated with it—remains unknown.[8]

Other inscriptions, including one from 112/111 BC recording the names of cult officials for each of the preceding ten years, bear witness to the city

6. Brocas-Deflassieux, *Béroia*, 78–82, 100, 102.
7. Tataki, *Ancient Beroea*, 450.
8. Tataki, *Ancient Beroea*, 447, 449.

The inscription attesting to Philip V's dedication of a stoa and its rents to Athena.

being home to a cult of the hero Heracles, organized as early as the third century BC, whose sanctuary is thought to have been in the northwest area of the city.[9] There was also a sanctuary of the healing god Asclepius located nearer the heart of the city, just south of the likely location of the principal agora.[10] Several inscriptions indicate that Asclepius was revered here at least since the third century BC in tandem with his daughter Hygeia and with Apollo, who also became associated with healing. Several Greek cities, most notably Corinth and Pergamum, had sprawling health resorts where the worship of this god took center stage. The process was essentially the same everywhere. The sanctuaries were equipped with sleeping chambers, and those suffering ailments of various kinds would come to the temple, sometimes for extended stays, hoping that Asclepius would communicate to them in a dream what they needed to do to be cured. The sanctuaries were also generally equipped with other amenities, such as theaters and, as here in Beroea, a thermal bath complex.[11]

A temple of Athena, goddess of wisdom and military strategy, once stood in the city, though no traces of the sanctuary itself have been found. An inscription, however, provides evidence that Philip V, king of Macedon from 221 to 179 BC, had built a number of columned porticoes with recessed

9. Brocas-Deflassieux, *Béroia*, 66–68, 98–99.
10. Brocas-Deflassieux, *Béroia*, 98, 100.
11. Brocas-Deflassieux, *Béroia*, 69–72.

An inscription bearing a sistrum (a kind of rattle), which was the signature instrument of the Isis cult.

shops on behalf of Athena. The rent paid for the shops became a source of regular income for the maintenance of Athena's temple and its cult. There was also a temple to Aphrodite, who was worshiped in Beroea not only as the goddess of love and sexuality but also as the goddess of moral virtue and grace. The Mother Goddess, often identified with and portrayed as Cybele, was worshiped at a large temple outside of the city but within the territory that fell within Beroea's jurisdiction. Inscriptions carved into the pillars of Cybele's temple bear witness to her devotees' belief that they had received answers to the prayers they had offered to her.

As in many other Greek cities, the worship of the Egyptian goddess Isis was practiced here, as attested by votive inscriptions that particularly credit her with protecting women through childbirth. Inscriptions also bear witness to a cult of Artemis; an active cult of Atargatis, the Syrian mother goddess, as early as the third century BC; and a sanctuary of Dionysus.[12]

A particularly large stele bears a unique inscription dating from the mid-second century BC. It bears the full text of the civic law regulating the election, privileges, and duties of the gymnasiarch, his assistants, the trainers, and the administration of the gymnasium.[13] The gymnasium was a staple institution, first throughout the cities of Greece and then throughout the Hellenized world. The remains of many gymnasiums contain lecture halls,

12. Tataki, *Ancient Beroea*, 469–70; Brocas-Deflassieux, *Béroia*, 77–78, 100.
13. Brocas-Deflassieux, *Béroia*, 87–88.

The stele bearing the rules for the regulation of the gymnasium in Beroea.

a running track, an exercise yard, and bathing facilities. There are important differences between modern notions of bathing and those in practice in Paul's time. While we look to soap and water to do the actual cleaning of our bodies, the ancients relied on olive oil, which they rubbed onto their bodies and then scraped off with metal tools called strigils, removing the oil, dirt, sweat, and no doubt some outer layers of skin. The program of the gymnasium was especially geared toward the young citizens in training, to pass on Greek values and cultural knowledge as well as to develop physical strength and skill. The kinds of athletic events typically practiced in the gymnasium—running, throwing the javelin, wrestling, and boxing—tended to be those most closely associated with military training, a throwback to the needs of the independent Greek city-states of the Classical period. What is most distinctive about the gymnasium law inscription from Beroea's Hellenistic period is that it envisions a program that is exclusively focused on the development of the body and martial skills rather than on a balance between the physical and the intellectual. This is probably a function of Macedonian cities maintaining citizen armies longer into the Hellenistic period than the Greek cities to the south did. The gymnasium and stadium are believed to have been constructed just south of the city's southern walls.[14]

The earliest inscriptional evidence for the Jewish community in Beroea, which figures so prominently in the episode in Acts, dates back only to the second and third centuries AD.[15] Our view of Roman Beroea is admittedly fragmentary on account of the living city that still stands on the site. The many churches in the modern city, however, continue to bear eloquent witness both to Paul's effectiveness and to the warm reception his first hearers in the synagogue there gave to his message.

Strigils from the Archaeological Museum of Amphipolis.

14. Brocas-Deflassieux, *Béroia*, 98–99.
15. Tataki, *Ancient Beroea*, 455.

9

ATHENS

Athens in the Ministry of Paul

According to the author of Acts, Athens was, somewhat surprisingly, not on Paul's missionary itinerary. He found himself here almost by accident after fleeing Beroea on account of the hostility of some number of Jews from Thessalonica who, having caught wind of Paul's team's activity in Beroea, sent representatives to undermine his work—and safety—there. The team, including Silas and Timothy, sent Paul ahead by sea to Athens, where he would await them (Acts 17:13–15). Paul's transport would have docked at one of the three ports in Piraeus, the satellite city that also functioned as Athens's principal harbor. Acts doesn't tell us why Silas, Timothy, and perhaps other unnamed members of the missionary team stayed behind in Beroea. Paul, however, suggests that they remained behind specifically to consolidate the work among the new believers in Thessalonica (and perhaps also Beroea), to make sure that Paul's hasty departure and the hostility of the local Jewish community did not undermine their fledgling faith (1 Thess. 3:1–3).[1]

What we do learn from Acts is that Paul found himself alone in Athens with some time on his hands. As one might expect, he had a look around. His response, however, was not typical of the thousands of tourists who still flock to this ancient city. The sight of the Acropolis and the agora with their

---

1. According to Acts, Silas and Timothy only caught up with Paul in Corinth (18:1, 5), and nothing is said about Timothy's return to Thessalonica unless we infer that this was part of the purpose for Paul's leaving him and Silas behind (17:14–15). First Thessalonians 3:1–3 could suggest that Timothy accompanied Paul to Athens and was sent back to Thessalonica from there at Paul's request, since Paul chose "to be *left* alone in Athens" (v. 1) rather than to *proceed* alone in Athens.

grand temples to Athena, Poseidon, Zeus, and others of the traditional Greek gods filled him with distress rather than awe and wonder: "His spirit was provoked within him, seeing the city full of idols" (Acts 17:16). And indeed, any tourist of the excavations of Greco-Roman Athens will come away with the same impression that Paul himself did at the end of his day of meandering through the city: "People of Athens, I see that in every respect you are extremely scrupulous when it comes to piety" (17:22).

The Archaeology of Athens

Athens was, as the name suggests, especially devoted to Athena. The Acropolis, the rocky outcropping overlooking the city, was particularly sacred to Athena, the city's patron deity. Images of Athena were at one time everywhere to be seen here. If Paul had followed the path to the Acropolis, one of the first things he would have noticed was a small temple dedicated to Athena Nike sitting on the brow of the Acropolis. Nike was the goddess of victory, frequently portrayed as a winged figure bearing a laurel wreath in her hands. In this ancient temple, however, she was identified with Athena, to whom the Athenians looked historically for their own victories, and here she was sculpted as having no wings—so that she could never forsake Athens. Friezes on the north and south sides (the long sides) depict Greeks fighting the Persians, commemorating the defeat of their inveterate enemies who had previously destroyed Athens in 480 BC under Xerxes I.

A low relief of Athena dating from the fifth century BC, dubbed the "Pensive Athena" (Acropolis Museum).

Worshipers and visitors ascended by means of a long ramp that is no longer extant. Had Paul taken this path, he would have passed a statue of Marcus Agrippa—Augustus's son-in-law, right-hand man, and until his early death, designated heir—standing atop a base 27 feet tall. An honorific inscription—"The people [honor] Marcus Agrippa, son of Lucius, thrice consul, benefactor"—acknowledged Agrippa's gift of a grand odeon (a concert hall)

The Temple of Athena Nike, seen from the rear (the front of the temple faces inward toward the Acropolis).

Views of the Propylaea from the west and east.

The Erechtheion seen from the west. The portion of the temple dedicated to Athena is approached from the east.

built in the agora.[2] The sacred spaces of the Acropolis were entered through an enormous gate surrounded by columned porticoes and covered with a bright marble roof, called the Propylaea. In this area once hung a gallery of paintings depicting scenes familiar from the Homeric epics and other mythical legends (Pausanias, *Descr.* 1.22.4–7).[3] A giant statue of Athena, known as Athena Promachos, Athena "Help in Battle," stood opposite the Propylaea, greeting visitors with her imposing presence as they emerged and letting them know on whose sacred ground they were standing. Now, however, only some decorative fragments of the base that once supported the statue remain.

One of the two principal temples atop the Acropolis is the Erechtheion. Built in the late fifth century BC, this was a double temple. One portion was dedicated to the worship of Poseidon (god of the sea) and his mortal son Erechtheus (after whom the temple was named); the other part was dedicated to Athena. The temple recalls in this way the myth of the city's naming, with the two deities each making a claim, in effect, to ownership. The city decided

2. Camp, *Archaeology of Athens*, 189.
3. Camp, *Archaeology of Athens*, 84.

in favor of Athena, but Poseidon continued to be duly honored in this city by the sea. The structure also was supposed to have altars to Hephaestus and Zeus and to house the tomb of Kekrops, the mythical king of Athens.[4] Perhaps the most distinctive feature of the Erechtheion is the group of columns on the south side depicting female devotees of Athena known as caryatids, maidens shown bearing baskets of offerings on their heads.

The most famous structure on the Acropolis is the iconic Parthenon, built in the fifth century BC and dedicated to Athena Parthenos, the "Virgin Athena." Within the Parthenon was a colossal statue of the goddess, estimated to have stood 40 feet tall (see the description of the statue in Pausanius, *Descr.* 1.24.5–7). The cult image was sculpted under the supervision of Pheidias in the mid-fifth century BC. He was the same artist who created the cult statue of the enthroned Zeus for the temple at Olympia, a statue that would be listed by ancient tourists as one of the seven must-see sights—or wonders—of the world. The triangular pediments on the east and west sides were once adorned with elaborate mythological scenes: on the west side, the contest between Poseidon and Athena for the devotion of the city; on the east, the side of the main entrance, the birth of Athena, who emerged fully grown and fully armed from the head of Zeus (Pausanias, *Descr.* 1.24.5). Friezes around the exterior perimeter of the roof also depicted scenes from mythology as well as a long

Steve Swayne / CC BY 2.0 / Wikimedia Commons

The Parthenon, viewed from the northwest.

4. Camp, *Archaeology of Athens*, 93–95; see also Pausanias, *Descr.* 1.26–27.

sequence depicting the Panathenaic procession. This was the highlight of the Athenian religious calendar, involving sacrifices of scores of oxen, public feasts, and, every four years, Olympic-style games, all in honor of Athena.

The only new building erected on the Acropolis during the Roman period was a shrine to the emperor Augustus and the goddess Roma. It was built in front of the entrance to the Parthenon. Henceforth all devotees of Athena would also acknowledge the power that had brought Greece under Rome's rule. The shrine was circular, about 25 feet in diameter, with a roof resting on eight columns. It was likely an open-air altar rather than a temple proper, as it appears to have lacked room for a sanctuary and cult images. As mentioned previously, the imperial cult, generally celebrating the deified personification of Rome itself alongside a particular emperor, was a widespread phenomenon throughout the Eastern Mediterranean, including Greece. It had its origins in the worship of benefactors and rulers—those whose gifts and power matched that of the gods and, therefore, merited gratitude and honor such as were given to the gods.

A small statue of Athena widely regarded as a miniature of the cult image that once stood in the Parthenon (National Archaeological Museum, Athens).

The names "Goddess Roma and Augustus Caesar" are clearly visible in the inscription from the architrave. Augustus is strikingly here called "savior,"

A segment of the Panathenaic frieze from the Parthenon. Athena and Hephaestus are seated while devotees examine the garment (a peplos) that would clothe Athena's cult statue and other accoutrements for the festival (The British Museum).

The remains of the shrine of Augustus and Roma with the Parthenon behind it.

The dedicatory inscription from the architrave of the shrine of Augustus and Roma. Note the third line of the text: *Rōmēs kai Sebastou sōtēros* (of Rome and Augustus, savior).

a title he won probably in connection with his victory in the civil wars that plagued the entire Mediterranean from Italy to Egypt from about 44 to 31 BC. Paul's message of a savior of a very different sort, who would nevertheless one day usher in a new order—a new kingdom with a resurrected Galilean as the head of state—was an overtly political one.

Athena shared her sacred space with other deities as well. Below the Acropolis on its north side were caves hallowed as sites sacred to Pan, Aphrodite, and Apollo. A number of temples sat on the path down the southern slope of the Acropolis. About halfway down this path one finds a temple and sacred area dedicated to Asclepius, god of healing (see the discussion of Asclepions in chap. 8).

At the base of the Acropolis sit the remains of the Theatre of Dionysus, the god of the vine, whose temple once stood just south of the theater. Almost nothing of the stage building survives, though a frieze in high relief celebrating scenes of Dionysus's life (dating from renovations undertaken under Hadrian in the early second century AD) remains. The worship of Dionysus included not only traditional rites and sacrifices but also dramatic performances of tragic plays as part of the annual Dionysia, the major festival in honor of the god. It was here, and in that religious context, that the famous Oedipus trilogy of Sophocles and the Oresteia trilogy of Aeschylus were first performed. The tragedies, whose plots always involved deaths, and the satyr plays that followed, were a kind of dramatic and symbolic sacrifice offered to Dionysus during the mornings of festivals, while comedies (such as those by Aristophanes and Menander) were performed in the afternoon to lighten the mood.

Athens boasted a grand temple to Olympian Zeus, the king of the gods. While only one cluster of 13 (and 2 additional) pillars out of an original

Asclepius with his staff and a serpent coiled around it (National Archaeological Museum, Athens).

View of the three-tiered Theatre of Dionysus, carved into the base of the Acropolis. Freestanding theaters would only come with the Roman invention of concrete.

A statue of Menander, a Greek comic playwright, from the area of the Theatre of Dionysus. In the centuries around the turn of the era, the epic poet Homer, the tragic playwright Euripides, and the comic poet Menander were the most widely read authors in school exercises, suggesting that those wishing to acquire the equivalent of first-century cultural literacy should begin with these three authors.

forest of 124 remain, they continue to dwarf visitors and remind them of the original grandeur of the cult site. While work on the foundations was initiated in the sixth century BC, the construction of the temple only started in earnest under the patronage of Antiochus IV of Syria—the king who is known for the brutal repression of Judaism in the Jerusalem of 167 BC, which gave rise to the Maccabean Revolt.[5] The structure was on its way to covering a footprint of 120 by 47 yards, but Antiochus's funds were too limited and his life too short to complete the project.[6] The temple would finally be completed almost three centuries later by Hadrian (ruled AD 117–138), perhaps the most "pro-Greek" of all the Roman emperors.

Perhaps the best preserved of all the temples from the period of Classical Greece is the Temple of Hephaestus and Athena Ergane. Hephaestus was the craftsman of the gods, often depicted working metal at a forge; as "Ergane," Athena was celebrated as the patron of pottery workers. It is perhaps appropriate, then, that this temple was erected at the northeastern edge of the main marketplace of the city, the agora. Panels of carved reliefs (called metopes) depicted the labors of Heracles and the exploits of Theseus.[7] The temple was reused as a church in the Byzantine period, which accounts for its marvelous state of preservation. Since it continued to be used and occupied, its resources were not quarried for other, newer buildings. Temples to Apollo and Ares also stood within the agora, as did an altar to Zeus.

---

5. See the narrative accounts of Antiochus's activity and the outbreak of revolt in 1 Macc. 1–3 and 2 Macc. 3–8 and the historical reconstruction in deSilva, *Judea under Greek and Roman Rule*, 29–41.

6. Camp, *Archaeology of Athens*, 174.

7. Camp, *Archaeology of Athens*, 102.

The Temple of Olympian Zeus, seen from the southeast. The distance between the cluster of pillars and the single pillars gives some sense of the original scope of the temple. The Acropolis is visible to the northwest.

The Temple of Hephaestus, seen from the southwest.

A small part of the Athenian agora with the Temple of Hephaestus in the background.

The city was thus, indeed, "full of idols," as the author of Acts tells us (17:16). And so, alongside preaching the good news about Jesus in the Jewish synagogue, Paul also took at once to open-air evangelism in the agora. Sprawling out below the Acropolis, the agora was the main center for commerce and government. Here were to be found the city's council chamber, courthouses, and mint. The agora had large areas of open space where merchants, craftspersons, and vendors of all kinds could set up their tables and awnings, but it was also bounded with large columned porticoes, some of which featured shops that merchants and craftspersons could rent. One, the Stoa of Attalus, has been thoroughly reconstructed to give visitors a sense of the grandeur of these gathering places.

Athens was at the center of the emergence of each of the major Greek philosophical schools. Socrates was a much-misunderstood citizen of Athens, whose constant questioning of his fellow citizens' understanding of things and probing of their critical-thinking skills led eventually to his alienation, conviction, and execution. He would be remembered as the father of philosophy, with every school claiming him in some respect as their hero. One of Socrates's most devoted students, Plato, founded his academy here, which would flourish for centuries. It was also in the columned porticoes—the stoai—of Athens's agora that the Stoic philosophy, founded by Zeno of Citium, took shape and took hold. Stoics were interested in every aspect of life and science but were especially famed for their ethics, which focused on strategies for mastering the desires, emotions, and feelings that could potentially lead a person away from choosing the virtuous course of action

A modern reconstruction of the Stoa of Attalus, so named because the second-century BC original was a gift of Attalus II, King of Pergamum, to the city.

in every situation (a problem for which Paul offered a distinctively different solution; cf. Gal. 5:16–25).

When Paul preached in the agora, his message attracted the attention of the Stoics present but also of the Epicureans: "Some of the Epicurean and Stoic philosophers who were present began to engage him: some were saying, 'What would this babbler wish to say?' but others, 'He appears to be a promoter of strange divinities,' because he was proclaiming the good news of Jesus and 'Resurrection'" (Acts 17:18), which some hearers misunderstood as the name of another strange god. Epicurus saw religion and belief in the gods and an afterlife as means of social control and enslavement, and he preached freedom from superstition. Philodemus, a later disciple of Epicurus, summarized the school's fundamental creed thus: "Nothing to fear from gods, nothing to feel in death, the good can be attained, the evil can be endured."[8] Although Epicurus himself was highly committed to a virtuous life as the best way to a trouble-free existence, many of his followers, freed from the fear of the gods and judgment, were not so high-minded and found here a license for indulgence, leading to the negative connotations that would adhere to the term "Epicurean." Public speakers and philosophers seeking to gain a following routinely used the agora as a venue for promoting their ideas or themselves and inviting people to sit with them in one of the colonnades for a more in-depth conversation, perhaps even leading to conversion.

During the early Roman period, a second agora was developed to the east of the ancient agora. A monumental entrance gate opened into the Forum of Julius and Augustus. The open courtyard and covered porticoes appear to have become the main commercial spaces for the city. At the eastern end of the forum stood an octagonal building called the Tower of the Winds after the carvings around its top, each representing one of the eight (not four!) winds and the seasonal changes they bring. Dating from the mid-second century BC, this early scientific marvel functioned as a water clock, a calendar (tracing the movements of the sun), a weather vane, and a planetarium all in one.

Paul's preaching in the agora, which captured the attention of some resident philosophers, led in turn to his being brought before the Areopagus. The Areopagus was a judicial body that had met in an open-air structure on the rocky outcropping known as Mars Hill (in Greek, *Areios pagos*), from which the council took its name. By Hellenistic and Roman times, the council met in a hall in the Athenian agora. Luke may understate the seriousness of the

---

8. This appears to summarize the first four sayings of Epicurus's "Principal Doctrines" (*Kyriai Doxai*). The text appears in *PHerc* 1005.4.10–14.

The western gate of the Forum of Julius and Augustus, erected in the late first century BC.

A view of the eastern half of the Forum of Julius and Augustus.

The Tower of the Winds.

situation in which Paul found himself. He was, in all likelihood, brought not to the physical space known as Mars Hill in order to preach more broadly to the Athenian people but rather before the judicial council known as the Areopagus, wherever they happened to be meeting around AD 50.[9] This council was charged with, among other things, investigating crimes of sacrilege against the gods. Their seemingly polite inquiry—"May we know what this new teaching is that you are presenting, for you are introducing some foreign things to our ears" (Acts 17:19–20)—may well have hidden a more official agenda, an initial investigation of this new message with a view to determining whether it should be allowed in the city at all. And such an agenda was not without some degree of menace. Socrates himself had been condemned to death by the Areopagus in the fourth century BC for introducing new gods (among other things), a suspicion also raised in regard to Paul: "He seems to be a preacher of strange divinities" (Acts 17:18; cf. Plato, *Euthyphr.* 3B; *Apol.* 24B; Xenophon, *Mem.* 1.1).[10]

9. Camp, *Archaeology of Athens*, 195.
10. Joshua Jipp ("Paul's Areopagus Speech") argues that Luke intends for his audience to recognize this parallel.

The Areopagus, seen from the ascent to the Acropolis.

Paul's ability to read audiences and situations is evident in the manner of his presentation of his message before the Areopagus. He claims that he is not presenting some new cult but rather promoting a time-honored deity that the Athenians themselves recognize, though only on some obscure altar as "an unknown god": "Athenians, in every way I see you to be exceedingly scrupulous where religion is concerned. For as I was passing through and looking at the objects you revere, I found also an altar on which stood the inscription 'To an unknown god.' What therefore you revere without clear knowledge, this I proclaim to you" (Acts 17:22–23).

As Paul's speech is represented in Acts, there are two rather bold barbs in his words. The word often translated "very religious" can, in fact, mean "very careful to observe all piety," but it can also be used in a derogatory fashion to mean "superstitious, [exceedingly] scrupulous." It is the term that Plutarch would later use when writing his essay on foreign cults (including Judaism) that he despises—a book title often rendered in English as *On Superstition*. The word rendered above as "without clear knowledge" can also mean "in ignorance." It might be argued that Paul would never risk insulting his audience with his opening lines—and he certainly doesn't do it blatantly—but he does go on to contrast the religious practice he sees going on everywhere in Athens with what even the Greek philosophers, at their best, would say about the nature of deity and the proper ways to think about and interact with deity. And so Paul continues:

> The God who made the world and all that is in it—this One, being Lord of heaven and earth, does not live in temples fashioned by hands, nor is he served by human hands as if needing anything (he himself giving life and breath and everything to all). He made from one [person?] every nation of people, for them to inhabit the whole face of the earth, setting the appointed seasons and the boundaries for their dwelling, so that they would search for God, if somehow they might reach out for him and find him who is indeed not far from each one of us. For "in him we live and move and exist"; as also some of your poets have said, "For we are also his offspring." Being God's offspring, then, we ought not to think the deity to be like gold, or silver, or stone, an impression made by the art and imagination of human beings. God, therefore, overlooking the times of ignorance, now commands all people everywhere to repent, even as he has set a day on which he will judge the world in righteousness through the man whom he has appointed, giving proof to all by raising him from the dead. (Acts 17:24–31)

Paul's presentation of his message aligns closely with Greek and Roman philosophers' criticisms of idols and other facets of popular religion. Many of the philosophers in the agora would have agreed that there is ultimately only one God, that he is the creator of all that is, that he stands in need of nothing from us (for example, the animal sacrifices are not *needed* by deity, as if for food), that his house is all of creation and not the stone buildings built as temples, and that images do injustice to him who transcends human and visible form. As support, Paul even introduces quotations from Greek philosophers and poets: the Cretan poet Epimenides, who wrote that in God "we live and move and have our being," and Cleanthes, the student and successor of Zeno of Citium, founder of the Stoic school, whose famous "Hymn to Zeus" includes the line "We are your offspring."[11] Since Paul was familiar with their own native critics of the traditional practice of religion and the sentiments of their own revered philosophers, the members of the Areopagus would have had to acknowledge that his message had deeps roots in Athenian tradition, even if Paul went on to lose most of his audience in his claim that a man had come back from the dead and would someday return as judge of all.

Athens was indeed a city in which many gods enjoyed long-standing reverence and worship and into which new cults entered only with difficulty. The

11. Keener, *Acts*, 446.

one exception to this was, of course, the cult of the Roman emperor, whose favor came to be every bit as important to the city as Athena's. It is perhaps not entirely surprising that Acts portrays Paul as having only modest success making inroads into this center both of classical civilization and of traditional religion. The fact that the author of Acts remembers and specifically mentions two by name—Dionysius the Areopagite (a member of that very council before which Paul had been brought) and a woman named Damaris—suggests that these conversions had staying power and probably eventually even led to the founding of a growing congregation in the symbolic center of the Greek world.

10

ROMAN CORINTH

Corinth in the Ministry of Paul

The city of Corinth was a major focus of the apostle Paul's work as a church planter and as a pastor. We know more about the Christians in Corinth, and more about Paul's relationship with this network of congregations, than we do about any other first-century Christian community. Acts 18:1–18 provides a rich description of Paul's initial visit to the city, a visit that spanned at least one and a half years (18:11), and perhaps even longer, depending on how one understands the hearing before Gallio to play into Paul's timetable in Corinth (18:12–18). Paul would visit Corinth on at least two more occasions after this founding visit (2 Cor. 1:15–17; 12:14; 13:1), and he would write no fewer than four letters to his converts there: (1) an early letter that has not survived (referred to in 1 Cor. 5:9–11), (2) 1 Corinthians, (3) a painful letter that has also not survived (referred to in 2 Cor. 2:1–4), and (4) 2 Corinthians.[1]

Each of these letters would have been carried and read to the congregations by one of the members of Paul's ministry team. Our 1 Corinthians was delivered by Timothy (1 Cor. 16:10). The painful letter was delivered by Titus, who no doubt had to use his personal diplomatic skills to help turn the tide there in Paul's favor (2 Cor. 7:13–14). As Paul writes our 2 Corinthians, he talks about Titus's eagerness to travel back to Corinth—no doubt bearing 2 Corinthians in his hands (2 Cor. 8:6, 16–18)—to oversee

1. The possibility that 2 Corinthians represents an edited collection of a number of Paul's letters has been a major focus of scholarly debate. For the arguments for and against this view, see deSilva, *Introduction to the New Testament*, 504–6, 510–13, and the literature cited therein.

the completion of the Corinthians' contributions to the important collection project that Paul had initiated among his Gentile churches on behalf of the poor in the Jewish churches in Judea. This was, for him, an important symbol of the solidarity of his congregations with the mother church in Jerusalem as well as the unity and reciprocity of all the churches in Christ. We learn from Romans 15:25–27 that these churches did in fact come through with their contribution to the collection, which also suggests that Paul and his Corinthian congregations were able at last to work through the difficulties that beset them. Paul wrote Romans from Corinth (Rom. 15:25–28; 16:23), sending it to Rome by the hand—and, in all probability, through the voice—of Phoebe, the patron and deacon of a house church in Cenchreae, one of Corinth's satellite port cities (Rom. 16:1–2). Paul would then set out from Cenchreae with the relief funds for Jerusalem, leading to the most trying phase of his career—his four-year imprisonment split between Caesarea Maritima and Rome itself.

The extensive excavations at Corinth coupled with the extensive biblical texts about or addressed to the Christian communities in Corinth make for particularly rich connections between the two, grounding many facets of the texts in the lived world of its recipients.

The Archaeology of the Roman Colony of Corinth

Corinth is a city whose history displays a dramatic before and after. It was a thriving Greek city with an ancient history, but the life of *that* city came to an abrupt and violent end in 146 BC as a consequence of its role in the Achaean League's revolt against the Roman Republic's intrusion into Greek affairs. Lucius Mummius, a Roman consul and part of the leadership of the Roman forces, allowed his soldiers to destroy Old Corinth's walls and defenses, plunder its treasures, massacre its male citizens, and sell many of its women and children as slaves (Pausanias, *Descr.* 2.1.2; 7.16.7–10; Strabo, *Geogr.* 8.6.23b; Dio Cassius, *Hist. rom.* 21). While Corinth was not left completely uninhabited in the decades that followed (Cicero, *Tusc.* 3.53), it ceased to be anything like a functioning city.

The city lay essentially in ruins for a hundred years until it was founded afresh as a Roman colony—the Colonia Laus Julia Corinthiensis—by Julius Caesar in 46 BC (Dio Cassius, *Hist. rom.* 43.50.3–5). "New Corinth" would have celebrated its centennial only after Paul's first visit was complete. The Roman character of the new city is dramatically displayed in the fact that 101 out of 104 inscriptions found at the site dating from the time of Julius Caesar through the time of Hadrian are written in Latin, with only the remaining

A satellite image of the isthmus of Corinth.

three written in Greek.[2] The new colony was first settled primarily with military veterans and freed persons ("freedmen")—former slaves who, though free, still occupied a social stratum below that of freeborn persons (Strabo, *Geogr.* 8.6.23c; Crinagoras, *Anth. Gr.* 9.284). As such, it was a city of opportunity for a newly landed class, merchants, craftspersons, and—something rare indeed in the ancient world—social climbers.

The city of Corinth stands on a narrow isthmus between the Aegean and Adriatic Seas, whence came Horace's epithet "twin-sea'd Corinth" (*Carm.* 1.7.2). It was well placed to profit from trade between the eastern and western Mediterranean. The city had two satellite ports: Cenchreae, 6 miles to the east, and Lechaion, 1.5 miles to the north. In Paul's day, ships bearing cargoes from the east across the Aegean could unload in Cenchreae. Their goods would be transported over land to the harbor of Lechaion on the west side of the isthmus, sitting on the Adriatic, where the cargoes would be loaded onto other ships heading for Italy. This facilitated trade between east and west by eliminating the long and often dangerous sea voyage around the whole of southern Greece.

Efforts were made to make trade and passage from east to west even more efficient as early as the Archaic period. In the sixth century BC, a path (called

2. Murphy-O'Connor, *St. Paul's Corinth*, 8.

the Diolkos) was laid out with great flagstones at the narrowest point of the isthmus, allowing smaller ships—whether military, merchant, or both—to be hauled across the 3.5 mile track on special carts (Strabo, *Geogr.* 8.2.1; 8.6.4). There were obvious limitations, but it served the needs of smaller vessels. In AD 67, the emperor Nero initiated an attempt to cut a canal across the isthmus along this road to open up a direct path for ships (Suetonius, *Nero* 19; Philostratus, *Vit. Apoll.* 4.24; 5.19). Flavius Josephus reports that the Roman general Vespasian, in charge of suppressing the Jewish revolt that erupted in Judea and Galilee in AD 66, sent six thousand Jewish prisoners of war from Galilee as slaves to labor on Nero's project (*J.W.* 3.540). The work proved too difficult, however, and the project was abandoned until modern engineering made it possible in the nineteenth century.

The costs of transporting the cargoes from port to port through the city, the import and export taxes on the goods passing through, and the incidental expenses of sailors and merchants that sought Corinth's entertainments and hospitality all contributed to Corinth's wealth. As Strabo, the important Greek traveler and author, observed, "Corinth is called 'wealthy' because of its commerce, since it is situated on the isthmus and is master of two harbors, of which the one leads straight to Asia, and the other to Italy; . . . and it makes easy the exchange of merchandise from both countries that are so far distant from each other" (*Geogr.* 8.6.20a, 22a).[3] The city was also ideally located for north-south land travel, as this same isthmus was the only land bridge between northern Greece and the entire Peloponnese. The geography all but predetermined that this would be the site of a thriving city.

The new Roman colony of Corinth was laid out in a typical grid pattern around a central forum across an area of about 0.5 miles (north-south) by 1.5 miles (east-west). Residential blocks were typically about 120 feet (east-west) by 240 feet (north-south), though some were 120 by 120 feet and some were 120 by 480 feet, depending on the spacing of the east-west roads from one another.[4] Most of the north-south streets (the *cardines*) were only 12 feet wide, and the east-west streets (the *decumani*) 20 feet wide. There was an affluent, desirable, and parklike residential area, called the Craneum, located southeast of the forum (Plutarch, *On Exile* 6 [*Mor.* 601b]).[5]

The central forum occupied a space of approximately 15,300 square yards, an uncommonly large area.[6] While many Greek cities and Roman colonies had both an administrative forum and a commercial forum, Corinth's forum

3. Translation from Murphy-O'Connor, *St. Paul's Corinth*, 53.
4. Murphy-O'Connor, *St. Paul's Corinth*, 21–22.
5. Murphy-O'Connor, *St. Paul's Corinth*, 22.
6. Murphy-O'Connor, *St. Paul's Corinth*, 27.

The Roman forum of Corinth.

Remains of shops at the west end of the forum's northern portico.

appears to have served both functions. The forum itself was marked off by columned, covered porticoes on all four sides, behind many of which sat rows of shops rented by artisans and merchants of every kind or shops converted to serve administrative functions in the new colony.

The South Stoa was laid out in the fourth century BC as a row of thirty-three two-roomed shops running over 300 feet in total length. When the colony was refounded, many of these shops were converted into civic offices, including an oval council chamber, a public fountain, an archive, and offices for the officials connected with the Isthmian games.[7] These Olympic-style games had been held every second year in the nearby city of Isthmia and brought tourists to the isthmus in droves. The games were celebrated in Corinth itself, however, between 40 BC and AD 50 before returning to Isthmia, possibly in

7. Murphy-O'Connor, *St. Paul's Corinth*, 28.

Remains of second-century AD shops at the southwest corner of the forum.

AD 50 or 51 (Paul's first year in Corinth).[8] The city's athletic facilities are not well excavated and are almost never visited, but there was a gymnasium complex and likely also a racecourse south of the Asclepion.[9] The ongoing presence of these games and officials in the city's life is a reminder of the prominence of athletic competitions in Paul's world and is a possible source of Paul's own use of athletic imagery—for example, his use of metaphors from boxing and foot races in 1 Corinthians 9:24–26. It is notable that the wreath given to victors in the Isthmian games was braided from withered celery (Plutarch, *Quaest. conv.* 5.3.1–3 [*Mor.* 675d–677b]), giving poignancy to Paul's contrast between the "rotting" wreath for which athletes compete and the "imperishable" wreath with which Paul and his fellow converts seek to be crowned for their victory over the impulses of the flesh (1 Cor. 9:25). The Corinthian Christians, many of whom would have been regular spectators of the Isthmian games, would also certainly resonate with Paul when

8. Murphy-O'Connor, *St. Paul's Corinth*, 13. The question of when the games returned to Isthmia admittedly remains open. See Harrison, "Paul and the *Agōnothetai*," 279–80; Winter, *After Paul Left Corinth*, 276–78.

9. Romano, "City Planning, Centuriation, and Land Division," 289; Murphy-O'Connor, *St. Paul's Corinth*, 34.

Several of the shops lining the forum's south portico (top) and the interior of the bouleuterion, the meeting hall of the city council (bottom).

he spoke of the "rules" governing athletic competitions and the potential for disqualifying oneself from the prize (9:27).

The forum was split into unequal northern and southern halves by a row of shops extending into the center from the eastern side. Halfway down this row, the series of shops was interrupted by a shrine to Ephesian Artemis, whose influence had spread to mainland Greece (Pausanias, *Descr.* 2.2.6). Near the center of the forum, in line with this row, stood the "tribunal" or

Statues of Augustus (center) and his adopted heirs, Caius and Lucius (left and right), from the eastern basilica (Archaeological Museum of Ancient Corinth).

bēma. This structure was probably most comparable to a rostrum, a platform from which orators would address the gathered citizenry on public occasions and a likely place for the Roman governor to make public appearances. At the easternmost side of the forum stood a basilica, a large columned hall that typically served judicial functions in Roman cities. It was adorned with statues of Augustus and his family, including his two grandsons, Caius and Lucius, who were originally slated to succeed him before their untimely deaths cleared Tiberius's way to the succession.[10]

As the city's economy grew, another large market area arose to the north of the main forum. This secondary forum consisted of forty-some permanent shops arranged around a central open space for the sale of wares and foods from portable kiosks. One row of these shops has been thoroughly excavated, revealing alcoves of a fairly standard 13 feet high by 13 feet deep, but varying between 9 and 13 feet wide, each with a large doorway of about 7 feet. They appear to have been fitted with lofts accessible by stone steps and wooden ladders. These lofts served as the makeshift residences for the artisans and merchants working in the shops below.

10. Murphy-O'Connor, *St. Paul's Corinth*, 28.

A row of shops in the secondary market north of the Temple of Apollo.

Paul was the pioneer of "tentmaker ministries." To support himself while in Corinth, he plied his trade as a leatherworker, a main product being leather tents. His words to his converts in Thessalonica could equally well have been addressed to the Corinthian congregations that he would plant: "You remember our labor and toil, brothers and sisters; we worked night and day, so that we might not burden any of you while we proclaimed to you the gospel of God" (1 Thess. 2:9 NRSV; see 1 Cor. 9:4–6, 12, 15–18; 2 Cor. 11:7–11; 12:12–13). Paul wanted to distinguish himself very clearly from the many marketplace and roadside preachers that his future converts regularly encountered at Corinth, as in any other major city, peddling one or another philosophy or religion as a means of profiting from those who would listen to and learn from them.

Paul likely spent most of his waking hours in Corinth working at his trade in one of the shops recessed behind the porticoes surrounding the main forum or the north forum (or perhaps in another such row of shops yet to be discovered).[11] He no doubt counted himself fortunate to have found Priscilla (or Prisca) and Aquila, fellow Jews, in Corinth already well established in their rented workshop, plying the same trade as his. When the emperor Claudius expelled the Jews from Rome in AD 49 (Suetonius, *Claud.* 25),[12] Priscilla and

11. For more on the conditions of Paul's craft, see Murphy-O'Connor, *St. Paul's Corinth*, 192–98.
12. Smallwood, *Jews under Roman Rule*, 210–16.

The Temple of Apollo.

the sun god; Necessity, a personification or deification of the idea of fate; and the Mother Goddess.

Perhaps the oldest surviving structure in downtown Corinth is the Temple of Apollo. It had a footprint of 27 by 58 yards, its roof supported by 38 massive Doric columns (6 at the front and back, 15 along each long side).[17] It was built around 550 BC on an elevated plateau, the site of an even earlier Apollo temple, and renovated early in the Roman period. It overlooked the surrounding Roman-period shops (both the new north market and the northern shops of the central forum), civic buildings, and porticoes, just as it had the Hellenistic- and Classical-era city of Old Corinth in past centuries. This was a physical and spatial symbol of the traditional Greco-Roman gods looking out over, and looking out for, the life of the city. For most of Corinth's inhabitants, this would have been a welcome reminder of the gods' sheltering presence.

Southwest of the Temple of Apollo (and west of the forum) stood a temple to Hera, the wife of Zeus and queen of the gods, once rising above the shops in the northwest corner of the forum. In the square north of the Hera temple and west of the Apollo temple was a public fountain, named the Fountain of

17. Pfaff, "Archaic Architecture," 112. The corner columns are included in the count for each side.

The scant remains of the Asclepion.

Glauke after the ill-fated princess of Corinth courted by Jason and poisoned by Medea (Pausanias, *Descr.* 2.3.6), a story that forms the basis of Euripides's tragic play *Medea*.

Corinth was also home to a well-known Asclepion, a sacred precinct dedicated to Asclepius, the god of healing, that included a sleeping area where "patients" would seek a dream vision of the god giving instructions for a cure or miraculously effecting the cure. Votive statues of the afflicted body parts were offered by those who believed themselves to have received healing by the god's intervention. The number and variety of these housed in the Archaeological Museum of Ancient Corinth bear witness to the many customers satisfied by the treatments offered in the Asclepion. The Asclepion was also something of a health spa, with recreational areas and multiple dining rooms that could be used by the local elites for entertaining, inviting their guests to dine at the god's table.[18] Indeed, social events throughout the city were almost always connected with honoring one local deity or another. Paul's converts in Corinth would have a difficult time getting along socially while also avoiding the tables of idols in every respect. How far *could* they go? Where *must* they draw the line? The

18. Murphy-O'Connor, *St. Paul's Corinth*, 189.

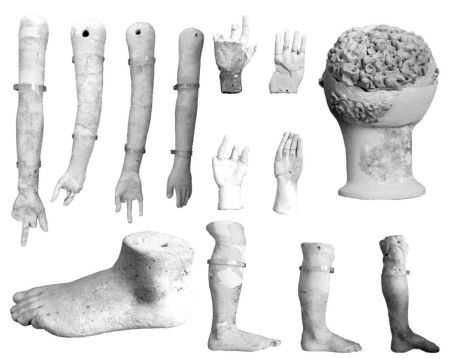

Clay models of body parts deposited in the Asclepion as testimonies to devotees' experiences of healing.

intersection of religion and all social activities in a Roman colony explains Paul's significant investment in dealing with these challenges in 1 Corinthians 8 and 10.[19]

Several smaller temples and cult sites stood within the forum itself. A temple of Tyche or Fortuna stood in the northwest area of the forum, south of the north stoa and its shops (Pausanias, *Descr.* 2.2.8). A head from a cult image of Tyche has been discovered on the spot. Temples of Venus (the mythical progenitrix of Julius Caesar and his line) and Apollo Clarios graced the southwest area of the forum (Pausanias, *Descr.* 2.2.8), at least the former dating from the time of Augustus. As already noted, a small shrine to Ephesian Artemis interrupted the central row of shops. According to Pausanias (*Descr.* 2.4.5), sanctuaries of Jupiter Capitolinus and Athena once stood in the vicinity of the theater, located some 200 yards northwest of the forum. Jupiter Capitolinus connected the cult in Corinth with the worship of Jupiter, Juno, and Minerva (Athena) in a grand temple on the Capitoline Hill

19. See also Murphy-O'Connor, *St. Paul's Corinth*, 186–90.

An inscription "to the divine Julius Caesar" (left) and the head of a statue of Julius Caesar (right) (Archaeological Museum of Ancient Corinth).

The Temple of Octavia, seen from the west.

in Rome, overlooking the Roman Forum. It appears to have been typical for Roman colonies to have such a temple, uniting them with the central cult of the mother city.

There were also some newer "gods" in Corinth. The Roman Senate pronounced Julius Caesar, who had refounded Corinth as a Roman colony, a god after his death in 44 BC. He was historically the first Roman to be granted that status, but many of his successors would come to be divinized as well. The cult of Julius Caesar, Augustus, and later emperors spread across the Mediterranean as an expression of loyalty and gratitude to the imperial family—and as a bid for imperial favors. A temple to Divus Iulius (the Deified Julius) was located somewhere in the city, probably in the area of the forum. A fragment of a dedicatory inscription "to the divine Julius Caesar" as well as several pieces of what might have served as a cult statue of Julius were found on site. Given Julius's personal interest in revitalizing and resettling Corinth (a policy advanced also by his immediate successor, Augustus), it is not difficult to imagine the inhabitants of New Corinth being quite enthusiastic promoters of the imperial cult in their city.

Another temple connected to the imperial cult was erected to the west of the forum, possibly for the worship of Octavia, the sister of the emperor Augustus and widow of Marc Antony, who had abandoned her in favor of his ill-fated union with Cleopatra VII (Pausanias, *Descr.* 2.3.1). Though little remains of the temple today, its sacred precincts originally covered an area as large as those connected to the Temple of Apollo. The temple itself had a footprint of 20 by 40 yards, surrounded by a courtyard occupying a space of about 80 by 140 yards, with porticoes running along three of its sides, leaving the central space visible from the forum below.[20] Olympic-style games held in honor of the reigning emperor were also inaugurated in 30 BC and held every fourth year in conjunction with the Isthmian games. Though these were technically an independent series of contests, the occasional linkage gave "international" profile to Corinth's games in honor of the emperor.[21]

Jews were historically known for their avoidance of participation in the worship of any gods beside the God of Israel. Many Greeks and Romans actually considered Jews atheists on account of their denial of the reality of any god but their own. Nevertheless, they were a long-tolerated oddity in the ancient world. Paul's Gentile converts, however, would have been seen quite differently: their neighbors would have regarded them as *betraying* the gods of their forebears and fellow citizens for the sake of their new and quite intentionally chosen devotion to a foreign cult. Religious rites were also native to the home. While the form these took in Roman homes differed from those performed in the homes of the Greek population, they would still have involved the worship of deities and spirit beings other than the God of Israel and would have placed Christian wives and slaves of non-Christian heads of

---

20. Romano, "City Planning, Centuriation, and Land Division," 286.

21. Harrison, "Paul and the *Agōnothetai*," 280. See also Winter, *After Paul Left Corinth*, 271–76, on developments in the imperial cult in the province of Achaia during Paul's dealings with the Corinthian Christians.

households in challenging situations, even at home.[22] It is no wonder that at least some converts would seek to make a case for "eating food sacrificed to idols" (1 Cor. 8:1–4) so as to secure smoother relationships with their neighbors and former associates. If they could just allow themselves to be seen frequenting the temples and joining their neighbors when invited to dinner in the temples' "fellowship halls," things would go much more easily for them. Paul, however, draws a sharp line: "What pagans sacrifice, they sacrifice to demons and not to God. I do not want you to be partners with demons. You cannot drink the cup of the Lord and the cup of demons. You cannot partake of the table of the Lord and the table of demons" (1 Cor. 10:20–21 NRSV). Christians must not compromise their witness that there is indeed only one God and one Lord.

However, Paul would give them some latitude when it came to buying meat from the marketplace. Corinth had its central macellum (meat market) in the northeast quarter of the downtown area, at least by the time of Augustus.[23] This area was approached from the northeast quadrant of the forum through an impressive three-arched gateway that opened onto the main road leading to the port of Lechaion, 1.5 miles to the north.[24] Perhaps still a gravel path

The Lechaion Road, looking north.

22. Ehrensperger, "Between Polis, Oikos, and Ekklesia." Ehrensperger also raises the emotional and personal difficulties of leaving behind *all* cultic interactions, when, prior to giving one's life to Jesus, one believed that the good graces of those gods and spirit beings determined one's own good and the good of one's city.

23. Harrison, "Introduction," 14.

24. Koursoumis, "Corinth," 55.

The Lower Peirene Fountain.

at the time of Paul's visit, it would eventually be paved and surrounded by colonnades and covered sidewalks on either side during the citywide renovations and restorations following an earthquake in AD 77.[25] Walking north through the gate, one would first pass by the Lower Peirene Fountain, an important public water source in Paul's time, on the right. The spring-fed reservoir could be accessed through the six archways at the southern side. Its large courtyard was a likely place for pleasant loitering, though again, the form in which visitors see it today represents a later rebuild of the Peirene Fountain that postdates Paul's visits.[26]

Further north from the Peirene Fountain sat the macellum. By the time Pausanias visited Corinth in the second century AD, this area had been converted into an enclosed area, which might have functioned as a shrine to Apollo (Pausanias, *Descr.* 2.3.3). Some portion of the meat sold here came from animal sacrifices that had been performed in the city's temples. This was an important regular source of revenue for those temples and, in peak holy seasons, one of the few times that meat would be more generally affordable. In 1 Corinthians 10:25, when Paul told his converts to "eat whatever is sold in the meat market without raising any question on the ground of conscience"

25. Murphy-O'Connor, *St. Paul's Corinth*, 29.
26. Murphy-O'Connor, *St. Paul's Corinth*, 29.

The first-century macellum.

(NRSV), he was likely referring to this well-known space. Paul claimed that the meat itself was not in any way "contaminated" by virtue of having come from a pagan sacrifice—though if eating such meat would contaminate the conscience of one's more scrupulous fellow Christians, Paul did command the more liberal Christians to abstain.

North of the macellum stood a bathhouse consisting at least of a frigidarium and tepidarium at the time of Augustus (the caldarium, or sauna, was either renovated or first added in renovations in the mid-first century) as well as the perfunctory latrine. Of the bathhouses discovered to date, this is the only one that securely dates back in its original form to the time of Paul's visit, though a Roman city of this size would have had several at that time.[27]

Because Corinth was a truly new city with no indigenous, landed elite, the military veterans and former slaves who had been settled here by Julius and Augustus had the possibility of significant upward mobility in the midst of a world where such social climbing was strikingly rare. They would become, within a few generations, the local elites, holding civic offices, gaining wealth through trade and business, and establishing a reputation that would have

27. Biers, "*Lavari est vivere*," 305–6.

The Erastus inscription (top) and an excavated portion of Erastus's pavement (bottom).

been impossible in many older established cities. Making a name for oneself—what Paul tends to refer to as "boasting," one of the more common verbs in 1 and 2 Corinthians—was not *just* a Corinthian thing, but self-promotion *was* uncommonly at home in Corinth.

Thus, for example, as Corinth grew, its citizens took on more public works and gained public recognition. When one citizen named Erastus was elected to the office of aedile (the office entrusted with overseeing public buildings and festivals), he showed his appreciation by paving an area northwest of the theater. An inscription on the site still provides perpetual testimony to his gift, his name, and his achievement of a coveted, if junior, local public office: "*Erastvs pro aedilitate s[ua] p[ecunia] stravit*" (Erastus paved this with his own money for the aedileship). It is tempting to identify this Erastus with the Erastus mentioned in Romans 16:23, who served as Corinth's city treasurer (its *oikonomos*, or "city steward") and who had become by then part of the Christian congregation in Corinth, though there are also considerations against it.

The Babbius Monument also exemplifies the self-promoting and self-congratulatory spirit of first-century AD Roman Corinth. Gnaeus Babbius Philenus was a freedman who rose to the offices of aedile, local priest, and duovir, one of the city's two chief magistrates. During the reign of Tiberius, Babbius, in his capacity as duovir, authorized the construction of this monument to himself as a testimony to his name, success, and generous benefactions to the city.[28] The monument originally consisted of eight columns arranged in a circle, each bearing an ornate "Corinthian" capital, all together supporting a cone-shaped roof. The same spirit of boasting, claiming honor, and calling for recognition would invade the Christian congregations in Corinth. But while boasting was at home in Corinth, Paul was adamant that *competitive* boasting was not to be at home in the church:

> What do you have that you did not receive? And if you did receive it, why do you boast as though you did not? (1 Cor. 4:7 NIV)

> Therefore, as it is written: "Let the one who boasts boast in the Lord." (1 Cor. 1:31 NIV)

> Since many boast according to the flesh, I too will boast. . . . Whatever anyone else dares to boast of—I am speaking as a fool—I also dare to boast of that. . . . If I must boast, I will boast of the things that show my weakness. (2 Cor. 11:18, 21, 30 ESV)

What counted for Paul was Christ alive in and shining through a believer. All that the believer did ought to point to Christ, his character, and his power (which, Paul says, is often most apparent when we have the least of which to boast; 2 Cor. 12:7–10): "I will boast all the more gladly of my weaknesses, so that the power of Christ may rest upon me" (12:9 ESV).

---

28. Harrison, "Introduction," 15.

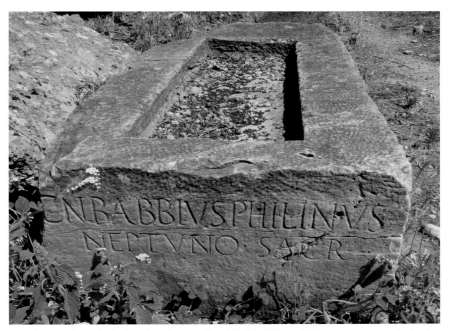

A portion of a fountain dedicated to Neptune (Poseidon) by Babbius Philenus, whose name is clearly visible on the inscription.

The Ports of Corinth: Lechaion and Cenchreae

Both of Corinth's seaports developed into small cities in their own rights. These ports were named after the two sons born to Poseidon (the god of the sea) and the nymph Peirene. As two of the principal natural water sources of the city of Corinth (the one located atop the Acrocorinth, the other north of the forum) were named after Peirene, it was perhaps natural to name the ports after her children, Leches and Cenchrias (Pausanias, *Descr.* 2.2.3).

Lechaion sits 1.5 miles north of Corinth. This was a major harbor installation, outclassed only by Ostia (the principal port of Rome) and Caesarea Maritima (the principal port of Herod's Judea). Two outer harbors were formed by the creation of three large breakwaters, or moles, extending out into the sea, of which almost nothing remains. An inner harbor of approximately 100,000 square yards, approached through the eastern outer harbor, was created by massive dredging operations, though it has long since been entirely silted up once again.[29] Temples to Poseidon and Aphrodite once stood in the region of the harbor (Pausanias, *Descr.* 2.2.3).

29. Murphy-O'Connor, *St. Paul's Corinth*, 16.

The harbor of Lechaion, seen from the Acrocorinth (top), and the remains of one of the moles from the outer Lechaion harbor (bottom).

A road on the south side of Corinth's forum branched off to the east and led to Cenchreae, not quite 6 miles away. The harbor of Cenchreae was created by building two large breakwaters around a natural inlet—a mole on the south side reaching over 100 yards into the sea to the east, and a mole on the north side reaching down almost 100 yards to the south. These formed a large horseshoe-shaped harbor of approximately 30,000 square yards with a wide mouth facing the southeast.[30] Though considerably smaller than Lechaion's

30. Murphy-O'Connor, *St. Paul's Corinth*, 16.

Remains of a tower and the foundations of several buildings from the north mole of Cenchreae's harbor.

The area of the ancient harbor of Cenchreae, looking north from the south mole.

harbors, Cenchreae was still sufficient for the high volume of traffic coming to and from Corinth on the Aegean. The entirety of both moles is now submerged.

The north mole of Cenchreae was once graced by a bronze statue of Poseidon similar to this one, discovered off the coast of Cape Artemisium in Greece (National Archaeological Museum, Athens).

A bronze statue of Poseidon and a temple to Aphrodite once graced the north mole (Pausanius, *Descr.* 2.2.3). Excavations to the north and northwest of the north mole have uncovered residential buildings, small industrial installations, and a large number of Roman-period underground tombs reminiscent of Macedonian tombs. These were carved into the subterranean rock-like apertures into the underworld and opened into large, somewhat rectangular chambers with two levels of niches. Bodies would be laid out to decompose in the larger niches on the lower level; smaller niches on the upper level held urns containing cremated bones. Traces of frescoed decorations can be seen on the interior walls of some of the tombs.[31]

Excavations around the edge of the harbor itself yielded signs of commercial buildings and piers. The remains of the south mole are dominated by a fourth-century Christian church, a testimony to the eventual triumph of the work of Paul and Phoebe in this port city. The outline of the main apse is

31. Evangelogiou, "Kenchreai," 35–36; Sarris et al., "Geological and Geophysical Investigations," esp. 4–5.

The late Roman Christian basilica and, toward the top right corner, the mostly submerged footprint of an apsidal structure believed to have been part of the first-century temple to Isis in Cenchreae.

clearly visible, flanked on the north by what appears to have been a rectangular hall and on the south by a columned portico. This church was built over the remains of a warehouse complex from the Roman period, the first of several such complexes extending out onto the now submerged south mole. Further out, underwater archaeologists discovered the remains of a complex of fish pools for storing live catches for sale or processing.

A shrine to Asclepius and a temple of Isis stood on the south mole (Pausanius, *Descr.* 2.2.3). While the former has not yet been discovered, the mostly submerged foundations of a rounded hall have been identified as part of Isis's temple, partially overbuilt by the fourth-century Christian church complex.[32] Isis was celebrated as a divine protector whose power could extend life beyond that which the Fates had allotted and offer a blessed afterlife as well. Hers was also a cult in which women could distinguish themselves as priestesses. An annual festival that opened the sailing season in Cenchreae each spring appears to have involved the launching of a new ship laden with offerings to Isis as a kind of firstfruits for the profitable season to come (Apuleius, *Metam.* 11.16).

32. Evangelogiou, "Kenchreai," 33, 35.

A cult statue of Isis (left) and a funerary stele of a priestess of Isis from Greece (right). Note the sistrum, a distinctive rattle used in the Isis cult, in the central figure's right hand (National Archaeological Museum, Athens).

Paul, along with Priscilla and Aquila, would leave Corinth for new mission fields by way of Cenchreae (Acts 18:18). The harbor city also became home to a Christian congregation that met in the house of a woman named Phoebe, whom Paul commends in Romans 16:1 as a benefactor and deacon of the congregation there. It was to Phoebe that Paul entrusted the delivery of the letter that contained his most mature theological expression of his gospel, the Letter to the Romans. It was in this context of commerce and cult, profit and paganism, that Phoebe dedicated herself to the support and nurture of a new faith that would come quite literally to supplant these older rites.

11

ROMAN EPHESUS

Ephesus in the Ministry of Paul

Few cities in the Mediterranean were more important centers of the Pauline mission than Ephesus, one of the principal cities of the Roman province of Asia (in what is now the westernmost part of Türkiye). Shortly after Paul had completed his work of church planting in Corinth (probably in AD 52), he traveled with Aquila and Priscilla to Ephesus. Paul stopped there only long enough to get the missionary couple settled as a kind of advance guard for his own future mission in the area (Acts 18:19–21). Apollos, a rhetorically gifted Jew from Alexandria, would encounter Priscilla and Aquila in Ephesus and be instructed by them in the gospel (18:24–26) before moving on to become a missionary and itinerant teacher himself in the circle of Pauline churches (see, e.g., Acts 18:27–19:1; 1 Cor. 1:12; 3:4–6; 16:12; Titus 3:13).

Paul returned to make Ephesus his home and base of operations for two or three years (AD 53–55)—long enough to allow him to become familiar, no doubt, with every yard of the public spaces of this city (Acts 19:1–20:1). He invested himself heavily in its evangelization. From Ephesus, members of his team or converts took the gospel to other cities in the province. Epaphras, for example, most likely set out from here to evangelize Colossae, Hierapolis, and Laodicea and also brought back word to Paul about these mission churches when his guidance was needed (Col. 1:7–8; 4:12–13). Paul's early letters to the Christians in Corinth—the "previous letter" referred to in 1 Corinthians 5:9–11 and 1 Corinthians itself—appear to have been written from Ephesus (see 1 Cor. 16:19–20). Timothy is remembered to have engaged in some

157

important follow-up work in Ephesus, perhaps at some point in Paul's later ministry (1 Tim. 1:2). Paul would meet with elders from the congregations in Ephesus on his fateful trip to Jerusalem that would end in his arrest and four-year imprisonment, though Paul chose the nearby port city of Miletus for the occasion (Acts 20:16–37).

The Archaeology of Roman Ephesus

Geography and Demographics

The Ephesus known to Paul was located near the mouth of the Cayster River (now the Küçük Menderes River) on the shore of a harbor with access to the Aegean Sea. The city stretched into the valley between two mountains, Mount Pion (the Panayır Dağ) and Mount Coressus (the Bülbül Dağ), its residential areas spreading up the lower slopes of both hills. The natural harbor, which had to be periodically dredged because of the silting caused by the Cayster River, made Ephesus a major node for trade and shipping between east and west (Strabo, *Geogr.* 14.1.24). The dramatic effects of the constant silting can be seen from the fact that the ruins of Roman Ephesus now sit landlocked 3 full miles inland from the Aegean shore.

The location of Roman Ephesus is the result of a decision made three centuries before Paul by Lysimachus, who succeeded to a piece of Alexander the Great's empire. A settlement had existed in the Homeric period (ca. eighth century BC) on the north side of the base of Mount Pion (near the now dried-up Coressus harbor). During the Classical period, the settlement had relocated to an area about 1 mile to the northeast, between the base of a third hill (the Ayasoluk) and the famous Temple of Artemis. Lysimachus chose Ephesus's final location to make it a major port city and fortified it with a perimeter wall about 6 miles in circumference.[1] Ephesus came to be a node on a highway running from north to south through Roman Asia; it was also the westernmost node on a series of highways that led east as far as India, most of that route being known as the Royal Road from the period of Persian domination (Strabo, *Geogr.* 14.2.29; Herodotus, *Hist.* 5.53–54). It was thus well positioned to prosper from trade over both land and sea.

The population of Ephesus is estimated to have reached somewhere between 150,000 and 225,000 in the early Roman period, making it the fourth or fifth largest city in the empire.[2] Immigration was an important factor in the growth of the city. At that time infant mortality was about 33 percent

---

1. Fairchild, *Christian Origins*, 7.
2. Murphy-O'Connor, *St. Paul's Ephesus*, 131; L. White, "Urban Development," 41.

during the first year and reached 50 percent by the fifth year; the growth of the population suggests, therefore, a steady flow of immigrants.[3]

There is no significant archaeological evidence for the presence of a Jewish community in Ephesus beyond a handful of inscriptions and other artifacts bearing common iconic Jewish decorations (for example, the menorah, shofar, lulav, and etrog).[4] There is, however, ample literary evidence, particularly in Josephus's *Jewish Antiquities*. Josephus documents the exemptions from military service, first of the Jews in Ephesus who were Roman citizens (*Ant.* 14.228) and then, from 43 BC on, of all Jews in the province of Asia (*Ant.* 14.225–27). He also records that Augustus affirmed the right of these Jewish communities to collect money and to transport it to Jerusalem for the maintenance of the Jewish temple and its sacrifices and personnel—a special exemption from the general prohibition of moving significant amounts of silver and gold across provincial lines for any but imperially sanctioned purposes (*Ant.* 16.167–68).[5]

Ephesus in the Time of Paul

After leaving Priscilla and Aquila in Ephesus to get established, Paul retraced his steps to Jerusalem, Antioch, and finally Galatia and Phrygia (Acts 18:22–23). When he finally returned to Ephesus, he would have entered through the Magnesian Gate, the major access point through the city's southeastern fortification walls. The road leading out from this gate connected Ephesus with Magnesia-on-the-Maeander about 15 miles to the east and thence to the ancient road that led all the way into Babylonia (Herodotus, *Hist.* 5.53–54).

A short walk would have brought Paul into the civic forum, the center of the city's government. Here he would have seen a largely open courtyard of about 525 by 190 feet surrounded by columned porches, the most magnificent of which would have been the Basilica Stoa, constructed around 11 BC by Sextilius Pollio.[6] This two-story, three-aisled portico was 50 feet wide, stretching the entire length of the civic forum on its north side. Its covered area, supported by 67 Ionic columns, would have been a popular place for city politicians and other members of the elite to meet and conduct business out of the sun or rain. The stoa was dedicated "to Artemis of the Ephesians; Emperor Caesar Augustus, son of a god; Tiberius Caesar, son of Augustus;

---

3. L. White, "Urban Development," 44–49.

4. Wilson, *Biblical Turkey*, 216. A menorah, for example, can be found carved into a marble block that is now in secondary use as part of the stairs leading up to the Library of Celsus (a second-century AD structure).

5. See further Trebilco, "Jewish Community in Ephesus."

6. Scherrer, "City of Ephesos," 5; Scherrer, *Ephesus*, 80.

The Basilica Stoa (top), together with the remains of the statues of Augustus
and Livia that once graced its easternmost alcove (bottom).

and to the Ephesian people" with larger-than-life statues of Augustus and
his wife, Livia, in an antechamber on its easternmost side.[7]

The city was well supplied with water, with significant amounts being
carried in by aqueducts, one of which was constructed as a gift to the city by

7. Price, *Rituals and Power*, 140, 255; Friesen, *Imperial Cults*, 95–96.

A portion of the Pollio Aqueduct visible to the south of the city. A Roman road once passed through the central arch.

the same Sextilius Pollio. One of the major water collection nodes, called a *castellum aquae* in Latin, was located on the south side of the civic forum. It would be distributed throughout the city through both stone and clay channels to public fountains and private residences. Several veins of clay water pipes have been uncovered beneath the pavement of the civic forum. The water system also supplied several bathhouse installations throughout the city, one of which was located in the east corner of the civic forum, though none have been sufficiently well excavated to reveal the various elements of a Roman bath experience—notably the warm bath, sauna, and cold plunge pool (tepidarium, caldarium, and frigidarium, respectively).

Several public buildings dominated the civic forum of Paul's day, three of which stood on the north side of the Basilica Stoa. The first of these was the

Stacks of segments of clay water pipes recovered from the civic forum. Fitted with male and female connectors, these were laid out end to end beneath the flagstones that paved the forum.

Some of the remains of the eastern bathhouse.

prytaneum, located in the northwest corner of the forum. This was the site of the city's sacred hearth—the symbolic fire kept perpetually burning. As a symbol of the city's hospitality, it would have been the place where state dinners were held and foreign dignitaries were entertained and housed. It also remained a place for the worship of several traditional Greek gods and goddesses, including, of course, Hestia, the goddess of the hearth. Inscriptions on the reerected pillars record the names of the priests—called *kouretai*—who served in this building, organized and subvented processions and festivals in honor of Artemis, and officiated in the mysteries of Ephesian Artemis, celebrated not far from Ephesus in a sacred grove on Mount Solmissos, near modern Şirince (Strabo, *Geogr.* 14.1.20). A fairly consistent record of these *kouretai*, along with the prytanis, who was the highest official connected with the prytaneum, can be reconstructed from the reign of Tiberius through the mid-third century AD on the basis of these inscribed pillars.[8]

A small temple of Artemis, the patron goddess of the city, stood next to the prytaneum. By the turn of the era, part of this temple had been rededicated also to the worship of Julius Caesar. It consisted of a courtyard of about 108 by 95 feet surrounded by colonnades on three of its sides; on the fourth side, a series of seven steps led up to the twin shrines, each housing a cult image of the god or goddess.[9] The blending of the imperial cult with the cult of Artemis was significant in Ephesus. Its elite were eager to demonstrate themselves pious in devotion and duty toward both Artemis and the Augusti, as Sextilius

8. Rogers, "Ephesian Tale," 81.
9. Price, *Rituals and Power*, 139, 254; Murphy-O'Connor, *St. Paul's Ephesus*, 190–91.

The remains of the prytaneum (top) with a close-up of one of the many column drums (bottom) bearing the names of the priests who both served and subsidized the cults of Hestia and Artemis in the city.

Pollio demonstrated with the dedication of his Basilica Stoa to Artemis and to members of the imperial family. A number of honorific inscriptions also feature the phrase *philartemis kai philosebastos*, affirming a benefactor to be a devotee (a *philos*, "friend") of both divine figures.

The shrine to Artemis and the Divine Julius in Ephesus's civic forum.

East of the twin shrines stands an odeon, a small theater suited for musical performances and poetical recitations. Unlike the larger theaters constructed primarily for dramatic presentations, these structures tended to be covered by wooden roofs. The current structure, which dates from the second century AD, also served as the meeting place for the civic council. As excavations have not been undertaken beneath this structure, it is not known whether it was built over an older structure that served as a council hall in Paul's time (which seems likely, as a bouleuterion, or council hall, was a standard feature of Greek and Roman cities) or whether the much larger theater served that purpose until the construction of this alternate venue.

The vast courtyard of the civic forum also became a kind of sacred precinct for a freestanding temple in its midst—a temple dedicated to the worship of Augustus and the goddess Roma. The worship of the Roman emperors had become an important expression of loyalty and gratitude to the chief patron of the world on the part of the citizens of Ephesus—as indeed for the whole province of Asia, whose cities vied for what they considered the privilege of constructing such temples to Roma and to members of the imperial family. This temple, sporting single rows of six columns front and back and ten

The second-century odeon in the civic forum.

columns on its sides, had a footprint of about 50 by 72 feet.[10] There would be no doubt in the minds of anyone entering the civic forum of Ephesus that the city's loyalties and interests were aligned with those of Rome, its emperors, and its vision for rule without end.

Paul would have left the civic forum by a single columned street beginning in its northwest corner and leading eventually to the commercial center of Ephesus. Archaeologists have named this street Curetes Street because it begins at the prytaneum where the *kouretai* carried out their duties. In antiquity it appears to have been known as the *Embolos*, the "Wedge," because it cut

10. Wilson, *Biblical Turkey*, 209. There is admittedly some debate as to which of the two cult sites in the civic forum was dedicated to the deified Julius and which to Augustus. Peter Scherrer ("City of Ephesos," 4–5) believes the double temple between the prytaneum and bouleuterion to have been dedicated to Augustus and Artemis, with the freestanding temple representing the temple Augustus ordered built for the divinized Julius and the goddess Roma in 29 BC, when Ephesus was made the capital of the province. Dio Cassius (*Hist. rom.* 51.20.6, trans. Cary) could be understood as providing support for this view when he writes of Augustus permitting "the dedication of sacred precincts in Ephesus and in Nicaea to Rome and to Caesar, his father," particularly as the object of Roman devotion, while Augustus permitted the local Greek population also to worship himself. Friesen (*Twice Neokoros*, 11n21; *Imperial Cults*, 101) and Price (*Rituals and Power*, 140, 254), on the other hand, believe the position reflected in the main text to be more probable.

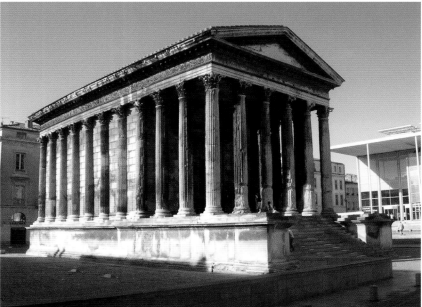

Little of the Temple of Augustus and Roma remains to be seen today beyond the foundations and a sampling of architectural fragments (top). In Paul's day, it would have closely resembled the Temple of Augustus and Roma still standing in Nimes, France (bottom).

diagonally across the city streets' grid pattern.[11] The street was lined with shops built into recesses behind the colonnades. It is remotely possible that Aquila and Priscilla secured one of these spaces to ply their trade, though other sites are more likely. Curetes Street would have been more akin to the Via del Corso in Rome or Fifth Avenue in New York City than to the strip malls where smaller businesses can afford to set up shop.

The street was also lined with statues set atop bases that bore inscriptions honoring public benefactors of the city (and thus, incidentally, bearing witness to the cultural importance of honoring them as such). One honorific statue base, for example, bears the inscription "The council and the citizenry honor the physician Alexander, son of Alexander." Grander honorary monuments were also to be found on the upper half of this street. One of these is a memorial built to Caius Memmius, a grandson of the dictator Sulla. What made Memmius deserving of such recognition beyond having an illustrious, if controversial, grandfather is unclear. This may have been sufficient. When Mithridates VI of Pontus sought to stave off Roman expansion in the early decades of the first century BC, he massacred many of the Roman residents of the province of Asia in the process (Appian, *Mith. Wars* 12.4.22–23; Valerius Maximus 9.2.4). Sulla played a major role in bringing Mithridates to heel and restoring the balance of power in the territories west of Cappadocia. Nevertheless, it is likely that Memmius himself, being a member of the ultra-elite, also served as a major benefactor of Ephesus during his lifetime. Another monument served as a tomb for local benefactor Sextilius Pollio, appropriately erected just beyond and below the west end of Pollio's Basilica Stoa.

At the base of Curetes Street stand two blocks of town houses, the second of which sits today under a protective Kevlar roof, having undergone significant restoration. The houses on this block give visitors a glimpse into the colorfully decorated interior spaces of ancient homes whose quality of preservation approaches that of homes in Pompeii. While the foundations of the houses date back to the first century BC, they remained occupied (and thus, modified) at least through the fourth century AD and thus reflect a later period in the form in which they have been recovered. Nevertheless, there is little in them that would not have been at home in the first century AD, as the residential blocks of Pompeii bear witness. This second block appears to contain six or perhaps seven individual units, most originally enjoying a second story (given the presence of the bases of staircases).[12] Two of these

11. Murphy-O'Connor, *St. Paul's Ephesus*, 192.
12. For detailed discussion, see Scherrer, *New Guide*, 100–113; Erdemgil, Evren, and Ozeren, *Terrace Houses in Ephesus*.

The view looking southeast down Curetes Street (top) and a view into one of the two-room barrel-vaulted shops that once lined it (bottom).

The peristyle courtyard of one of the Terrace Houses, originally surrounded by interior rooms (top), and a view into the highly decorated spaces of another house (bottom).

individual units measure about 4,000 and 7,000 square feet—lavishly spacious by modern standards and all the more so by ancient standards. The size of these dwellings, the provisions for indoor plumbing (and even private bathhouses complete with saunas), and the elaborate decorations that adorn them in the way of frescoes and mosaics show these to be the houses of the rich and powerful citizens of Ephesus. Paul seems to have made a point of bearing witness to members of this class, or perhaps the next highest echelon, in the various cities in which he sought to plant churches, since securing such patrons, whose homes would be large enough to serve as meeting places for the congregation, was essential to the movement's long-term success.

More tomb monuments were to be found at the base of Curetes Street. The tomb monument of Arsinoë IV, a half sister of Cleopatra VII of Egypt, once sat in front of the second block of apartments. Toward the end of Arsinoë's failed run as a rival claimant to the throne, she sought asylum in the Artemision but was dragged out from the sacred precincts and killed by Marc Antony's soldiers in 41 BC to advance Cleopatra's interests in Egypt (Josephus, *Ant.* 15.89; cf. Dio Cassius, *Hist. rom.* 48.24.1–2; Appian, *Bell. civ.* 5.1.9).[13] The monument was octagonal in design. While little remains on the site itself, some architectural fragments have been taken to the Ephesos Museum in Vienna and positioned to give some idea of the stately grandeur that once marked the tomb monument (see photos on p. 172). The impetus—and the money—for the construction of the monument remain unknown, leading some to speculate that the monument was funded by Octavian himself after he and Antony began to fall out, as a means of memorializing the latter's act of sacrilege against the temple of Artemis. A monument also once stood at this crossroads to honor Androclus, the legendary founder of Ephesus (see Pausanias, *Descr.* 7.2.6–9; Strabo, *Geogr.* 14.1.3).

Although adjacent to a bath complex that likely postdates Paul's visit, and thus probably also Paul's time in Ephesus, there is an excellent example of an ancient public latrine across Curetes Street from the Terrace Houses. Modern visitors are always surprised at how little privacy and personal space the ancients required for such functions. Latrines were frequently positioned in close proximity to bathhouses so that as the water in the latter was changed, the runoff could flush the latrines.

Less expensive blocks of multistory apartments, or *insulae*, climbed Mount Pion on the other side of Curetes Street, with the first floor generally consisting of shops or workshops. One of the narrow side streets leading north up Mount Pion led to a large residential complex, the original foundations of

---

13. Murphy-O'Connor, *St. Paul's Ephesus*, 45–46.

A decorated room featuring simple frescoes of the nine muses (top) and a floor sporting a finely detailed mosaic of Neptune and his bride, Amphitrite, riding an oversized seahorse (bottom). This mosaic was probably the decorative centerpiece of a dining room (a triclinium).

which date back to the first century BC but which continued to be renovated and used through the fourth century AD. It is tempting to speculate that this might have served as the home and (unofficial) administrative center for the governor of the province of Asia (the civic forum serving as the official

The base and some architectural fragments of the tomb monument of Arsinoë (top) and the architectural and decorative remnants re-creating one of the original eight faces of the monument (bottom) (Ephesos Museum, Vienna).

One of the public latrines in Ephesus. This installation, with seats lining three of the room's four sides, could accommodate forty-eight users. Note the channel in front of the seats, through which water constantly flowed. Sponges on sticks were provided for personal hygiene.

locus for public administrative business) after Ephesus became the capital of the province under Augustus. Such a location would have been symbolically strategic, as the complex overlooked—and could be seen to overlook—the Great Theater of Ephesus, the commercial forum, and the activity streaming to and from the harbor.[14]

Curetes Street opened at its base into a public square that also afforded one point of access to the commercial center of Ephesus—the Tetragonos Agora, the "Square Market." The agora could be entered here from its southeast corner through a magnificent gate built by Mazaeus and Mithridates, two freedmen of the house of Augustus. An inscription in both Greek

14. Murphy-O'Connor, *St. Paul's Ephesus*, 198.

The south gate to the commercial forum (top) and a close-up of the dedicatory inscription (bottom).

The commercial forum and the street leading from Curetes Street to the theater, seen from the highest Terrace Houses.

and Latin dedicates the structure to the honor of their former master and perpetual patron (Augustus), his wife (Livia), Marcus Agrippa (at the time, Augustus's heir apparent), and Julia (daughter of Augustus and wife of Agrippa).[15] At the same time, it has brought recognition to Mazaeus and Mithridates for two millennia. The magnitude of the structure attests to the wealth that could be amassed by well-placed imperial freedmen during this period.

During the reign of Augustus, the commercial agora itself doubled in size to the dimensions of 15,000 square yards. There were sixty or so permanent workshops and stalls, built from stone, surrounding the inside perimeter on three sides. Columned porches on all four sides would have provided an ideal venue for buying, selling, or open-air preaching. These porticoes were impressive two-story structures with stairs at the corners giving access to the upper floor. A side street running north from Curetes Street alongside the agora and past the Great Theater also gave access to the upper story of these porticoes through a basilica built during the early years of Nero's reign and dedicated to Ephesian Artemis, Nero, Agrippina, and the people of Ephesus.[16] The vast open courtyard of the commercial forum would, of course, have also been filled with vendors' carts and tents. This would have been the likeliest place among those so far excavated for Aquila, Priscilla, and Paul to have set up shop for their long stay in Ephesus. Statues of public benefactors, including members of the imperial household, graced the complex. In AD 43, for example, an association of Roman merchants commissioned an equestrian statue of Claudius, recently

15. Harrison, "Epigraphic Portrait of Ephesus," 32–35.
16. Scherrer, *Ephesus*, 142.

A view of the southeast area of the commercial forum (top) and some of the shops lining the east side of the forum (bottom).

risen to the throne.[17] It bears mention that inscriptions attest to the presence of a slave market in the city as well, though its location remains uncertain.[18]

17. Scherrer, "City of Ephesos," 8; Scherrer, *Ephesus*, 142.
18. Harrison, "Epigraphic Portrait of Ephesus," 37–38.

From the commercial agora one could find one's way to the harbor by two paths: one through a gate in the west side of the agora that opened onto a street leading west to the harbor, another through a gate on the north side that led eventually to a broad thoroughfare running between the Great Theater and the harbor. This street was 36 feet wide and a third of a mile long. It led past storehouses and more venues for vendors and merchants to conduct their business or inspect cargoes and eventually to the harbor itself, which in Paul's day, was one of the busiest seaports of the Roman Empire. This was a major node in the flow of goods from the east to Rome. As such, it was also carefully regulated. A massive inscription was found on a slab, standing taller than a human being, that details the customs regulations of the harbor as well as penalties for smuggling and other infractions.

There were advantages and incentives for merchants and shipowners to put themselves in Rome's service. One inscription in Ephesus reads, "No one is liable to pay tax for goods carried in service to the people of Rome, nor for goods conveyed for religious purposes."[19] The emperor Claudius went so far as to provide insurance for ships dedicated to delivering grain to Rome, should the ships be lost at sea, a major incentive in a risky industry (witness the four shipwrecks to which Paul was subjected as a passenger; Acts 27:39–44; 2 Cor. 11:25). An inscription above the entrance to the somewhat pretentious tomb of one Flavius Zeuxis, a merchant and sea captain from Hierapolis, boasts of his making seventy-two successful trips around Cape Malea, the southern coast of Greece, to Italy (most likely using Ephesus as his port) in trade with Rome. He was thus part of the trade system that catered to the demands of the center of the empire. The Ephesian harbor indeed afforded a distinctive view into the Roman imperial economy, which directed a disproportionate percentage of the world's goods—both luxury items and staples—toward the empire's heartland.

At the east end of Harbor Street stands the Great Theater of Ephesus. Originally constructed during the Hellenistic period, it was expanded to its present dimensions over the course of a century, beginning in about AD 40. At its peak, the theater could have accommodated between twenty-one thousand and twenty-five thousand spectators.[20] Not much remains of the stage building save for its foundations. When the theater was fully functional, most spectators' view of the harbor would have been completely obscured by the stage and its multistory backdrop. It is here that the author of Acts locates the riot that probably convinced Paul that it might be time

19. Kraybill, *Imperial Cult and Commerce*, 66.
20. Fairchild, *Christian Origins*, 22.

The broad street leading to the now silted and swampy harbor, seen from the top tiers of the theater.

to move on from Ephesus (Acts 19:23–20:1). That episode is instructive from a number of angles: the economic interests that were inseparable from questions of religion and conversion, the ease with which civic pride could be connected with the worship of a particular deity and harnessed against a foreign cult, and Paul's team's apparent degree of effectiveness in

The Great Theater, seen from the street leading to the harbor (top) and from the interior (bottom).

this city, such that anyone connected commercially with the Artemis cult would feel—or at least fear—the economic pinch of a drop of interest in the celebrated goddess.

The street that ran north from Curetes Street past the Great Theater continued further north to a gymnasium complex that began just diagonally across from the theater. This same road led eventually to a vast U-shaped stadium. During the Hellenistic period, this was a simple earthen stadium

The fully reconstructed theater in Aspendos of Pamphylia. The stage building of the theater of Ephesus would have resembled the one seen in this theater.

The palaestra, or exercise yard, in front of the gymnasium and bath complex northwest of the theater.

like the one at Olympia in Greece. It was reconfigured in stone with typical stadium seating over arched passageways during Nero's reign.[21] The stadium was home to the *Ephesia*, an annual series of games drawing competitors from throughout the province and involving both athletic and artistic competitions, including music and dance.[22] Another principal egress from the city's fortifications could be found behind the stadium—the Coressian Gate, from which the great Artemision, the city's pride, would have been clearly visible in the distance.

Ephesus and Artemis

As in every major city in the Roman world, the residents of Ephesus were devoted to many deities. For example, the worship of the Phrygian mother goddess and symbol of fertility, Cybele, is attested in a shrine that stands on the far north side of Mount Pion. Her cult myth involved, according to one version at least, the madness and self-castration of her lover, Attis, after he had broken faith with her—an act that was thenceforth to be replicated by her eunuch priests (Ovid, *Fast.* 4.241–44). Mysteries were celebrated in honor of Demeter and her daughter Persephone, whose story was closely related to the agricultural cycle of each year.[23] Extensive evidence of private devotion to Aphrodite, Dionysus, and Isis was discovered in houses throughout the city. An altar was dedicated to the Egyptian deities Serapis, Isis, and Anubis as early as the third century BC.[24] A monumental temple would be erected to Serapis, probably in conjunction with his consort Isis and their son, Harpocrates (Horus), just west of the commercial forum in the second century AD.

Ephesus was known throughout the region, however, as a city specially devoted to Artemis. While Artemis was worshiped in many of the cities of Asia Minor (for example, at Magnesia, Didyma, and Sardis), Ephesus was home to her greatest temple. Today, very little remains of the Artemision, since throughout the Byzantine, medieval, and Ottoman periods the perfectly cut stones of the derelict temple were quarried for new buildings. In Paul's time, however, the great Temple of Artemis was one of the seven wonders of the ancient world—indeed, the crowning marvel among them according to the traveler Antipater of Sidon (*Anth. Gr.* 9.58). It was a major destination for pilgrims and tourists from across the Mediterranean. With a footprint of 220 by 425 feet, the Artemision covered four times more ground than the

21. Fairchild, *Christian Origins*, 23.
22. Murphy-O'Connor, *St. Paul's Ephesus*, 199.
23. Rogers, "Ephesian Tale," 72.
24. Walters, "Egyptian Religions in Ephesos," 284.

Two of many votive steles dedicated to Cybele at Ephesus. She is flanked by Zeus and perhaps by Attis, her lover. She holds a patera, a shallow bowl used in ritual offerings of wine, and is accompanied by one or more lions, the animals that drove her chariot.

Parthenon in Athens. Double rows of columns 6.5 feet in diameter and 65 feet high stood around the temple's perimeter, supporting its roof. These were arranged in rows of 8 on the shorter sides and 20 on the longer sides, to a total of 127 columns (Pliny the Elder, *Nat.* 36.21.95–97; Vitruvius, *De arch.* 3.2.7).[25] A grand altar stood about 100 feet in front of the temple itself. Worship and offerings were conducted decorously in front of, and not within, the house of the goddess. A shrine to Augustus may also have been incorporated into this famous Artemision in the early imperial period.

In addition to being the most prominent religious site in the area, the temple also served major commercial functions. It was the ancient equivalent of a bank, using the proceeds from the lands owned by the goddess as capital to be lent out at interest and serving as a sacred depository for major sums of money, both for private and for public funds (Caesar, *Bell. civ.* 3.33, 105; Dio Chrysostom, *Rhod.* 54–55; Aelius Aristides, *Or.* 23.24).[26] Its activities were supported by an immense staff of priests, functionaries, and temple slaves.

The Artemision sat less than 1 mile from the Coressian Gate (the northern gate of Roman Ephesus) and about 1.25 miles from the Magnesian Gate (the city's eastern gate). A calendar of regular sacred processions featuring

25. Murphy-O'Connor, *St. Paul's Ephesus*, 116–18.
26. Murphy-O'Connor, *St. Paul's Ephesus*, 65.

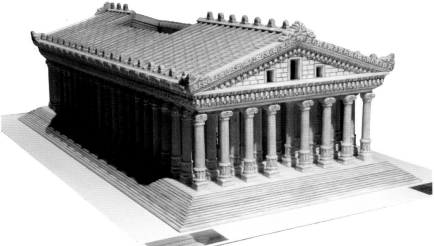

The scant remains of the once great Artemision (top) and a model of the temple based on the description in Pliny the Elder (bottom) (Ephesus Archaeological Museum).

Artemis connected the city with her temple. One itinerary brought the sacred images of Artemis and other cult images and paraphernalia from the temple to the Magnesian Gate, through the civic agora, down Curetes Street, past the Square Market and theater, and out the Coressian Gate, to return thence to the Artemision. Over 250 participants might have been involved in the typical sacred procession, carrying the images on platforms, singing, and carrying out various offerings at sacred locations throughout the city (Xenophon of Ephesus, *Eph*. 1.2–3).[27]

27. Knibbe, "*Via Sacra Ephesiaca*," 153–54.

A single column drum sculpted with life-size figures in low relief. Death (far left) and Hermes (right) are escorting either Alcestis or Eurydice (center left) to the underworld (The British Museum). Similar mythical scenes would have adorned many of the lower column drums in the Artemision.

Architectural fragments housed in the Ephesos Museum in Vienna give some sense of the ornamentation that decorated the great altar in front of the temple proper.

We may be more familiar with Artemis, or Diana, as she is portrayed in the Greek or Roman art of Europe—as a huntress goddess, often with bow at the ready and deer at her feet. Although Greek-style images of Artemis were found in private homes in Ephesus, this was not her public face in Asia Minor. Cult statues show her as a mother goddess flanked by two deer, her chest covered with symbols of fertility. It is debated whether the dozens of protuberances on the cult figure's front should be understood as breasts (so Minucius Felix, *Oct.* 23.5), eggs, or even the testicles of bulls. It is clear, however, that at an early stage the more ancient worship of a regional fertility goddess was melded with the worship of Artemis. She wears a peculiar headdress on which several buildings are represented—perhaps representing the city of Ephesus itself, with Artemis as its personal patron and protector.[28] Representations of the cult statue or the facade of the Artemision itself (with the cult statue plainly visible within) appear frequently on provincial coins from the first and early second centuries AD, which proudly bear the legend "Diana Ephesia." Such coins bear witness to the city's pride in their identification with their patron goddess.

Inscriptions found throughout Ephesus demonstrate the importance of Artemis (as well as the Roman emperor) for the life of the city. One typical inscription begins with a dedication to both Ephesian Artemis and Augustus. Artemis was so closely linked with the prestige and

Artemis (or Diana) in her typically Greek form (top left) and Artemis as represented throughout Asia and its neighboring provinces (right). This cult image was found buried beneath the prytaneum, likely a miniature version of the cult statue housed in the great Artemision.

28. Murphy-O'Connor, *St. Paul's Ephesus*, 21.

The inscription honoring Vibius Salutaris for establishing and subventing a new religious procession celebrating Artemis, the imperial gods, and the various tribes of the Ephesian people (Rogers, "Ephesian Tale," 87).

well-being of the city that the city laid special claim to her as, in some sense, their own, as the use of the adjective "Ephesia" with either "Diana" or "Artemis" demonstrates. They also claimed to be the *neokoros* of Artemis, the city selected (perhaps by the goddess herself) to be the guardian and custodian of her primary dwelling place. Acts 19:35 attests to the use of this title, as do coins from the Ephesus mint (though by AD 90 Ephesus would be prouder and louder about its appointment as *neokoros* of the temple of the Flavian emperors, becoming thus a provincial center for the imperial cult under Domitian). The inscription goes on to honor a member of the Ephesian elite named Vibius Salutaris as "*philartemis kai philosebastos*" (a friend of Artemis and friend of Augustus). What gives Vibius honor in this city is his piety toward the civic cults of Artemis and the emperor.

In such a city, Paul was destined to run into trouble. His proclamation of one, and only one, God threatened the city's very identity and its claim to fame, not to mention the livelihood of the concessioners, like Demetrius, whose trade depended on the reputation and worship of Artemis of the Ephesians. Demetrius, a maker of souvenir silver replicas of the goddess Artemis, rallied thousands

An inscription from Miletus honoring Marcus Antonius Apollodorus, an Asiarch.

of Ephesus's citizens to gather in the theater to protest Paul's activity. As one sits in its stands, one can almost still hear the echoes of the chant they took up for two whole hours: "Great is Artemis of the Ephesians!" (Acts 19:34 NRSV). One final detail of this narrative merits notice. In another testimony to Luke's care for appropriate local detail, he refers to the officials that seek to dissuade Paul from entering the theater as "Asiarchs" (Acts 19:31). This is indeed the title given to those who served on the provincial council of Asia (the *koinon Asias*), whose responsibilities included the promotion and subvention of the imperial cult, among other duties. It is well represented in local honorary inscriptions.

The congregations Paul and his team planted would continue to grow in this city in the decades following Paul's departure. The Letter to the Ephesians addresses these congregations—and potentially all the congregations in the region—a minimum of five years after Paul had left the city. The Christians in Ephesus emerge prominently again in Revelation as one of the seven congregations addressed by that text (Rev. 1:11; 2:1–7). By then, the point of conflict between the Christians and their Ephesian neighbors had moved away from Artemis and more fully toward the worship of the emperors, with the latter becoming an even more pronounced focus for civic pride and identity.[29] Ignatius of Antioch, the bishop-martyr under Trajan (emperor from AD 98 to 117), wrote to the Christian assemblies in Ephesus around AD 112 on his way to martyrdom in Rome. The eventual triumph of Christianity in Ephesus is

29. See deSilva, *Discovering Revelation*, 49–50.

dramatically illustrated in the remains of the Church of Mary the Theotokos ("the Mother of God"), which was built around AD 500 within the southern portico of the massive temple of Hadrian, which had by then been dismantled down to its very foundations.

12

COLOSSAE, LAODICEA, AND HIERAPOLIS

The Churches of the Lycus Valley in the Ministry of Paul

While Paul based himself in Ephesus along with Priscilla and Aquila, other members of his team worked to take the gospel to other cities in the region. Epaphras, himself a Christian convert native to Colossae, appears to have been primarily responsible for planting and tending churches in Colossae, Hierapolis, and Laodicea during this time. Paul directly testifies to this effect, in regard to Colossae at least, speaking of the Colossian converts' reception of the gospel "as you learned it from Epaphras, our beloved fellow slave, who is a faithful servant of Christ on your behalf" (Col. 1:7). Paul had, in the meanwhile, received some information from Epaphras about the congregation in Colossae, not least a report about their "love in the Spirit" (1:8). But Epaphras's scope of labor and concern extended to the Christian assemblies in at least two other cities of the Lycus River valley. Paul reports, "Epaphras . . . is always wrestling in his prayers on your behalf, so that you may stand mature and fully assured in everything that God wills. For I testify for him that he has worked hard for you and for those in Laodicea and in Hierapolis" (4:12–13 NRSV). These three cities stood in close proximity to one another. Traveling from Colossae to Laodicea involved a walk of a little more than 10 miles; from Laodicea to Hierapolis was fewer than 10 miles. The inter-relationships between these congregations not only are to be inferred from their close proximity to one another but were explicitly promoted by Paul. He

189

instructs the Christian believers in Colossae to "greet the brothers and sisters in Laodicea as well as Nympha and the assembly meeting in her house; and when the letter is read among you, cause it also to be read in the assembly of the Laodiceans—and you yourselves read the one from Laodicea" (4:15–16).[1]

It seems highly likely that Philemon, another of Paul's converts, was also connected with the Christians in Colossae. There are also indications that the letter addressed to him and to the assembly that gathered in his house was sent at the same time as the letter to the Colossian assembly or assemblies. First, Paul is surrounded by the same people as he writes both letters: Epaphras, Mark, Aristarchus, Demas, and Luke send greetings in both, with only Justus missing from Philemon (Philem. 23–24; cf. Col. 4:10–14). Paul speaks of Onesimus, a slave in Philemon's house, as "one of your own" when writing to Colossae (Col. 4:9). Archippus, who is greeted as a member of Philemon's circle in Philemon 2, is addressed directly in Colossians 4:17. Onesimus is traveling with Tychicus to Colossae, quite possibly bearing both letters (Col. 4:7–9; Philem. 10–12).

Colossae

Given the importance of Colossae as the site of a congregation to which Paul directly addressed a letter and that was founded by one of Paul's associates, it is astonishing that the ancient city Colossae has remained completely unexcavated for so long.[2] The visitor to the site is still greeted by a largely undisturbed double mound on which the city's acropolis and more important public buildings once stood and by vast modern orchards and cultivated fields that cover, no doubt, the major streets, forums, and residential districts of the ancient city.

Archaeologists believe that a sacred area would have occupied the highest parts of the mound (the northwest area). The crater of a small theater once capable of seating about nine hundred viewers can still be seen at the center east of the mound, though almost all the blocks used for its nine to twelve rows of seating have been repurposed over the centuries.[3] Some postulate that an agora once stood upon the lower larger flat space on the south portion of the mound. If this is true, it would more likely have been

---

1. The authorship of Colossians is, of course, a matter of debate among scholars. See the discussions in Sumney, *Colossians*, 1–9; Moo, *Letters to the Colossians and to Philemon*, 28–41; McKnight, *Letter to the Colossians*, 5–18.

2. Excavations began in earnest at last in 2021 under the supervision of Bariş Yener of Pammukale University in Denizli.

3. Standhartinger, "City with a Message," 241.

An aerial view of the unexcavated acropolis of Colossae.

Courtesy of Alan Cadwallader

a civic agora or administrative forum. An acropolis is an inconvenient place to situate a commercial market, from the point of view of both suppliers and consumers.

At present, little can be discerned from the scattered and sparse architectural fragments littering the surface. Small finds, reliefs, and inscriptions tell us that Men (the moon god) and Cybele (the mother goddess), together with her consort, Attis, were worshiped in and around the city. Blocks with carved reliefs of Zeus and his thunderbolt in the necropolis reveal both reverence for the god and the invocation of his protection over graves. Coins from Colossae feature the head of Zeus or Apollo on the obverse; another coin features Asclepius and his daughter Hygeia on the reverse, also suggesting that cults of these gods existed somewhere within the ancient city. The diversity of Colossae's pantheon essentially reflects that of other cities of Roman Asia, Phrygia, and Galatia.

Every ancient city had its hinterlands, the farming of which provided at least some of the inhabitants' subsistence. Colossae was well situated near the Lycus River to take advantage of it, through a system of water channels, for the steady irrigation of crops as well as the provision of water for the city's residents and industries. Vitruvius (*De arch.* 8.3.14), a contemporary of Augustus, bears witness to the involvement of Laodicea and Hierapolis in the regional wool industry, breeding and raising sheep with a distinctive glossy violet-black wool, and one might also add Colossae as well. All three cities were significant hubs of producing wool and textiles as well as dyeing and processing them. Finally, like all ancient cities, Colossae had an area designated as its necropolis, which has been explored, informally at least, for the various types of tombs (and signs of relative affluence of the families involved), for what can be known about occupations from reliefs, and the like. The frequent appearance of small livestock and agricultural products on grave steles reinforces the largely agricultural nature of the city's economy.[4]

Even though excavations have begun, we have three reasons not to get our hopes up that the results will come anywhere close to what we have for Corinth or Ephesus. First, of course, the settlement of Colossae, while a major city in the Persian period, was no longer a major city in the Hellenistic and Roman periods.[5] This was due, in large measure, to the foundation and growth of Laodicea and Hierapolis in such close proximity. Second, most of the surface remains have already been repurposed and lost. A large field of precut masonry blocks was irresistible to every succeeding generation of residents and settlers in the vicinity. For example, a group of large ashlars thought once to have belonged to a Byzantine-period church, perhaps even the cathedral of St. Michael the Archangel, now stands arranged as an animal pen in a field not far from the mound. And this relates to the third reason: any remains that are found are more likely to belong to the late Roman or early Byzantine period and not to the early imperial period, which would be of greater interest to students of the New Testament. This is due largely to the frequency and severity of earthquakes throughout the Lycus valley, some of which were so devastating (like the earthquake of AD 60 during Nero's reign) that very few monumental structures survived to remain in use (Eusebius, *Chron.* 2.154; Orosius, *Adv. pag.* 7.12).[6] This proved true as well for the neighboring cities of Hierapolis and Laodicea. Almost everything of interest dates from the Flavian period or later, often *centuries* later.

Laodicea

Colossae's neighbors to the west and the northwest (Laodicea and Hierapolis) have been substantially excavated and give a much better sense of the lived spaces of the Roman cities of the Lycus valley—and thus some context for thinking about the Christian communities that were founded by Epaphras

---

4. Standhartinger, "City with a Message," 246.
5. Standhartinger, "City with a Message," 240–41.
6. Standhartinger, "City with a Message," 243.

The late Roman version of the principal east-west thoroughfare through Laodicea.

in these three cities and that fell within Paul's scope of concern. The Christians in Laodicea gathered for worship, prayer, and instruction in the house of a woman named Nympha, whose hospitality was essential to the new community's flourishing. Paul wrote a letter to the church in Laodicea at about the same time that he wrote Colossians, instructing these two churches to exchange and read each other's letters. Paul's letter to the Christians in Laodicea is lost, unless, as some scholars argue, the so-called Letter to the Ephesians began its life in some fashion as Paul's letter to Laodicea.[7]

The city was founded by Antiochus II Theos, ruler of the Seleucid Kingdom from 261–46 BC, and named in honor of his first wife, Laodice. It was ideally situated at the intersection of two major roads, one of which came in from Ephesus to the east and extended westward through the whole of what is now Türkiye. The portion of this major east-west road that fell within the city walls and bisected Laodicea is clearly visible as a result of excavations. Excavations on both sides of this road are ongoing, particularly northward into the residential and small industrial areas of the city. These finds, however, date from the late Roman and Byzantine periods rather than the early imperial period of Paul and Epaphras's time. A second major road, one oriented essentially north to south, led to Pergamum to the north and Perge and the seaport city of Attalia on the Mediterranean shore to the south. Adjacent

7. See Muddiman, *Epistle to the Ephesians*, 20–32, 302–5, where a case is made for regarding Ephesians as a pseudepigraphic expansion of a recoverable Letter to the Laodiceans.

The public square, surrounded by columned porticoes.

to the main east-west street is a square once surrounded by porticoes, 32 yards wide and somewhat greater in length. It was accessible only by steps and thus closed to vehicular traffic. This dates to the turn of the era and may have served multiple purposes, from commercial activities to a staging area for festival processions.

Laodicea was thus well positioned to thrive from trade, including the export of its signature garments made from the glossy black wool of locally bred goats. Its commercial forums were once bustling centers of commerce. The central agora, likely the site of the city's oldest market, measures about 115 by 65 yards, though archaeologists are not certain that it achieved this size by the first century. Laodicea also gained considerable wealth through its services as a banking center. In the Greek and Roman periods, temples served not only as centers for the worship of the gods but also as repositories for the wealth of a city, its institutions, its private citizens, and foreigners. This symbiosis arose not only because temples were generally well constructed and well fortified but because of the strong social taboos against violating the sanctity of holy space. Stealing money from a neighbor's house was just theft, but removing goods from a temple was sacrilege against the gods and called down on the temple-robber the curse of human beings and gods alike. Given these economic conditions, the residents of Laodicea appear to have prospered during the early imperial period. The historian Tacitus, writing in the early second century, recalls that after the devastating earthquake of

The central marketplace of Laodicea.

AD 60 the Laodiceans were able to decline imperial aid and rebuild their city using their own resources, which was remembered as a source of pride for the city (*Ann.* 14.27).

Laodicea enjoyed all the amenities of a Greco-Roman city. In the first century, it already enjoyed a theater (the "West Theater"), carved in Hellenistic fashion into the west slope of a hill. It was capable of seating an audience of about eight thousand. A stadium—one of the three largest in Roman Asia— would be built during the reign of Titus and a second theater, with a capacity of twelve thousand, in the second century AD. The city also no doubt had bath complexes and public fountains, all fed by aqueduct and the city's water distribution system, though all the baths and fountains (nymphaea) hitherto excavated date from the third century AD and later. To really appreciate the layout and features of a Roman bath, one must look to Pompeii, where first-century bathhouses have been marvelously, if tragically, well preserved.

Surprisingly few temples have as yet been identified in Laodicea. Archaeologists have excavated a sprawling temple complex near the heart of the city, thought to have been used as a center for the cult of the emperors from the second century AD on. Laodicea was among the twelve cities of the province of Asia vying for the honor of hosting the provincial temple for the cult of Tiberius, though it was passed over as lacking sufficient size and resources at that point in its history (Tacitus, *Ann.* 4.55). It was finally awarded the honor of

The West Theater before and after excavation.

being named a *neokoros* city under Elaga-
balus in the early third century AD, with
this temple perhaps being renovated for the
occasion. A colonnade that runs between
the two theaters in the northern area of the
city probably marked the location of two
temples from the late Hellenistic and early
Roman periods. Inscriptions discovered in
the area suggest that the temples were dedicated to Athena and to Zeus. Coins attest
that the city's patron deity was Zeus, so
there was very likely a temple to Zeus present from early on in the city's history. These
two temples, however, were dismantled and
their materials incorporated into a grand
Christian basilica erected on the spot in
the period after Constantine. A statue of a
priestess of Isis suggests a cult to the Egyptian goddess, and perhaps the larger trio of
Isis, Serapis, and Horus (Harpocrates), at least by the second century AD.

A pillar bearing carvings of a menorah, lulab, and etrog, with a cross later superimposed upon the menorah.

Literary sources suggest that the city had a significantly large Jewish population (numbering in the thousands in the mid-first century BC), though almost no archaeological witness to their presence has yet been uncovered. One
exception is the rough carving on a pillar showing a menorah, a palm branch,
and a shofar, though the date of the carving is uncertain. The pillar was reused
in a Byzantine-period church with a bold cross engraved above the earlier
symbols. Indeed, what most strikes the visitor to the excavations in Laodicea
is the strong presence of Christian churches, basilicas, and decorations—
monuments to the triumph of the faith that Epaphras brought to the city
and that Paul nourished, at least through his writings, at a very early stage.

Hierapolis

Like Laodicea, Hierapolis has been rather thoroughly excavated, though,
once again, many of the discoveries postdate Paul's lifetime. Hierapolis was
founded by the Seleucid kings of the third century BC. As did both Colossae and Laodicea, Hierapolis also passed into the hands of the kingdom of
Pergamum in 188 BC, the year that Rome put a stop to the westward expansion of the Seleucid king Antiochus III. Hierapolis's streets were laid out in
the grid pattern typical of Hellenistic cities, a layout that would continue to

Travertine (marble) cascades formed by the hot springs immediately southeast of the city of Hierapolis.

determine the shape of the city for centuries to come. When the last king of Pergamum, Attalus III, died in 133 BC without an heir, he bequeathed his kingdom to Rome in his will.

Like Colossae and Laodicea, Hierapolis was heavily involved in the industry of producing, processing, and dyeing wool. The mineral-rich water from the thermal springs of Hierapolis had the property of fixing dyes and making wool colorfast (Strabo, *Geogr.* 13.4.14). These thermal springs were also sought out for their healing properties in antiquity, even as the modern spa hotels drawing on the same waters attract tourists today. Also like Colossae and Laodicea, the city that Epaphras would have known suffered major damage from the earthquake of AD 60. Significant rebuilding, renovations, and expansions took place under the Flavian emperors, especially under Domitian, through the second and third centuries AD.

Hierapolis was especially devoted to Apollo, and a temple to this god existed in the city from at least the reign of Tiberius.[8] Apollo was the patron god of the city, something made clear by representations of the city on

8. Riit, *Epigraphic Guide to Hierapolis*, 92.

A menorah carved into the lintel of a tomb.

only material clues to date, as Jewish tombs often featured religious symbols from the cultic life of the temple, the menorah being the most common. This is all the more disappointing as the presenting challenge behind Paul's letter to the Christians in neighboring Colossae appears to have involved an ascetic movement among the Jewish community that was having broader appeal on account of its rigor and its promise of opening devotees up to the worship in which the angels themselves participated, not entirely unlike the ascetic practice that led the Essenes at Qumran to believe that they were rendered worthy to join the angels themselves in the worship of God.

Epaphras prayed for, and perhaps even planted, the Christian congregation in Hierapolis; others, like Philip the Evangelist (see Acts 8:4–13, 26–40), were remembered to have watered it. Indeed, local tradition holds that Philip was martyred for his work there. A fifth-century shrine marks the traditional site of his execution. The church in Hierapolis would have long-lasting fruits. It would produce the early second-century bishop and scholar Papias and would continue to grow into the fourth and fifth centuries, when the church was sufficiently powerful to suppress local pagan cults—for example, by filling in the shrine to Hades and closing, at last, the portal to the underworld (as Christ, indeed, could be said to have done).

PART 3

ENDINGS

A mission of great importance to Paul that did *not* involve evangelism was the transportation of a significant collection of relief aid from his Gentile converts to the Christians in Jerusalem in AD 57 or 58 (Rom. 15:25–27). This was, for him, a sign of the unity of his mission churches with the mother church in Jerusalem as well as a token of his faithfulness to his agreement with the Jerusalem apostles to "continue to remember the poor" (Gal. 2:10). Luke is strangely silent about this collection project as the primary motivation for Paul's trip to Jerusalem (see the passing mention in Acts 24:17), though he appears to recount this voyage in great detail in Acts 20:4–21:17.

The trip appears, however, to have led to a riot against Paul in Jerusalem that led, in turn, to his imprisonment in Caesarea Maritima for two years followed by detention under house arrest in Rome for another two years (Acts 21:27–28:31). This is where Luke leaves off in his narrative of the expanding mission of the early church in general and the story of Paul in particular.

Was Paul released from custody in Rome at the end of his two-year period of house arrest? This is commonly affirmed, often in tandem with the conviction that he did make his planned missionary journey to Spain between AD 62 and his eventual execution prior to Nero's death in AD 68.[1] The

---

1. Clement of Rome is the earliest witness to such a journey, writing around AD 95 (1 Clem. 5.6–7). It is impossible to tell whether this is based on genuine historical knowledge of such a mission or on an inference from Rom. 15:23–29. In favor of this additional chapter in the ministry of Paul, see Schnabel, *Early Christian Mission*, 2:1271–83.

reprieve also makes room for missionary work on Crete, possibly in connection with additional visits to congregations that Paul and his team had already founded.[2] But as Luke thought it sufficient to bring his presentation of the ministry of Paul to an end with the apostle's arrival in Rome, we will here follow his lead.

2. Schnabel, *Early Christian Mission*, 2:1183–87.

13

MILETUS

Miletus in the Ministry of Paul

While Paul is on his way to Jerusalem to deliver the collection for the impoverished church there—and to begin his yearslong trial that would eventually take him to Rome—he makes a brief stop in Miletus (Acts 20:13–16). He does this to avoid having to make a longer stop in Ephesus, which would mean spending some time visiting his congregations there, since he is anxious to get to Jerusalem. He sends word, however, to the elders of the Ephesian churches to meet him in Miletus, where he delivers what might prove to be his last words to the church that was so central to his ministry in the region (20:17–38).

Miletus appears again in Paul's itinerary later in his life. As he writes his second letter to Timothy, one that bears all the evidence of being written in the shadow of impending martyrdom, he recalls that he left one of his teammates, Trophimus, ill in Miletus (2 Tim. 4:20). It may well be that, by that point, there was a Christian congregation in that city to whose members Paul could entrust his ailing partner.

The Archaeology of Miletus

Miletus was a formidable city in the sixth and fifth centuries BC. It led a revolt after the Persian conquest and paid for it with near-total destruction in 494 BC. Rebuilding commenced by 479 BC under the direction of the city's own Hippodamus, the urban planner credited with perfecting the grid-like system of roads that would become the hallmark of Greek and Roman cities

The base and remaining architectural fragments of the round harbor monument and the western wing of the Harbor Stoa. The design once featured Tritons (half men, half fish) holding oars and rudders, dolphins, and the carved prows of ships.

ever after.[1] Miletus was incorporated into the Roman Empire in 133 BC as a result of the natural death of King Attalus III of Pergamum, who bequeathed his kingdom to Rome.[2]

Paul arrived by ship in AD 57 or 58, docking in one of Miletus's four harbors. As a result of centuries of silting, Miletus now sits 5 miles inland—a fate shared with Ephesus, the major port city to the north. The largest of the harbors, flanked by statues of lions at its mouth, thus known as Lion

1. Wilson, *Biblical Turkey*, 265; Niewöhner, *Miletus/Balat*, 7, 9. Hippodamus did not *invent* the pattern, as several cities were laid out in grid patterns prior to his time, but he improved on it by using it to determine the width that various streets in the city would need to be for optimal traffic flow in public versus private areas (Niewöhner, *Miletus/Balat*, 29).

2. Niewöhner, *Miletus/Balat*, 20.

Harbor, would have landed Paul on the northeast part of the city. On disembarking, he would have seen a striking monument standing 25 feet above the harbor's inner shore. Originally built in the second century BC, the harbor had already been economically rededicated on several occasions to honor new Roman heroes. In 63 BC, it had been dedicated to Pompey the Great for his ridding the sea of pirates; later, it was reinscribed with a dedication to Augustus in celebration of his victory over Marc Antony at Actium in 31 BC.[3]

Behind the Harbor Stoa was the north agora, which had occupied that location, strategically close to the docks of the Lion Harbor, since the fifth century BC.[4] Like most such marketplaces, it featured an open area surrounded by rows of stone-built shops fronted by long columned porticoes.

Walking east from the harbor and through a monumental gate built during the first half of the first century AD, Paul would have been struck next by the sight of a giant open-air temple dedicated to Apollo, portrayed here with dolphin iconography to recall Apollo's role as the protector of sailors. The sacred area, established in the sixth century BC, measured about 170 by 200 feet. By the time of Paul's visit, it was fronted on its west side by a beautiful gateway and surrounded by columned porticoes. Originally it housed only a large altar (along with smaller circular altars and

A decorative carved tripod—a common symbol of Apollo and his oracular mouthpieces—discovered in the bouleuterion in Miletus but thought to have once topped the harbor monument (Pergamonmuseum, Berlin) (see Bayhan, *Priene*, 103, 105).

decorative exedrae, which were large semicircular benches adorned with statues standing atop the tall backs of the benches), but a circular shrine with a

3. Niewöhner, *Miletus/Balat*, 52–54.
4. Bayhan, *Priene*, 102; Wilson, *Biblical Turkey*, 270.

A short segment of the Sacred Way connecting Miletus and Didyma.

cult image of Apollo appears to have been erected by the first century. The sacred area was also a place for displaying important civic documents in the form of inscriptions, becoming also in this way a kind of archive.[5]

The worship of Apollo was as important in this region as the worship of his sister Artemis was in Ephesus. Half a century after Paul, the emperor Trajan would honor Miletus by repairing the 12-mile road connecting its sanctuary of Apollo to the monumental Temple of Apollo at Didyma to the south. Priests and worshipers would travel this Sacred Way as part of an annual festival honoring Apollo at both sites, probably culminating at Didyma. One hundred and twelve columns, each 50 feet high, originally surrounded and supported this temple. Its interior, too, was probably mostly open to the sky: a large courtyard within a temple, with a small sanctuary within the courtyard for the cult image of Apollo.[6] With a footprint of 168 by 358 feet, it was the Greek-speaking world's fourth largest temple.[7] It was also the home of one of Apollo's principal oracles; the other two

5. Bayhan, *Priene*, 101–2; Niewöhner, *Miletus/Balat*, 61–64.
6. Bayhan, *Priene*, 129–31.
7. Wilson, *Biblical Turkey*, 274.

A view of the exterior of the Temple of Apollo at Didyma.

were consulted at Delphi in Greece and at Claros, about 13 miles northwest of Ephesus.

As Paul continued past Miletus's sacred precincts of Apollo, he would have walked alongside the newly constructed Ionic Stoa, a covered portico with thirty-five columns that extended several hundred feet alongside the Sacred Way with spaces for nineteen shopkeepers to set up their businesses. Inscriptions show this stoa to have been the gift of one Tiberius Claudius Sophanes, built in AD 50.[8] It would be extended even further south in the century to follow.

Behind this stoa sat a large bath complex recently donated to the city by Cnaeus Vergilius Capito, governor of Asia and Egypt during the latter half of Claudius's reign (AD 41–54).[9] This was a complete Roman bath experience with cold pools, saunas, warm pools, and an exercise yard. To the south of the Capito Baths, approached through the Ionic Stoa, sat a courtyard surrounded by columned porticoes and fitted with five rooms on its sides, dating from the second century BC. It is unclear whether this served as part of a small gymnasium complex or an administrative center.[10]

8. Bayhan, *Priene*, 97–98.
9. Niewöhner, *Miletus/Balat*, 69–72.
10. Bayhan, *Priene*, 93; Niewöhner, *Miletus/Balat*, 75–76.

The Ionic Stoa, seen from the Sacred Way.

Diagonally across from the south end of the Ionic Stoa, Paul would have spotted the bouleuterion, or city council chamber. This was a semicircular hall with rows of seats where the leading citizens debated public policy. Only nine rows are still (mostly) in place, though originally there were twice as many, suggesting a seating capacity of 1,200 to 1,500.[11] The council chamber was approached through a large square courtyard, in the middle of which stood a rectangular structure (30 by 23 feet) that appears to have been an imperial cult site, perhaps a monumental altar similar to the Altar of the Augustan Peace on the Campus Martius (Field of Mars) in Rome. Miletus had also built a temple to the emperor Gaius (Caligula) during his lifetime, though it was surely repurposed after his death and the Roman Senate's de facto condemnation of his memory (Claudius vetoed the formal act of the Senate in this regard).[12]

If Paul approached close enough to examine the inscription recording the dedication of the complex, he would have experienced a chill. The bouleuterion

11. Bayhan, *Priene*, 94; Niewöhner, *Miletus/Balat*, 90–91.
12. Wilson, *Biblical Turkey*, 265.

The inscription naming Antiochus (IV) Epiphanes in connection with the construction of the bouleu-terion, with the surviving rows of seating in the council chamber itself visible on the top left.

bore an inscription honoring Antiochus IV Epiphanes, ruler of the Seleucid Empire from 175 to 164 BC, most likely for his subsidizing the construction of the council chamber (perhaps as a favor to the two Milesian citizens named in the inscription who also had served in the Seleucid government).[13] Under Antiochus IV, and with his full authorization, Jerusalem had been refounded as a Greek city in 175 BC, the first of a series of events that led eventually to the desecration of the Jerusalem temple—what came to be spoken of as the "abomination of desolation" (see 1 Macc. 1:54; Dan. 11:31; 12:11)—and the persecution of the faithful Jews who resisted his "improvements."

South of the bouleuterion was the principal agora of the city, dating from the Hellenistic period. Two of its four colonnades—those on the east and south sides—had spaces for permanent shops or businesses. The vast court-yard of 538 by 643 feet would have accommodated an army of vendors and their kiosks.[14] Paul and his traveling companions, of course, were only in this city long enough to send for, and to say goodbye to, a select group of leaders from the Christian community in Ephesus—not to set up shop, as it were, for long-term mission work. It is difficult to imagine the apostle to the Gentiles, however, not spending at least some of his handful of days in the city either strengthening a Christian church that had already been planted or sowing the seeds of one that might blossom later by preaching in such public spaces as this marketplace.

Like most major cities, Miletus also had a theater. As in Ephesus, the Miletus theater overlooked a harbor—the city's second harbor and another

13. Niewöhner, *Miletus/Balat*, 91.
14. Bayhan, *Priene*, 90; Wilson, *Biblical Turkey*, 272.

The bases of pillars and walls marking the footprint of a Hellenistic-period warehouse, a massive structure of about 178 by 15 yards, as well as the north edge of the south agora.

The Miletus theater. The remains of the first level of the stage building are clearly visible on the right.

possible point of entry or departure for the apostle. During the Hellenistic period, the theater could seat 5,300 people; renovations and expansions during the Roman period increased its capacity to 15,000.[15] This theater had a special covered area front and center for dignitaries, who enjoyed seating in stone chairs carved with backs rather than enduring long performances on the typical backless benches.

Various associations and groups within the city also claimed certain sections as their own reserved seating. An inscription of particular interest is one that appears to claim a small area of the theater's seating for people attached in some form to the Jewish community. The syntax of the inscription most naturally reads, "The place of the Jews, the ones who are also God-fearing," which could be understood in a number of ways: (1) the Gentile adherents of the synagogue who continued to frequent the theater; (2) local Jews (probably along with Gentile adherents) whom the inscriber also describes as "God-fearers," not being clear on the distinction between Jews and God-fearers.[16] Either way, it is an interesting witness to the use of the term "God-fearers" in the second century AD and to some degree of integration of the community that identified as Jewish in the larger cultural life of the city.

A temple of Dionysus once stood to the east of the theater, likely built during the Hellenistic period, though it was leveled to make room for a church in the seventh century AD.[17] Had Paul had occasion to walk south of the theater—along what would have been the shore of a second ancient harbor—he would have come to the city's stadium and principal gymnasium complex, the result of a generous donation by King Eumenes II of

The "God-fearer" inscription from the Miletus theater.

15. Bayhan, *Priene*, 68; Niewöhner, *Miletus/Balat*, 31–33.
16. It is common to translate the inscription as "the place of the Judeans and God-fearers," but this would require correcting the order of the words actually inscribed, though it is indeed not impossible that the inscriber made a mistake.
17. Niewöhner, *Miletus/Balat*, 44–48.

Pergamum,[18] and thence to a temple to Athena, first built in the early fifth century BC.[19] According to Acts, however, Paul came to Miletus with more of a retrospective than a prospective glance. He was there just long enough for his messenger to travel to Ephesus, gather the elders, and bring them back with him to Miletus—perhaps a three-day task if traveling between the cities by boat, six (hard) days if traveling by foot—so that he could do what he could to secure his work in Ephesus for the future through their commitment to diligent oversight in the years and decades that would follow his own death.

18. Bayhan, *Priene*, 80–81; Wilson, *Biblical Turkey*, 269. Some prefer to regard the expansive gymnasium as yet another marketplace (e.g., Bayhan, *Priene*, 80). The archaeology is not entirely clear on this point, though the fact that both the "agora" and the stadium measure 100 yards in length may suggest that the former space was indeed also designed for athletic practice.
    19. Bayhan, *Priene*, 78; Wilson, *Biblical Turkey*, 269.

14

RHODES

The next ship that Paul took to move closer to Jerusalem from Miletus made stops on the island of Cos (a little more than 40 miles south of Miletus) and then on the island of Rhodes (a voyage of perhaps 75 additional miles; Acts 21:1). It was typical for most ships to hug shorelines and make frequent anchorage for greater safety and easier navigation, for the offloading and on-loading of cargoes, and for refreshing supplies. Local tradition places Paul's landing halfway down the eastern coast of the island, in a harbor at Lindos, one of the ancient city-states on the island of Rhodes.

The sacred sites on the city's acropolis watched over the larger settlement, which was closer to sea level. If Paul landed in one of the Lindos harbors, he might have taken himself on a tour of the city, as he did when he arrived at Athens. Halfway up the path to the acropolis, he would have seen a Greek galley—a trireme, so named after the three rows of oarsmen—carved into the cliff face as part of a monument to the military commander Agesander, in honor of a naval victory in 180 BC.[1] At that time the commander's statue stood in a niche carved into the wall. Continuing his climb, Paul would have entered the acropolis itself through a gate in the Hellenistic wall and would have been greeted by the sight of an expansive colonnade built in the second century BC, stretching about 250 feet in length.[2] At the midpoint of this colonnade, steps led up to the highest level of the acropolis, through an impressive gatehouse, or propylon, and into the courtyard in front of the Temple of

1. Fant and Reddish, *Guide to Biblical Sites*, 114.
2. Fant and Reddish, *Guide to Biblical Sites*, 114.

The so-called St. Paul's Harbor at Lindos, a natural harbor cut off from the sea, apart from a narrow entrance located at the bottom left of the harbor in the photo (here obscured by the edge of the cliff of the acropolis).

The Hellenistic-period portico atop the Lindos acropolis, part of the impressive complex surrounding the Temple of Athena.

Athena, boldly placed against the edge of the cliffside. The present remains date to the early Hellenistic period, the last of a series of renovations and reconstructions.

The Temple of Athena at Lindos.

The acropolis was a showplace for Rhodian religion and the Rhodian elite. The whole was once decorated with statues of gods and of civic benefactors. Several distinctive monuments called exedrae can still be seen here. These were semicircular stone benches erected in honor of an illustrious family, such as Pamphilidas, a third-century BC priest, and his family. Statues once stood on the perimeter of a bench immortalizing Pamphilidas and select members of his line. A similar monument was erected closer to the Temple of Athena to the emperor Tiberius and the imperial family.

Aside from tradition, however, there is little reason to suppose that Paul's ship made its layover in the harbor of Lindos. Harboring at the principal city of Rhodes, called by the name of the island, would have made much more sense. Located on the northern part of the island, it would have been the natural stopping point for a ship arriving from Cos and bound for the southern coast of Türkiye (the port of Patara; Acts 21:1).

The Rhodes harbor was celebrated in antiquity for the Colossus of Rhodes, a bronze statue of the sun god, Helios, originally standing about 100 feet tall. The statue was erected in thanksgiving for the defeat of Demetrius Poliorketes, son of one of the warring successors of Alexander the Great, who had laid siege to Rhodes in 305 BC. The sale of the siege engines and other supplies left behind by Demetrius provided the funds for the construction of the colossus.

Once numbered among the seven wonders of the world, it collapsed during an earthquake in 226 BC, little more than fifty years after its completion. The common depiction of the colossus as standing astride the harbor of Rhodes is certainly incorrect. The earthquake caused the statue to collapse onto dry ground, where it was still visible to admiring tourists for centuries before being broken up and melted down in the early Arab period. If it originally stood astride the harbor, it would have collapsed into the water and been lost to view.

Like Lindos, the city of Rhodes also had a splendid acropolis. Part of the facade and the entire foundation of the Temple of Apollo can still be seen today. Apollo, also connected with the sun, was an appropriate deity to highlight for the city that considered Helios its patron god. Herod the Great allocated substantial funds for the reconstruction of this temple after it burned down in a fire (Josephus, *J.W.* 1.424). This was but one of his many benefactions to Greek cities, a principal means by which he made a name for himself (and a positive reputation for Judea) throughout the Eastern Mediterranean.[3] He had a special heart for Rhodes, however, since it was there that he, a refugee from his own country, met Marc Antony and gained his support for a return to Judea as king of

A larger-than-life-size statue of Helios from the second century AD, the deity represented also by the Colossus of Rhodes.

the Jews (Josephus, *J.W.* 1.280). Next to the Apollo temple stood a temple to Apollo's twin sister, Artemis. Only parts of the foundation remain to be seen. These twin temples overlooked a large stadium, the site of the Rhodian games. A gymnasium was once located beyond the stadium, a place where foreign competitors would stay and train for several weeks before the games. A small odeon also once graced the site.

3. Richardson, *Herod*, 201–2.

The Temple of Apollo on the acropolis of Rhodes.

The largely reconstructed stadium situated just below the Temples of Apollo and Artemis.

Paul's conscience would no doubt have been pricked in Rhodes, just as it had been in Athens, as he saw the devotion of the city's inhabitants to their "gods." His mission, however, did not permit him to remain in the city for one hour more than was necessary for his ship to offload any cargo and take on any new supplies it would require for the next leg of the journey. No doubt the fact that he and his traveling companions were carrying a sizable sum of money added to the urgency, since they would have desired to deliver the relief funds before any mishap could overtake them. The ship would land at Patara on the southern coast of modern Türkiye, about 60 miles east of Rhodes. There Paul and his companions would arrange for passage on another ship that would take them closer to their destination. This one would pass by Cyprus and dock at Tyre, apparently to remain there a week—allowing Paul and his team to connect with a Christian community in that important port city—before heading south to Ptolemais and finally to Caesarea Maritima (Acts 21:2–8).

TYRE

Tyre has a long history of intersecting with the biblical story, beginning with King David and King Solomon arranging to secure building supplies and skilled artisans from King Hiram of Tyre for the construction of David's palace and of the Solomonic temple in the tenth century BC (see 2 Sam. 5:11; 1 Kings 5:10–11). The schedule of the merchant vessel on which Paul and his companions had booked passage included a week's layover in Tyre, which they used as an opportunity to connect with the Christian community there (Acts 21:3–6). Excavations in Tyre (modern Sour) have focused to date on uncovering and restoring the city as it existed in the second and third centuries AD, after it received major facelifts under Hadrian and Septimius Severus. Thus very little of the Tyre that Paul would have seen in the first century is visible today. This is a pity since, according to Josephus (*J.W.* 1.422), Herod the Great subsidized the construction of halls, porticoes, temples, and agoras in Tyre—a similar level of beneficence to what he lavished upon Berytus (Beirut).[a]

a. Richardson, *Herod*, 201.

15

JERUSALEM

Paul arrived at last in Jerusalem, essentially returning to the place he began in the narrative of Acts. Paul himself, however, provides few details about his own upbringing. From his letters we would never know of his connection to Tarsus as his native city nor suspect that he had enjoyed extensive training in Jerusalem during his youth and young adult years. All that information comes secondhand through Luke, as does the report of Paul's preaching in the synagogues in Jerusalem for a short while after his conversion—before he had to leave Jerusalem for his own safety even as he had fled Damascus just before (Acts 9:26–30). Luke previously recounted Stephen's provocative proclamation of Jesus in the "Synagogue of the Freedmen," with Greek-speaking Jews from the Roman provinces of Cyrenaica, Egypt, Cilicia, and Asia reportedly present (6:8–10). These diaspora Jews were also the source of the charges against Stephen that led to his execution by stoning. While Luke does not specify the venue, one might suspect that Paul also chose synagogues for Greek-speaking Jews when he promoted Jesus as the Messiah among "the Hellenists" in Jerusalem for a short time.[1]

An important inscription attesting to the existence of synagogues serving the Greek-speaking Jewish community in the first century AD was discovered in a cistern in the residential district just south of the Temple Mount (see photo on p. 226). This inscription commemorates the substantial monetary contribution made by "Theodotus, the son of Vettenos, priest and *archisynagogos*, son of an *archisynagogos*, grandson of an *archisynagogos*" to

---

1. On the tension between the accounts in Acts (9:26–30; 26:19–20) and Paul's own account of his presence and activity in Jerusalem at about the same time (Gal. 1:18–20, 23), as well as possible ways to reconcile a good portion of the tension, see deSilva, *Letter to the Galatians*, 165–67.

The Theodotus inscription (Israel Museum).

build a "synagogue [*synagōgē*] for the reading of the Law . . . and the study
of the commandments, and a guesthouse and rooms and water installations
for hosting those in need from abroad, it . . . having been founded by his fathers, the presbyters, and Simonides."[2] The fact that the text was inscribed in
Greek suggests that the synagogue was frequented particularly by repatriated
Greek-speaking Jews from the diaspora as well as by those visiting Jerusalem
from the diaspora for whatever reason, but especially for the major pilgrim-
age festivals of the Jewish liturgical calendar. The guest rooms were likely
offered to such pilgrims. The inscription also attests to the use of the title
archisynagōgos, "president of the synagogue," encountered also in the Gospels
and Acts (see, for example, Luke 8:49; 13:14; Acts 13:15; 18:8, 17), a title that
appears sometimes to denote an active role in leadership, sometimes to serve
as an honorific for a local benefactor, probably in many cases to denote both.[3]

Paul speaks of a further meeting in Jerusalem with James, Peter, and John
that he considered to be of great importance as it won for him their recognition of the validity of his calling and work and established some basic guide-
lines for the coexisting missions of Peter and Paul (Gal. 2:1–10). Whether
this was the same visit as, or a visit prior to, the one that Paul and Barnabas
made for the conference that adjudicated between Paul's practice and the
Judaizing teachers' demands (Acts 15:1–29) is a highly debated question.[4]

2. Quoted in Levine, *Jerusalem*, 395.
3. Magness, *Archaeology of the Holy Land*, 288.
4. Concerning the positions in this debate and one possible solution, see deSilva, *Letter to
the Galatians*, 48–58.

Luke mentions in passing yet another brief visit that Paul made to greet the brothers and sisters in Jerusalem en route to Antioch as he returned from his mission to Macedonia and Achaia (Acts 18:22). We can be certain that Paul, together with a number of his team, made a visit to Jerusalem in AD 57 or 58. In Romans 15:25–29, Paul speaks of this trip, which he was about to undertake to convey the money collected among his predominantly Gentile converts for the relief of the poor among the Christ-followers in Jerusalem and Judea. In all likelihood, this is also the fateful trip recounted in Acts 21:17–36 that resulted in Paul's arrest, two-year detention in Caesarea Maritima, and eventual transfer to Rome.

According to Acts, James, the half brother of Jesus and leader of the Jerusalem church, urged Paul to take public action to discredit the rumors, widespread among the law-observant community of Jewish Christ-followers in Jerusalem, that Paul himself was an apostate from the Mosaic law and led other Jews into similar disregard for the Torah. This action would take Paul to the temple, where he would perform all that was appropriate for a law-observant Jew as well as subsidize the sacrifices that he and four fellow Jews would make at the end of seven days, marking the completion of a vow they had taken.

The broad steps on the southern side of the Temple Mount leading to the twin gates and internal stairways that delivered temple-bound traffic to the middle of the court, which was open to all races. These steps and entrances were a part of Herod's innovations to the complex.

Well-preserved shops once sheltered by Robinson's Arch and the grand staircase, which allowed foot traffic to enter the temple complex at its southwest corner. The street on which these shops sit is a Herodian or early Roman north-south street that ran alongside the western retaining wall of the Temple Mount in Paul's time.

Paul's presence in the temple, however, had the opposite effect. Jews visiting Jerusalem from the Roman province of Asia brought an allegation against Paul that they had seen him take Trophimus, an Ephesian Gentile convert to Christianity, beyond the outer court that was appropriate for Gentile God-fearers and visitors into the inner courts of the temple that were set apart solely for Jews and full converts. This was a jealously guarded boundary. Greek-speaking Jews wrote narratives in which God defended this boundary himself against encroachment on the part of Gentiles (see 2 Macc. 3:22–40; 3 Macc. 1:16–2:24) and in which the ability of Gentiles to cross with impunity on a particular occasion demonstrated God's anger against the nation (2 Macc. 5:15–20). Herod had fitted his renovated temple complex with a chest-high balustrade a few yards out from the inner courts of the temple with openings at regular intervals. Beside these openings he had warnings inscribed on blocks: "No member of another race may enter within the barrier and perimeter around the sanctuary. Whoever is caught will be the cause of his [or her] own subsequent death" (see Josephus, *Ant.* 15.417; *J.W.* 5.193–94; 6.125).

Two mikvahs from the immediate vicinity of the temple complex. Paul and his companions would have performed lustrations in one of the many such mikvahs surrounding the temple, if not in one of the larger pools provided for this purpose for the hordes of pilgrims heading for the sacred precincts, in conjunction with their visit to the temple (Acts 21:26).

The sole surviving complete exemplar of the inscription warning foreigners not to cross the perimeter fence separating the outer court, which was open to people of all ethnicities, from the inner courts, which were exclusively reserved for Jews (Istanbul Archaeological Museum).

Paul's reputation for disregarding the law of Moses, according to Luke's report at least, made this allegation sufficiently credible to stir up a riot against Paul in those very temple courts, resulting in Paul's being taken into Roman custody, led into the Antonia Fortress at the northwest corner of the temple complex, and soon thereafter delivered to the governor Antonius Felix in Caesarea Maritima.

16

CAESAREA MARITIMA

Caesarea Maritima in the Ministry of Paul

Caesarea Maritima, or "Caesarea by the Sea," is a familiar location in the story of the early church as told in the book of Acts. It was here that the centurion Cornelius resided and was visited by Peter, resulting in a watershed event that would lead the church to include Gentiles in its mission henceforth (Acts 10:1–48; 11:1–18; 15:7–11). It was here that King Agrippa I, a grandson of Herod the Great, would be struck dead by God's unseen hand (12:20–23). Paul would become very familiar with Caesarea. After his conversion and his initial attempts to promote his newfound understanding of Jesus's place in God's drama of salvation, the disciples in Jerusalem spirited him away to Caesarea for his own protection, getting passage for him on a ship bound for his home city of Tarsus (9:30). He would land again at Caesarea after his so-called third missionary journey and travel overland to Jerusalem to greet the believers there before heading to Antioch-on-the-Orontes (18:22–23). He would put in to port at Caesarea yet again as he journeyed a final time to Jerusalem, presumably bearing the collection for the poor among the believers in Judea (21:8–16). This visit would lead, of course, to his arrest in Jerusalem and detention in Caesarea for no fewer than two years, during which time his case would have preliminary hearings before the Roman governors Felix and Festus and Herod's great-grandson Agrippa II.

The Archaeology of Caesarea Maritima

Before there were either Herods or Caesars, a much smaller and less grand Hellenistic city stood on this spot. Founded in the fourth century BC by Strato (Abd-Astarte), king of Sidon, the small city came to be known as Strato's Tower.[1] The city was built to provide a convenient rest stop for sailors in the business of the maritime trade between Sidon and Egypt as they made their way down the coast from port to port. A small harbor had been constructed on its north side. The jetty, or mole, that once served as a breakwater has been crushed by the waves over the centuries. The "tower" for which the town was named may have been a landmark or even a light-house on the promontory on which Herod would later build his seaside vil-la.[2] North of this promontory an artificial harbor was dug inland, providing a second, southern harbor for the seaport town. Strato's Tower is mentioned in the Zenon Papyri, the archives of a certain official named Zenon, who sailed from Alexandria to Strato's Tower to begin his inspection tour of the province on behalf of Ptolemy II Philadelphus and his finance minister, Apollonius, in 259 BC. The Hellenistic town was almost certainly fortified with walls and towers. According to some archaeologists, the remains of a tower and wall on the north side of the site date from the second century BC, perhaps built particularly to defend the coastal Gentile town from the newly established and actively expansionist Hasmonean dynasty, which had wrested control of Judea from the Seleucid dynasty. Others prefer to regard these structures as part of Herod's own fortification of the city.[3] The northern gate gave access to a residential area, very little of which has been excavated.

The Hasmonean king Alexander Jannaeus successfully annexed Strato's Tower along with the other coastal cities of Palestine by 103 BC, opening the cities up to Jewish inhabitants and significantly improving Judean access to maritime trade (Josephus, *Ant.* 13.334–37). Henceforth, it would be a city for Greeks and Jews, a combination that would foster significant tension during the next century and a half. When Pompey the Great intervened in the civil wars that had erupted between the two sons of Alexander Jannaeus—Hyrcanus II and Aristobulus II—from 67 to 63 BC, he not only stripped the title of king from the last Hasmoneans but also stripped away the territories they had conquered during the eighty years of their domination.

---

1. Holum et al., *King Herod's Dream*, 27.
2. Holum et al., *King Herod's Dream*, 27–28.
3. The former view is expressed in Porath et al., "Caesarea," 1658; Holum et al., *King Herod's Dream*, 53. The latter seems to be the view of Netzer, *Architecture of Herod*, 99.

The remains of a round defensive tower, typical for the Hellenistic period, and the perimeter wall at the northern end of Caesarea. A second round tower once stood on the opposite side of the central gate.

By 31 BC, however, the political face of both Rome and Judea had changed. Octavian, soon to be called Augustus, had become the undisputed ruler of the Roman Empire and Herod the Great his loyal client king over Judea. Octavian increased Herod's territories to include the seacoast cities, a sign of his confidence in both Herod's loyalty and his competence. Herod found that Strato's Tower had fallen into disuse and disrepair (Josephus calls the town "dilapidated," *J.W.* 1.408), setting the stage for his most ambitious building program next to the Temple Mount in Jerusalem itself. The principal features of the city were put in place between 22 and 10 BC, a remarkably short time for such a significant change to the landscape and seascape.[4]

Herod would make of Caesarea a major Mediterranean seaport, facilitating the sale of the produce of his land across the Roman world, the import of luxury goods from abroad, and the collection of taxes and customs that would be levied in a busy center of trade. Pottery vessels found throughout the site testify to a trade network connecting Caesarea with every region around the Mediterranean. To accomplish this, Herod undertook the construction of a vast artificial harbor. In the words of Josephus, "The king triumphed over nature and constructed a harbor larger than the Piraeus," the primary port

4. Holum et al., *King Herod's Dream*, 72.

Aerial view of the harbor of Caesarea. The natural promontories that marked the middle harbor are still visible. The moles that bounded Herod's outer harbor appear as deteriorated rubble beneath the surface of the sea in the upper portion of the picture. The arrow in the top right marks the entrance to Herod's outer harbor. The arrow in the bottom center marks the front of the platform of Herod's Temple of Augustus and Roma. The inner harbor would have occupied the lawn and much of the area of the buildings to the right of it.

of Athens (Josephus, *J.W.* 1.410, trans. Thackeray). The portion of the harbor visible today—the result of repeated rebuilds of Herod's middle harbor during the Byzantine and Crusader eras—represents only one-third to one-fourth of the total area of Herod's triple harbor. Herod's middle harbor consisted of about 240 square yards of sea area protected in the main by natural promontories to the north and south that remain visible today.

To create the outer harbor, Herod had a breakwater constructed that extended another 220 yards west from the southern promontory of the middle harbor and then turned north for another 330 yards to isolate the whole harbor area from the sea and its pounding surf. He also created a second breakwater that extended about 200 yards west from the northern promontory.[5] These moles were sufficiently wide to allow for exterior fortification walls, a broad promenade, and loading and unloading areas. An entrance was created for ships on the north side in the northwest corner, where the winds and waves were the calmest. The breakwaters were constructed mostly of concrete rather than cut rocks. Herod's engineers used the Roman invention

5. Raban, "Maritime Caesarea," 287.

of hydraulic cement (cement that hardened underwater), a combination of stone rubble, lime, and a special volcanic ash (pozzolana) imported from Italy. Massive wooden forms were built and floated out into place. The mixture was then dumped into them, sinking them into the sea. The castings typically measure about 40 cubic yards, though some reach a volume of 160 cubic yards.[6] Unfortunately, the sea would soon neutralize Herod's achievement. Within a century, parts of the breakwaters collapsed as the sands subsided and became an additional hazard to ships. In the following centuries, the Herodian breakwaters sank into the sand and were broken down by the waves, visible now merely as murky shadows reaching out to sea below the surface.

Herod's desire to honor his political patron, Augustus, for the gift of this territory is everywhere evident. He named the harbor itself Sebastos, the Greek equivalent of Augustus. The city was renamed Caesarea to honor the same man. Herod went beyond this, and beyond what any law-observant Jew would countenance. On the most prominent place in the area of the harbor, visible for a great distance out to sea and dominating the harbor itself, he built a grand temple to Augustus and the goddess Roma. The artificially extended platform rose about 11 yards above street and harbor level. The temple itself had a footprint of 50 by 30 yards and rose another 23 yards in height. It was surrounded by a broad courtyard of about 100 by 110 yards, bounded by colonnades in the Corinthian order on three sides, leaving the front of the temple in plain view of the harbor and the many ships putting into port—perhaps, Herod imagined, in plain view of his patron across the sea in Rome.[7] The temple was approached by a broad staircase (22 yards wide) from a landing at the innermost harbor. Little of note survives of this temple beyond its massive foundations and a few architectural fragments, in large measure because it was deconstructed to provide room and materials for an octagonal church built on the site around AD 500.[8] It appears to have been grander than either of the temples to Augustus and Rome that Herod built in Samaria or in the vicinity of the grotto of Pan near Banias (the city that would come to be known as Caesarea Philippi after Herod the Great's death). According to Josephus, within the temple stood two cult images: "A colossal statue of the emperor, not inferior to the Olympian Zeus, which served for its model, and another of Rome, rivalling that of Hera at Argos" (Josephus, *J.W.* 1.414, trans. Thackeray).

---

6. Netzer, *Architecture of Herod*, 100–101.
7. Netzer, *Architecture of Herod*, 103–6.
8. Porath et al., "Caesarea," 1666–67.

The platform on which once sat Herod's monumental temple to Augustus and Roma. A modern stair-case covers the remains of the ancient approach to the platform (itself cut in half in the Byzantine period). The lawn would have been part of the inner harbor and its quay in the Herodian and early Roman period.

Herod's cult image of Augustus probably resembled, on a much larger scale, this seated statue of Augustus from a shrine in Herculaneum, Italy, which depicts the emperor in a regal seated pose reminiscent of the famous cult statue of Zeus in Olympia, Greece, often named one of the seven wonders of the ancient world (left). The cult image of the goddess Roma likely resembled this second-century AD statue of Roma housed at the Capitoline Museums in Rome (right).

One of a series of warehouses discovered south of the harbor. This one was converted into a shrine for the cult of Mithras in the third century AD.

Herod provided a Roman-style marketplace, or forum, for his city as well. This has not been positively identified but likely stood in the area just north of, and in the shadow of, the Temple of Augustus and Roma. Herod would also have provided the city with scores of warehouses for the storage of grain, amphorae of wine and olive oil, and other cargoes bound for ports west on the Mediterranean, though none identified so far can be confidently dated to the Herodian or earliest Roman periods.

Herod also provided Caesarea with all the accoutrements of Roman culture. In the southernmost area of the city, Herod had a theater constructed (likely the first in his territory) sufficient to accommodate four thousand viewers.[9] This would be the venue for Agrippa I's display of hubris that, according to Josephus, led to his demise (Josephus, *Ant.* 19.343–50; the location in Acts 12:20–23 is unspecified). Between the theater and the harbor sat an expansive hippodrome, a long oval stadium for chariot racing. The arena itself, apart from seating, occupied a space of 330 by 55 yards. A long central divider, called a *spina*, created a circuit around which the chariot drivers would have

---

9. Netzer, *Architecture of Herod*, 112–15.

The southern bend of the hippodrome.

to travel seven times. The course was purposefully too narrow for the number of chariots involved, resulting in spectacular crashes, particularly around the turns. Archaeologists disagree concerning the arrangements for the seating. Some believe that it was provided in the usual configuration along the two long sides and the southern bend, though the western seats have been thoroughly demolished by the sea over the centuries.[10] Others suggest that there never was seating on the seaside wing, perhaps to allow for a less obstructed view of the ocean.[11] This was likely the venue in which Herod celebrated the inaugural games of the city sometime around 10 BC—games that were to take place every five years thereafter in honor of the emperor.

On the promontory between the theater and the hippodrome Herod built his seaside palace. Almost nothing survives of what was no doubt once a magnificent structure. The outline of a swimming pool with dimensions of about 40 by 22 yards is still clearly visible. A statue or other ornamental structure once stood in its center. The pool was surrounded by columned porticoes on every side, with the king's private chambers constructed behind

10. Netzer, *Architecture of Herod*, 116.
11. Porath et al., "Caesarea," 1658.

the pool on elevated foundations, all of which has long since been crushed by and submerged into the sea. Finely decorated rooms for entertaining guests and other functions stood on the inland side of the pool.

The palace was approached by land through an expansive courtyard surrounded by roofed colonnades, covering a space of approximately 70 by 46 yards. On the north side stood a large reception hall of 16 by 18 yards—the sort of "audience hall" (Acts 25:23) that would have well served judicial functions like Paul's hearing before Festus, Agrippa II, and Berenice. The hall

The footprint of Herod's promontory palace. The dining room dominates the bottom center of the photo, the swimming pool the upper center.

A multicolored, geometric mosaic, typical in Herodian architecture, marked the centerpiece of a large triclinium (dining room). Three dining couches would have flanked the mosaic, with the space toward the pool left open to view.

was surrounded by other rooms of various sizes, the precise function of each now eluding archaeologists on account of their greatly deteriorated (eroded) condition.[12] It is not clear to what extent the remains currently visible reflect Herod's initial plan or later modifications, from the period after Judea came under the direct governance of Roman prefects and procurators in AD 6.[13] After AD 6, it is likely that provisions were made for barracks for the Praetorian guard as well as holding cells for prisoners in close proximity to, if not as part of, this compound, though Herod surely had some such facilities on this location for his own bodyguard.

Most of the streets as well as the residential and small business districts of Herod's time are unrecoverable due to the ongoing development of the site during the Byzantine, Muslim, and Crusader periods. Herod assigned hinterlands to Caesarea that extended 21 miles north-south and as wide as 17 miles east-west for a total of 350 square miles.[14] This made a great deal of arable land available both to the city (which would derive income from the produce of civic lands) and to the military veterans who were settled there and given grants of land as part of their pension. On the basis of both the acreage within the Roman-period walls and the population that could be supported by the cultivation of the hinterlands, some estimates place the city's population at about fifty thousand by AD 66.

One of the most basic needs of a large population is sufficient water, which was provided by the iconic aqueduct that runs along the beach to Caesarea from water sources to the north. In its current form, it is a double aqueduct. The inland channel was built first, probably under Herod for his new city.[15] The second, seaside channel would be built later (around AD 130) under the emperor Hadrian. With the addition of the second channel, the aqueduct carried eight hundred thousand gallons of water per hour from springs south of Mount Carmel to the city of Caesarea.[16] Herod's engineers also took careful thought for the sewage and drainage systems of the city, with rainwater being carefully channeled into sewers and both rainwater and sea surges being harnessed to flush waste.

Herod the Great died in 4 BC, and his immediate heir, Archelaus, proved incompetent and was removed a decade later. Judea thus came under the

---

12. Netzer, *Architecture of Herod*, 110–12.

13. See Porath et al., "Caesarea," 1658, versus Netzer, *Architecture of Herod*, 110–12.

14. Holum et al., *King Herod's Dream*, 75.

15. Jerome Murphy-O'Connor (*Holy Land*, 243, 249) disagrees with the consensus, regarding the presence of two wells in the praetorium as evidence that the aqueduct was not yet functional in Herod's time. He assigns the first channel of the high-level aqueduct to the Roman procurators of the mid-first century.

16. Levine, *Roman Caesarea*, 30–36.

The high-level double aqueduct.

administration of Roman prefects beginning in AD 6 (called procurators after AD 44). Caesarea—as the major port in the region and thus the major hub for communications with Rome or the Roman governor of Syria and for sea trade—became the capital of the subprovince. The prefects spent only a minority of their time in Jerusalem. Most of their administrative duties were performed at Caesarea, including the supervision of taxes and customs, judicial functions, and the strategic positioning of the six cohorts of auxiliaries (five infantry and one cavalry, numbering about three thousand in total, according to Josephus, *J.W.* 3.66) entrusted with keeping the peace in a reluctant region. Herod's seaside villa, together with the administrative buildings overlooking the villa, became the praetorium of these Roman officials. It was in this praetorium that, according to Acts, Paul was kept under guard for two years under the procurators Antonius Felix and Porcius Festus (Acts 23:35).

About five years after Paul was shipped out from Caesarea to Rome to stand trial in Nero's courts, the Gentile residents of Caesarea would rise up against their Jewish fellow citizens and slaughter thousands of them. This would, in turn, become a major impetus for the Jewish revolt against Rome. Caesarea would serve first as Vespasian's and then Titus's headquarters as they prosecuted the suppression of the rebellion. For its support and hospitality, the city was rewarded with the privileged status of a Roman colony: Colonia Prima Flavia Augusta Caesariensis. This honor would no doubt have greatly pleased Herod the friend of Rome, but the circumstances that led to it would have grieved Herod the king of the Jews.

A spectacular find in the area of the theater of Caesarea is this inscription bearing the partial name of Pontius Pilatus, or Pilate. Pilate appears to have donated the funds to build a shrine or some other such monument to Tiberius in Caesarea. The inscription also supplies his proper title: prefect of Judea.

17

MALTA

Malta in the Ministry of Paul

As a result of appealing for his case to be heard in Rome, Paul began a long and arduous sea voyage from Caesarea Maritima, past Cyprus, and along the southern coast of Türkiye. At Myra, Julius, the centurion in charge of Paul and his fellow prisoners, secured passage on "an Alexandrian ship," quite likely one of the hundreds transporting grain from Egypt to Rome (Acts 27:6). Because ships depended on the winds and currents for navigation, Alexandrian ships could cross the Mediterranean directly from Rome to Egypt on their return trips but essentially had to hug coasts on the outbound voyages to Rome. This ship took the company around the southern coast of Crete, anchoring temporarily at Fair Havens. As it was late in the season, when sailing became increasingly hazardous, the centurion in charge of the prisoner transport and the captain in charge of the ship were keen on finding a more suitable harbor in Crete than the somewhat exposed harbor of Fair Havens in which to spend the winter months.[1] Paul warned them, however, of the danger of pressing any farther. He had been shipwrecked at least three times before, according to 2 Corinthians 11:25, so he had some firsthand experience of the fickleness and danger of the Mediterranean Sea. The captain pressed on nevertheless and, encountering unexpected and violent weather, the ship was driven away from Crete and into the open sea.

1. The ship carrying Paul and his fellow prisoners only reached Crete after the Day of Atonement ("the Fast," Acts 27:9), which falls between September 14 and October 14. From the conditions at sea, one might presume that it fell later within that span that year.

St. Paul's Islands and the mouth of St. Paul's Bay.

After passing through more than 500 miles of storm-tossed waters, Paul's ship came to Malta, a small island of about 20 by 9 miles, lying just 50 miles south of Sicily. The coastline of Malta alternates between forbidding cliffs, rocky approaches, and natural harbors. We will probably never know exactly where Paul made landfall. Local tradition identifies an area known today as St. Paul's Bay—immediately south of St. Paul's Islands—as the "bay with a beach" (Acts 27:39 NRSV), which looked like a promising landing from the sea. The approach, however, was far more treacherous than the sailors anticipated. The bow of the ship lodged itself on an underwater reef while the pounding surf broke up the stern. All hands had to abandon the ship and swim to shore.

The Archaeology of Malta

Archaeological remains from the Greek and Roman periods are regrettably sparse. An inscription from the early imperial period bears witness to the presence on the island of a temple to Persephone, the reluctant wife of Hades, Greek god of the underworld. According to the inscription, the temple had been renovated by an imperial freedman named Chrestion, who served as overseer of an early emperor's personal estates and interests on Melita and Gaulos (modern Malta and Gozo), perhaps those of Augustus himself.[2]

Acts relates that Paul and his traveling companions were received hospitably by the inhabitants of the island. It was perhaps Paul's miraculous survival of the bite of a viper that brought him to the attention of a Roman named

---

2. Bonanno, *Malta*, 203–4; Mercieca, "Proserpina Temple"; Busuttil, "Chrestion Inscription."

Publius, who is called "the first man of the island" (Acts 28:7). An inscription from slightly later in the first century names another Roman, Lucius Castricius Prudens, "first among the Maltese," bearing independent witness to the use of this title.[3] It probably represents not an official position so much as an informal recognition of the chief patron or person who enjoyed the highest dignity on the island. This same inscription bears witness to an active cult of the Roman emperor on the island during the first century, naming Prudens as a priest of the Divine Augustus. A further inscription names a certain Lutatia as a priestess of Augustus's wife, Julia (Livia) Augusta.[4]

Several Roman-period villas have been found on Malta, such as might have belonged to a "first man" like Publius. The so-called Domus Romana just outside the wall of modern Mdina is the most thoroughly excavated and best preserved.[5] It was built in the late second century BC and continued to be occupied through the time of Paul's shipwreck. This upscale villa was located in the midst of a larger residential neighborhood, many of whose residents lived in considerably more modest dwellings. A narrow road ran through this neighborhood, deep ruts bearing silent witness to the decades of heavy cart traffic that once traversed it. Little remains besides the footprints of these homes, some of their foundations having been carved directly into the underlying bedrock. Water channels attest to the importance the residents attached to gathering all possible runoff rainwater into their cisterns for use especially during the long dry season of April through August. Olive presses and a number of stone basins indicate the light industry that took place in and around the villa as residents processed some of the most basic necessities of life.

Like the nearby residences, not much of the upscale villa survived above the floor level, but the floors that did survive attest to the wealth of the family that once lived here. The villa, like most affluent Greek and Roman homes, was arranged around a courtyard once surrounded by columns that supported a roof covering areas on all four sides of a large space open to the sun. The mosaic floor of the courtyard features a variation on the traditional meander pattern with an unusual three-dimensional effect. Within this is a much simpler and more traditional border design of geometric waves such as can be found in places as diverse as Pompeii's villas and Herod the Great's bathhouses. The center features a traditional scene of two birds perched on a basin or birdbath.

3. Bonanno, *Malta*, 204.
4. Bonanno, *Malta*, 205.
5. Bonanno, *Malta*, 308–17.

The mosaic floor of the Domus Romana's peristyle courtyard.

Fragments of columns and the decorative stone frieze and molding of the peristyle.

The other, more public rooms of the house, such as the triclinium (or dining room) and the tablinum (the head of the household's office and receiving room), were also decorated with a variety of mosaic designs, including a border motif featuring garlands and tragic masks as well as other intricate geometric patterns. The residents of this particular villa appear to have had a penchant for more exotic deities, such as Isis, a statue of whom once graced an inner room.

One peculiarity of this villa is the fact that it housed not merely busts but life-size statues of the emperor Claudius and members of his family, including his daughter Claudia Antonia. These suggest a personal connection with the imperial family such as might have been appropriate for "the first man of the island," particularly one bearing a Roman name like Publius. Though once again we cannot pinpoint Paul to this location, Paul and certain of his traveling companions were entertained for three days in a villa like this one, where Paul healed Publius's father and others who had learned of his ability to mediate divine healing.

Another Roman villa built and operational prior to Paul's visit was discovered close to St. Paul's Islands, a little more than a 1-mile walk from St. Paul's Bay and less than a 5-mile walk from the bay with a beach just north of St. Paul's Islands.[6] Acts does not say, however, that Paul was taken to the most conveniently located villa but to the one that belonged to "the first man of the island," and the Domus Romana is still only an 8-mile walk from the farther of the two bays mentioned above.

According to Lucian of Samosata, a writer from the second century AD, Malta was a regular stopping point for commercial ships carrying grain from Alexandria to Rome (*The Ship* 9). Alexandria was the principal seaport of Egypt, the breadbasket of the empire. When the winter season had ended and the sea

Statues of Claudius (left), emperor for much of Paul's active ministry (AD 41–54), and his daughter (right) found within the Domus Romana.

6. On the villa at San Pawl Milqi, see Bonanno, *Malta*, 298–99.

was opened once again for traveling (Pliny the Elder, *Nat.* 2.47), the centurion in charge of the prison transport secured passage on another Alexandrian ship that was already wintering on Malta when Paul and his fellow travelers arrived (Acts 28:11). This was quite possibly a grain supply ship—one that bore the "Twin Brothers" as its figurehead. These were the demigods Castor and Pollux, immortalized in the constellation Gemini. Even though they were twins, the myth speaks of each having a different father: Castor was the natural son of Leda and her husband, King Tyndareus of Sparta, but Pollux was the offspring of the Greek god Zeus, who, appearing in the form of a swan, had impregnated Leda almost at the same time. When Castor was killed in a battle, Pollux prayed to his father to divide his own immortality between them so that they might remain together. As a result, they were elevated to the stars for half of the year (the six months that Gemini is visible in one hemisphere) and spent the other half together in the underworld. They were particularly regarded as the protectors of sailors (hence the propriety of this particular Alexandrian ship's figurehead) and were frequently the objects of worship, even in the heart of the Roman Forum itself (see Strabo, *Geogr.* 1.3.2.). This ship would bear Paul and his fellow prisoners to the Italian port of Puteoli, whence he would travel by land to Rome.

18

PUTEOLI

The Alexandrian ship that carried Paul and his fellow prisoners stopped for three days at Syracuse on the southeastern coast of Sicily and one day at Rhegium on the toe of Italy before arriving at Puteoli, the principal port city for the large grain ships whose cargoes were destined for Rome despite the fact that these cargoes would still have to be transported about 145 miles over land to arrive at Rome.[1] These ships kept a steady supply of grain coming from Egypt throughout the sailing season to the residents of Rome, who enjoyed a daily dole as one of the benefits of living in the empire's heart. Claudius had already begun construction of a new harbor at Ostia, a great artificial harbor with a mouth facing the south, but this would only be completed during Nero's reign—certainly by AD 64, the year a coin minting celebrated the port on its reverse. It would be some time, however, before Ostia eclipsed Puteoli.

Puteoli's acropolis stood immediately to the east of the port. At only 100 feet in elevation, it was not the most imposing acropolis, but it made the usual statement about the importance of traditional religion in the city, having once been studded with temples. Prominent among these was a temple dedicated to Augustus, the remnants of which have been incorporated into the modern Cathedral of St. Proclus Martyr—a none-too-subtle statement concerning the triumph of the gospel of Jesus over the gospel of Augustus.

---

1. Glen L. Thompson and Mark Wilson painstakingly trace out and explore the relevant archaeological evidence surrounding Paul's land journey from the port of Puteoli (modern Pozzuoli) to Rome in *In This Way We Came to Rome*.

The harbor of Puteoli. The modern breakwater incorporates the remains of the ancient mole, extending no less than 330 yards, built under Augustus.

A first-century fresco from a villa at Stabia on the Bay of Naples believed to display the port of Puteoli as Paul would have encountered it.

As Paul and his guard disembarked and entered the city, they would likely have passed the busy macellum, the principal market for the city, which sat at

The interior of the Cathedral of St. Proclus Martyr, showing the ancient columns and portions of the architrave of the Temple of Augustus.

a central location on the shore of the harbor.[2] A central courtyard was surrounded by two stories of shops and porticoes, with an additional single-story quadrangle of shops surrounding that in turn. To enhance traffic flow, the entrances to adjacent shops alternated opening onto the inner and the outer courtyards. The whole complex appears to have been dedicated to Serapis. His consort, Isis, and their son, Harpocrates (Horus), might have been included in the central shrine, as it was common to encounter the trio together. Given the heavy and constant traffic between Alexandria and Puteoli, it is not altogether surprising to find these particular Egyptian deities featured so

2. The macellum currently visible appears to date back only as far as the Flavian period. Paul would have seen an earlier iteration of the same (Maiuro, *Phlegraean Fields*, 28).

The macellum viewed from the southwest (that is, from the direction of the harbor).

prominently. For the convenience of customers, merchants, and sailors alike, the macellum was equipped with large public latrines in the northeast and northwest corners of the inner quadrangle of shops, each likely designated for a particular gender.

The residents of Puteoli loved their entertainments as much as the residents of next Roman town did. To the northeast of the bath complex sit the scant remains of an amphitheater from the time of Augustus. This facility was not able to keep up with the tastes of the residents for a variety of spectacles, and so a new and larger amphitheater was built just southwest of the older one during Vespasian's reign. It is a sign of the prosperity of Puteoli that the city was able to undertake this at its own expense, creating an arena that nearly rivaled the Colosseum in Rome. There were thirty-nine rows of seats divided into three tiers, all crowned by a columned portico running the circumference above the top tier. The whole was splendidly decorated with the same quality and designs of carving one would find in Rome itself. The real marvel of engineering in this amphitheater, like its sister in Rome, lies beneath its surface. Beneath the sand of the arena sat the storage cells for exotic animals and all the tackle needed to steer their cages and release them into the arena above for hunts or beast fights. Here gladiators and condemned prisoners could also await their own ascent up the ramps into the bright sun and the clamor of the spectators.[3]

As a major port city, Puteoli was a hub of intersecting cultures. Alongside the cult of the Greco-Egyptian gods, cults of the Phrygian mother goddess Cybele and the Syrian Jupiter Heliopolitanus, worshiped famously at a colossal temple in Baalbek in modern Lebanon, also flourished here. Flavius Josephus attests also to the presence of a significant Jewish community in this city (*J.W.* 2.103–4; *Ant.* 17.328–29). This might have been the seedbed of the Christian community that Paul encountered there, among whom he stayed—under close guard—for seven days before his guards set out with him for Rome (Acts 28:14). As a major port city to which ships from Palestine, Syria, and Egypt regularly traveled, Puteoli experienced a steady stream of land travel between itself and Rome, which was home already to a number of Christian congregations. Thus it is no surprise that Paul should have found devotees of the new faith in Puteoli. In addition to providing him with encouragement and hospitality, their presence would have reminded him that without him as well as through him the Christian movement was growing throughout the empire—a process that would not be hindered by the outcome of his own trial, whatever the verdict.

3. Maiuro, *Phlegraean Fields*, 39–50.

19

ROME

Rome in the Ministry of Paul

Paul addressed what is arguably his most substantial letter to the Christians in Rome, written while he was still in the region of Corinth. We learn that he sent it to the house churches in Rome through Phoebe, a deacon and patron of the assembly in Cenchreae, as he himself was heading to Jerusalem to deliver the collection for the poor among the Judean Christians—the visit that was to result in his arrest, his two-year incarceration in Caesarea Maritima, and his voyage to stand trial in Rome (Acts 21:15–28:31; Rom. 15:25–27, 31; 16:1–2). It had been Paul's plan to visit the Christian assemblies in Rome (Rom. 1:11–13; 15:23–24, 28–29, 32), though undoubtedly not under these conditions. This was, nevertheless, the manner in which a word spoken twice by the Lord to Paul earlier in Acts found fulfillment (Acts 19:21; 23:11).

Upon Paul's arrival at last in the capital city, we see him only in his own rented dwelling, meeting with local leaders of the Jewish community, all the while with a Roman guard on duty (Acts 28:16–31). We learn nothing from Acts of his interactions with the Christian assemblies already firmly rooted in Rome, nor of his activities after this period. Some speculate that Paul did, in fact, make his hoped-for missionary trip to Spain, returning to Rome a second time to stand trial and finally face execution late in Nero's reign. Others speculate that Paul never regained his freedom and thus did not leave Rome before his execution. In 2 Timothy, we learn that a man named Onesiphorus successfully navigated the urban jungle of Rome to bring relief and support to Paul during his imprisonment—or *one* of his imprisonments—there (2 Tim. 1:16–18).

The origins of the Christian communities in Rome are shrouded in mystery. According to Luke, Jewish pilgrims from Rome, and perhaps Gentile God-fearing pilgrims as well, were present at Pentecost to hear Peter's inspired proclamation of the good news (Acts 2:10–11). Some of these pilgrims may have been won to the new movement and eventually taken word of the Christ-followers' confession and way of life back to Rome with them. The list of greetings that Paul sends along with his letter, however, is also a list of associates and relatives of Paul who may themselves have been instrumental in building up the Christian community there, if not planting some sizable portion of it themselves (Rom. 16:3–16). The notices of the "hard work" of many of these sisters and brothers may refer to their church planting and nurturing activity in Rome, as is at the very least the case for the Mary lauded in Romans 16:6.

Rome was perhaps the most permanent home for Aquila (originally a native of Pontus in northern Türkiye) and Priscilla. This important missionary couple lived there for an undisclosed period prior to the emperor Claudius's expulsion of Jews from Rome because of some disturbances caused by a troublemaker named "Chrestus," according to Suetonius (*Claud.* 25.4; Acts 18:2). While "Chrestus" is attested as a slave's name in the period, it is tempting to believe that Suetonius misunderstood the cause of these disturbances, which were really the result of inner-Jewish conflict over claims concerning

A grave inscription bearing witness to the use of "Chrestus" as a slave name in the Roman world: "Chrestus, accounting officer of Norbanus Flaccus and Norbanus Balbus."

"Christus" or "Christos." It was this expulsion, dated to AD 49, that brought Priscilla and Aquila to Corinth and, thus, into Paul's orbit. This important couple found their way back to Rome prior to Paul writing his letter to the churches there, in which he sends fond greetings to his old partners in mission (Rom. 16:3–4).

We learn surprisingly little about the conditions of Roman Christians from Paul's letter—no doubt because he himself had not yet been to the city or interacted with more than a few dozen Christians who would find themselves present in Rome at the time of his writing (Rom. 16:3–16). The one issue that emerges clearly from Romans is the existence of tensions between the Jewish Christian and Gentile Christian members of the assemblies there, reflected most clearly in Paul's direct advice (14:1–15:13) but also in his careful insistence that neither Jew nor Gentile has preferred standing—or is decisively laid aside—in God's saving interventions in Christ (Rom. 1:1–4:25; 9:1–11:32).

The Christian movement grew sufficiently large to be noticed by Nero and his informants and to be selected for scapegoating in the aftermath of the great fire of AD 64 that destroyed two-thirds of the city. Christians must have also lived in sufficiently high tension with their neighbors for this scapegoating to be greeted without resistance—and perhaps even with pleasure—by the general population of the city (Tacitus, *Ann.* 15.44). According to Eusebius, Nero ordered the execution of two central figures in the early Christian mission who were present in Rome—Peter and Paul (*Hist. eccl.* 2.25)—though, strangely, he says nothing of the fire.

The Archaeology of Rome

Geographic Overview and Central Forum

The geographic location of Rome enabled the city to grow in importance over the centuries. Located primarily on the eastern shore of the Tiber River, in a great bend of the river as well as at a juncture where several established ancient land routes crossed at a low point, Rome was well placed for trade by land and water and would later be in an excellent position to coordinate communications and movements throughout a larger empire. The Tiber River emptied into the Mediterranean about 20 miles west of Rome near Ostia, which would become a major port for Rome's sea trade.

The seven hills across which the city eventually spread—the Palatine, Capitoline, Quirinal, Viminal, Esquiline, Caelian, and Aventine—provided a defensible position for a growing settlement and, later, city. Virgil, Ovid, and Martial all speak of the city as *urbs septicollis* (a seven-hilled city) in

A view of the Tiber River as it snakes through the city of Rome.

their poetical works (Virgil, *Georg.* 2.535; *Aen.* 6.784; Ovid, *Tristia* 1.4.69; Martial, *Epigr.* 4.64.11). Plutarch and Varro both refer to an obscure festival called Septimontium connected with the growth of the city to encompass the seventh hill (Plutarch, *Quaest. rom.* 69 [*Mor.* 280d]; Varro, *Ling.* 6.24). All but the Caelian were enclosed within the city's walls in the Republican period (indeed, by the fourth century BC).[1] By the time of Augustus, however, the city had outgrown its walls (most of which had either fallen into disrepair or been hidden as the city literally grew up around and against them on both sides). Rome's transition from a walled city to an open city with no need of defensive fortifications was a result of Augustus establishing the Roman peace—his bringing an end to the civil wars and pushing back the frontiers of potentially hostile forces so far from the city of Rome as to render walls superfluous. The legions on the distant frontiers became, as it were, the city's "walls."

1. Connolly and Dodge, *Ancient City*, 108.

The city of Rome was the beating heart of the empire that encompassed the lands around the entire Mediterranean. It was also a parasitic and insatiable consumer of the world's goods. The grandeur of Rome came from its siphoning off the resources and wealth of its conquered territories and vassal states around the Mediterranean. Though Rome didn't have "emperors" until the late first century BC, it had an empire as early as the beginning of the second century BC, when it began to take over the lands of Greece and North Africa. The public architecture of the city was designed above all to impress, to create a visual image that matched its leaders' propaganda about its greatness, its eternity, its achievement. Brick and marble everywhere gave eloquent testimony to Rome's grandeur, power, and wealth.

If Rome was the heart of the empire, the Roman Forum was the heart of Rome. Here the politics and piety of the city blended to proclaim that Rome's power was the result of the gods' beneficent purposes. Official public orations and addresses were made from a rostrum in the center west of the forum. This was a large, elevated platform adorned with the prows of defeated warships (Latin, *rostra*). Legal proceedings, both civil and criminal, were heard

Overview of the Roman Forum. The footprint of the Basilica Julia, the remaining column bases marking out the narrower side aisles and the broad central hall, is visible middle right, with the podium and three remaining pillars of the Temple of Castor and Pollux standing at its eastern end, just right of center. The imperial palaces of the Palatine Hill overlook the forum from the top right.

The brick substructure of the Curia Julia, once covered with a thick veneer of marble.

in the basilicas—expansive, columned, covered buildings like the Basilica Aemilia on the north side of the forum and the even grander Basilica Julia on the south side, both of which also provided offices for several governmental functionaries. Julius Caesar, first a member of the triumvirate that included Sextus Pompeius and Marcus Licinius Crassus and, later, the sole surviving autocrat, undertook the construction of the latter basilica, funding the operation with spoils from the conquest of Gaul (including the proceeds from selling tens of thousands of prisoners of war into slavery). Next to the Basilica Aemilia, the Senate—composed essentially of Rome's male millionaires from its most distinguished families—met in the Curia Julia, the Roman Senate house, to decide Roman policy to the extent that Julius and his successors, the emperors, would allow them. Julius prepared for the renovation of this structure, though his assassination in 44 BC left it to his successor, Octavian (later named "Augustus" by the Senate), to execute.[2]

Julius also began the first major expansion of the Republican-era Roman Forum, building the Forum of Caesar north and northwest of the Curia Julia. This created additional public spaces for offices, meetings, and the conducting of the business of empire, all under the watchful shadow of a new temple to

2. Guidobaldi, *Roman Forum*, 15; Claridge, *Rome*, 71.

A partial view of the Forum of Caesar, showing the remains of one of the column-lined porticoes and several of the recessed rooms that served a variety of official personnel and functions.

Venus Genetrix.[3] The epithet of the goddess refers to the myth of Venus falling in love with the Trojan Anchises and giving birth to his son Aeneas, the mythical hero of the Roman people whose story is told in Virgil's *Aeneid*. But Julius Caesar also traced the mythical ancestry of the Julii family line back through the line of Aeneas to the goddess, making his new forum a blatant witness to his own propaganda.

The business of the Roman Forum took place under the watchful eye of the gods. A temple toward the east end of the forum was dedicated to Vesta, the goddess of the hearth. Six virgin priestesses tended the sacred fire that represented the hearth not just of a single family but of all Roman people—the larger family of which the emperor himself was the head (as pater patriae, "father of the fatherland"). These Vestal Virgins lived in a villa adjacent to the temple. Their celibacy during their thirty-year term as priestesses bought them freedom from being under a man's authority and often significant influence with the emperors and their court.[4]

A temple to Castor and Pollux stood between the Temple of Vesta and the Basilica Julia to the west. Castor was an important precedent for a mortal

3. Claridge, *Rome*, 163–68.
4. Guidobaldi, *Roman Forum*, 55–57; Claridge, *Rome*, 105–8.

The podium and three re-erected pillars of the Temple of Venus Genetrix.

The remains of the Temple of Vesta.

The courtyard of the villa of the Vestal Virgins. Both the temple and the villa were destroyed in the fire of AD 64 and were quickly restored by Nero.

becoming divine and no doubt eased developments for the worship of the emperors in Rome after their deaths.

The iconic Temple of Saturn, the mythical father of Jupiter, Neptune, and Pluto (in Greek, *Hadēs*), stood near the west end of the forum at a slight elevation (that is, on the beginning rise of the Capitoline Hill). It was originally erected before the period of the Republic.[5] Today the front six Ionic columns still stand, along with their architrave and a small portion of the pediment. This temple served also as the treasury of Rome, guarded by the ancient god. A legend written on the architrave commemorates the rebuilding of the temple after a disastrous fire. The first line of this inscription—*Senatus populusque Romanum* (The Roman Senate and people)—is incidentally the source of the famous acronym SPQR, seen everywhere in Rome and on things Roman. A temple to Concordia, reaching back to the early Republic but rebuilt after a fire in AD 10, stood to the north of the Temple of Saturn, and a portico honoring the "counseling gods"—the twelve Olympian deities—was added to the west.[6]

Overshadowing all from atop the Capitoline Hill to the west of the forum stood the Temple of Jupiter, Juno, and Minerva, the foundations of which are still visible within the Capitoline Museums. Representations on a number

---

5. Guidobaldi, *Roman Forum*, 30; Claridge, *Rome*, 83–84.
6. Claridge, *Rome*, 80, 83; Guidobaldi, *Roman Forum*, 29.

The remaining front facade of the Temple of Saturn.

of coins and carved reliefs suggest that the temple had four columns at its front during the late Republic and early imperial period but was rebuilt more grandly under Vespasian, spreading to a size that required the support of six columns.[7] Jupiter Capitolinus was the quintessentially Roman deity, and Roman colonies (like Ostia, Corinth, and Philippi) typically had their own "Capitolium"—a temple to Jupiter, Juno, and Minerva—connecting their civic worship with that of the *metropolis* (the "mother city") of Rome. When Hadrian refounded Jerusalem as a Roman colony in the early 130s AD, he built a shrine to Jupiter Capitolinus, likely in the civic forum on the west

7. Compare a coin minted under M. Volteius during the Republican period (78 BC), showing the facade of the temple with four columns and three pairs of bronze doors opening to each of the three sacred areas (cellae) of the divine trio (https://www.britishmuseum.org/collection /object/C_1902-0503-159, last accessed July 30, 2024) with a sesterce minted under Vespasian, showing the restored temple with six columns, this time also showing the doors open to reveal the three cult images within ("Sale: CNG 69, Lot: 1557," Research Coins: Feature Auction, Classical Numismatic Group, LLC, June 8, 2005, www.cngcoins.com/Coin.aspx?CoinID=66125, last accessed July 30, 2024).

side of the city. Hadrian gave the colony the name Aelia Capitolina, the first term coming from his own family name, the second a mark of devotion to the Capitoline god Jupiter.

This archaeological witness to the vital religious life of the city of Rome helps us to grasp the countercultural—indeed, the revolutionary—nature of Paul's proclamations concerning idolatry. Paul foregrounds this in the opening paragraphs of the body of his letter to the Christians in Rome, where idolatry—taking the worship due to the one and only God, the God of *Israel*, and giving it instead to all these human-made images—is the source of all the moral chaos that plagues human society. It was not the reflection of core civic virtues—piety, giving the gods their due, showing solidarity with one's fellow citizens in petitioning and thanking the gods as a community—that the majority of Rome's residents believed it to be (Rom. 1:18–32). Like other

A low relief of Marcus Aurelius sacrificing incense or wine before the Temple of Jupiter Capitolinus. A bull and his slayer stand ready for the next liturgical act (Capitoline Museums).

early Christian missionaries and, indeed, like many Hellenistic Jews, Paul believed that all this alleged piety had served only to incur the wrath of the one true God and to alienate human beings from God's favor.

Rome beyond the Forum

If the business of the forum happened under the watchful eye of the gods, it happened also under the watchful eyes of the living emperors and their families, whose palaces spread across the sides and top of the Palatine Hill to the south of the forum. On the western Palatine sat the houses of Augustus and Livia along with an older temple to Magna Mater (the Great Mother Goddess), which Augustus renovated, and a new temple to Apollo, built by Augustus in honor of the god whom he credited with his victory at Actium (Virgil, *Aen.* 8.698–713).[8] Tiberius would build his palace, the Domus Tiberiana, to the north of these structures, directly overlooking the forum. This would be rebuilt by Nero and expanded by Hadrian, such that the visible remains postdate Paul's visit.

On the south side of the Palatine Hill sat the Circus Maximus, the most famous racetrack in Rome. The racecourse would have at one time been surrounded with stone stadium seating raised a safe distance above the action of the chariots.[9] The distinctive feature of circuses or hippodromes was the central *spina*, which made an open space into an oval track. As mentioned previously, the most dangerous parts of the chariot races were the sharp turns at either end, the occasion for many spectacular wrecks that were no doubt part of the draw of these events. The *spina* was a prime location for displaying pieces of political propaganda. It was not out of a desire merely to decorate that Augustus placed in its very center one of the obelisks of Ramses II that he imported from Heliopolis in Egypt in 10 BC; it was a prominent reminder of his defeat of Marc Antony and Cleopatra VII in 31 BC, whose alliance threatened the unity of the empire.

A second significantly developed district within the city of Rome was the Campus Martius, the Field of Mars, so named because it was once the site for Rome's military training exercises. This would have been before the southern half of the field was developed into another religious, political, and entertainment district. Four small temples from the earlier Republican period stood near the center of this area. Pompey the Great, once a partner and then a defeated rival of Julius Caesar, had built a theater, expansive portico, and public latrines west of these temples. Pompey's complex also featured a second

---

8. Claridge, *Rome*, 126, 135–44; Harrison, "City of Rome," 5.
9. On the Circus Maximus, see Connolly and Dodge, *Ancient City*, 176–81.

The (largely unexcavated) Circus Maximus.

The *spina* from the circus (or hippodrome) in Roman-period Tyre.

The Pantheon, the temple honoring "every god." Its present form reflects Hadrian's rebuilding of the temple, which had been destroyed by fire twice before (AD 64 and AD 110).

meeting venue for the Roman Senate (it was here that Julius Caesar was assassinated in 44 BC). North of the four temples, Marcus Agrippa, Augustus's right-hand man, had built a public bath complex and, further to the north, a monumental temple that was later incorporated by the emperor Hadrian into the famous Pantheon.[10]

East of these stood a large parklike area used for the regular voting of the *plebs*, or ordinary citizens of Rome. South of this stood a columned portico built by Augustus in honor of his sister, Octavia, surrounding the sacred precinct of two temples to Jupiter and Juno. Just south of that, Augustus built a second theater in this district in honor of his then heir apparent, Marcellus. Augustus also allowed his friend L. Cornelius Balbus, a victorious general, to build a smaller theater and portico north of the Portico of Octavia in honor of his pacification of Libya.[11] These theaters would have featured performances of Roman comedy such as those written by Plautus and Terence, tragedy such as Seneca wrote, bawdy farces, and pantomimes.[12]

10. Pescarin, *Rome*, 64–65; Claridge, *Rome*, 226.
11. Claridge, *Rome*, 247.
12. See further Connolly and Dodge, *Ancient City*, 182–89.

Southwest of the Roman Forum on the banks of the Tiber is the Aventine Hill, which had grown to become an important quarter for merchants and manual laborers. This was the major offloading area for shipments coming up the Tiber from the port of Ostia at the river's mouth, with wharves and warehouses lining the Tiber at this point.[13] The Aventine was also one of several sites where great amounts of grain were stored to keep the citizens of Rome supplied with their daily rations of wheat for baking bread. An ironic monument to the massive amounts of supplies that passed through the port here is the so-called Monte Testaccio, a 120-foot-high mountain made entirely from the discarded amphorae and other clay vessels used (chiefly) to bring olive oil to Rome from Spain and North Africa.[14] Other large market areas were to be found alongside the Tiber north of the Aventine, including a vast livestock market and a produce market. We must never forget the economic realities required to support the population of one million in this city at the heart of an empire, a population that, as far as the Roman elites were concerned, the provinces existed to serve and supply.

Augustus's Transformation of Rome

One Roman story that particularly merits attention—and one that can be plainly read from the architectural landscape of early imperial Rome—is the story of Octavian, who would become known as Augustus, Rome's first emperor. The story of Augustus is to Rome what the infancy narratives of Matthew and Luke are to the Gospels. Augustus's birth was, in the words of an inscription by the provincial council of Asia Minor, "the beginning of good news." This inscription, the Priene calendar inscription, employs a form of the Greek word *euangelion*—the word rendered "gospel" or "good news" in English translations of the New Testament!—to talk about the significance of Augustus, who was lauded as a god and bringer of peace for the world.[15] It is noteworthy that the inscription used this language at least eight decades before Luke would write his Gospel. As Luke begins to tell the story of Jesus's birth, he reminds his readers that these events happened under the shadow of Augustus, emperor of Rome from 31 BC to AD 14. This is more than just a date to help readers know how long ago the story took place. It is a subtle invitation to read the story that would follow—the story of a Son of God who would be a savior to the people and usher in a reign of peace and well-being for all nations—over against the story of Augustus, who had been painted in these

13. Claridge, *Rome*, 403–5.
14. Connolly and Dodge, *Ancient City*, 127; Claridge, *Rome*, 402.
15. For the full text and discussion of this inscription, see Danker, *Benefactor*, 215–22.

specific hues. Luke's view of which
story is true, of course, is clear from
the beginning. God's own angels announce the birth of *this* savior and
affirm the promise of peace that *this* Son
of God will bring to the world.

Octavian was adopted by Julius Cae-
sar, who had no legitimate son of his own, even
though Octavian's biological parents were still
living. Such an adoption of an adult was essentially Julius's way of naming Octavian his successor and heir. After Julius was assassinated,
Octavian vowed to avenge his death and punish
the conspirators led by the senators Brutus and
Cassius. Octavian promised to build a monumental temple to Mars Ultor, or Mars the Avenger,
beside the Roman Forum if he returned victorious—a vow he would begin to fulfill just five
years later in the context of creating a massive
expansion of the public forum to the north of
the Roman Forum and perpendicular to the
Forum of Julius, with his Temple of Mars
Ultor as its showpiece.[16] Most of the new
Forum of Augustus, finished around 2 BC,
stretches under a modern thoroughfare and
is therefore not excavatable, but at the time
it provided significant new venues for judicial
proceedings and government business.[17]

Octavian's partnership with Marc Antony, another loyal client of Julius Caesar,
outlived the conspirators and assassins by only a decade. Antony's alliance
with Cleopatra VII, Egypt's last queen, proved to be a fatal mistake. Octavian
emerged as the protector of Rome's interests and enjoyed the strong support of
the Senate and people of Rome, while Antony and Cleopatra were represented
as threats to the empire's unity, the eastern half of which was allegedly being
ceded to a foreign queen. Antony was labeled a traitor to his own people.
A triumphal arch, of which only the bases and one or two column capitals

A posthumous statue of Augustus
from the villa of his widow, Livia,
in Prima Porta. He is depicted in
military dress but barefoot—as
is typical for gods (Vatican
Museums).

---

16. Connolly and Dodge, *Ancient City*, 111.
17. Dumser, "Urban Topography of Rome," 141; Claridge, *Rome*, 177–80.

The podium and several columns of the Temple of Mars Ultor (top; note the wall behind the temple separating the Forum of Augustus from a less desirable residential neighborhood) and a statue of Mars (bottom; Capitoline Museum).

The northern exedra of the Forum of Augustus.

remain, was built in 29 BC to celebrate Octavian's victory over Marc Antony in the naval battle near Actium two years before.[18] This arch was erected near the center of the Roman Forum adjoining the Temple of Castor and Pollux and the newly built Temple of the Deified Julius Caesar.

The rise of Augustus to sole power was celebrated as the beginning of a new golden age of peace and stability. "Peace" became the watchword of the new regime, the source of the legitimacy of Augustus's power. Perhaps the most significant monument to the *Pax Augusti*—the "Augustan Peace"—is the Altar of the Augustan Peace, once erected in the northern portion of the Field of Mars. This monument was commissioned by the Senate in 13 BC in honor of Augustus's "pacification" of Spain and Gaul.[19] The altar itself is housed at the top of a flight of steps inside a nearly square monument of 40 by 36 feet. A carved relief on the two shorter sides of the Altar of the Augustan Peace displays a religious procession in which Augustus and his extended family take conspicuous part, along with senators, lictors, and a variety of priests.

18. Guidobaldi, *Roman Forum*, 37; Claridge, *Rome*, 101–2.
19. Claridge, *Rome*, 207.

The Altar of the Augustan Peace, with a detail of a panel showing a religious procession. Augustus stands second from the left, his head draped in the manner of a Roman priest, with Marcus Agrippa following behind him.

After his victory over Antony and Cleopatra at Actium in 31 BC and the suicide of the pair, Augustus had several Egyptian monuments transported to Rome as trophies and placed in prominent locations as perpetual reminders of his successful end to the civil war and foreign threat. A second obelisk from the time of Ramses II was erected in the Field of Mars and used as the needle of a solar meridian, a kind of sundial that marks out the progression of a solar year, allowing the civil calendar to keep in step with the solar calendar. A long strip of metal was laid out beside the obelisk and engraved such that at noon every day the shadow of the tip of the obelisk pointed to the date and indicated important seasonal transitions, like the solstices and equinoxes. The inscription on the obelisk, dated to 10 BC, declared, "The emperor Caesar Augustus, Son of the Deified one, Chief Priest, with Egypt restored to the power of the Roman people, gave this as a gift to the Sun."

Augustus also selected a site in the northernmost part of the Field of Mars (*Campus Martius*) for his mausoleum. This was a great round marble-faced brick tomb with a diameter of almost 100 yards and a height of perhaps 50 yards when it was still complete. It would become the site of a massive city-block-long inscription celebrating the achievements of Augustus's career and his many benefactions to the Roman people, written by Augustus himself shortly before his death—the *Res gestae divi Augusti* (Things accomplished by the Divine Augustus). The "Altar of the Augustan Peace," the horologium, and Augustus's mausoleum with its massive inscription created a triad of monuments to his legacy of peace.

The brick substructure of the once marble-clad Mausoleum of Augustus.

The reverse of a denarius commemorating the divinization of Julius Caesar. The legend reads *Divus Iulius,* "Deified Julius," and shows the comet that was interpreted as the new god ascending to his place in the heavenly pantheon.

An essential claim to legitimate power for Augustus was his adoption by Julius Caesar, and thus his inheritance not only of Julius's estates and wealth but also of the loyalty of Julius's client base. The Senate had declared his adoptive father to be a god after his assassination, which improved the legitimacy of Augustus's rule tremendously.

In 29 BC, Augustus erected a temple to the deified Julius in the heart of the Roman Forum. Only parts of the podium remain, including the temple's most distinctive feature: a concave area in the front of the podium surrounding the site where the body of Julius was cremated.[20] This temple became a constant reminder of the power that stood behind Augustus's leadership of the empire. The triumphal Arch of Augustus, in what was surely no accident, adjoins this temple on its southern side. Temples would be erected to the deified Julius throughout the Roman world,

The podium of the Temple of Divus Julius.

20. Guidobaldi, *Roman Forum*, 36; Claridge, *Rome*, 100–101.

particularly in the Eastern Mediterranean (as in Ephesus and Corinth), often in conjunction with the goddess Roma. As the adopted son of Julius, Augustus became *divi filius*, "son of the deified one," a title included in almost every public inscription. In Greek, the fine distinction between a *deus* and a *divus*, between a god who had always been a god and a mortal who had become divine, was lost, and the emperor was simply "a son of a god."

Given this ideological environment, it is impossible to miss the politically subversive ramifications of the early Christian proclamation concerning Jesus, the anointed one. From its first sentence, Paul's letter to the Christians in Rome throws down the gauntlet in the midst of the empire's capital city by celebrating a "gospel" or "good news" that has come to the world thanks to another Son of another God—who, as it happens, is also the *only* genuine God. The "good news of God's Son" (Rom. 1:3) contested the story presented (and widely embraced) as the good news brought to the world by virtue of Augustus, son of the god Julius. Where Augustus's achievements and blessings for the world were foretold in the "prophetic" sections of the *Aeneid*—a work written by Augustus's court poet, Virgil—the good news that has come in Jesus was "proclaimed as good news in advance through his prophets in the holy writings" (Rom. 1:2). And where Augustus was declared divine after his death by the Roman Senate, this Jesus "was appointed Son of God in power through the spirit of holiness on the basis of resurrection from the dead" (1:4)—quite a bit more impressive than Augustus's "apotheosis by vote."

This Jesus is also, for Paul, "our Lord," who, along with the Father God, is the source of favor and peace. It was not politically innocent to claim the title—and the authority—of "Lord" for a man crucified on Roman authority under Augustus's successor, Tiberius. To confess Jesus as Lord and to affirm that God raised him from the dead (Rom. 10:9)—that is, to say that God established this Jesus as his Son through the resurrection from the dead (1:4)—was to confess that one's ultimate allegiance was to a man executed as an enemy of the Roman order. Nor was it politically innocent to claim that "faithful obedience" or "the obedience of faith" (1:5) belongs by right to this one Lord and the one God whom he represented and on whose behalf he acted.

It is noteworthy that the Christians in Rome who read Paul's letter would find nothing therein that reinforced the alleged importance of the public story of Aeneas of Troy, the destiny of Rome foretold by the gods, or the realization of those promises in Augustus. Rather, the story that really matters for all of humanity, according to Paul, is the one that begins with Adam, runs through Abraham and Moses, and climaxes in Jesus Christ, in whom the one God's provisions for peace and salvation have truly been given.

The Porta Maggiore and its water channels. The structure bears inscriptions acknowledging the emperor Claudius for the completion of this branch of the aqueduct system and the emperors Vespasian and Titus for its renovation and expansion.

Claudius (Vatican Museums).

Tiberius, Caligula, and Claudius appear to have altered the cityscape of Rome very little in comparison to Julius and Augustus, though Claudius significantly improved its water supply with a new aqueduct, part of which can be seen in the Porta Maggiore, a great gate on the eastern side of the city of Rome supporting several water channels (only incorporated into the city's walls in the third century AD). The Senate would vote divine honors to Claudius, after which a massive temple complex was built to him southeast of the Roman Forum.

Living Life in the Center of Empire

We have focused thus far on essentially the grand public areas of Rome—the political, religious, and judicial spaces of Rome as well as the places of public entertainment. But Rome was a city of approximately one million people, and the largest part of the cityscape was occupied by their residences, workshops, and supporting structures, like the ancient fast-food joints and taverns that sustained them and the hundreds of smaller bath facilities that kept them feeling civilized.[21]

The most elite Romans lived in private homes that might span half or all of a city block, with some of the frontage rented out to shops of one kind or another, often with living quarters—think of little more than a loft—above the shop for the renters. The elite domus itself was largely a single-story residence with a high ceiling, its rooms arranged around an open atrium in the front half and an open columned courtyard in the rear half. These openings would provide the greater part of the light and ventilation.

The majority of the population would have lived far more modestly in *insulae*, essentially apartment blocks with the lowest story devoted to workshops, taverns, or other businesses. Apartments on the second floor would have been relatively comfortable; apartments decreased in size (including the height of the ceilings!) and in number of rooms as one went above that. While many *insulae* would not have climbed above a third story, the remains of a six-story apartment block can be seen on the west side of the Capitoline Hill, and there is some evidence that a few topped out at eight stories.[22] Most of the residents on the upper floors would not have had the means for cooking or easy access to water, with the result that they would have purchased all their meals at local *thermopolii* and *tavernae* and used the public latrines and other facilities exclusively, save for a chamber pot. One particularly unsavory

---

21. These smaller bath facilities would increasingly be surpassed and replaced by the monumental facilities built under Trajan, Caracalla, and Diocletian in the centuries to follow.
22. See further Storey, "Housing and Domestic Architecture."

The atrium (top) and peristyle courtyard (bottom) of the House of the Menander, a town house of an ultrarich family, in Pompeii.

Part of the Insula dell'Ara Coeli, likely the middle floors of one of the few discovered and excavated tenement blocks in the city of Rome. The fresco and marble slab on the left side of the photo shows part of the complex to have been converted into a Christian church in the fourteenth century.

residential area was the Subura, immediately northeast of the Forum of Augustus, which Augustus cordoned off with a 30-foot-high wall. These *insulae* would likely be more the world of the house churches that gathered in Rome to hear Paul's letter and bid for support for his ongoing mission to the West (Rom. 15:23–29), though the possibility exists that a *few* elite families were won to the new faith and opened up their domus to the assembly.

An important aspect of Paul's letter to the Roman Christians and, indeed, an important aspect of their congregational life is the presence of Jewish Christians in their midst. Unfortunately, although there are substantial literary witnesses to the presence and to the fortunes of the Jewish community in Rome, there are almost no archaeological witnesses to their presence above the ground.[23] Rather, historians have relied on the epigraphic—or inscriptional—evidence to be found in the subterranean burial complexes of the Jewish community used throughout the Roman period. Iconography makes it fairly easy to determine which sites were used by the Jewish community for burial. Scores of epitaphs are engraved also with religious symbols—above all the distinctive seven-branched candelabra, the menorah, which was associated

---

23. On the origins and history of the Jewish community in Rome, see Smallwood, *Jews under Roman Rule*, 128–43, 201–19; Leon, *Jews of Ancient Rome*.

The *thermopolium*—that is, the "fast-food" establishment—of Vetutius Placidus in Pompeii.

with the temple in Jerusalem. These inscriptions reveal the presence of at least eleven distinct synagogues in Rome: a "synagogue of the Hebrews," which is most likely the oldest synagogue, given the general name; a "synagogue of the Agrippensians," named in honor of either Marcus Agrippa (Augustus's right-hand man and, through his close friendship with Herod, a protector of Jewish rights) or one of the first-century AD kings of Judea (Agrippa I or Agrippa II), both of whom spent significant time in Rome and might be presumed to have formed bonds with the Jewish community there; a "synagogue of the Augustesians," a name bearing witness to the high regard in which the Jewish community held Augustus, who affirmed and protected Jewish rights (to follow their own laws, to collect and send money to the temple in Jerusalem, to be exempted from military service, which would conflict with both the honoring of the Sabbath and the avoidance of idolatry) throughout the empire; as well as several others that appear to have been named after the districts in which they were located.[24]

The Jewish community, either in whole or in substantial part, was subjected to sporadic evictions from the city of Rome due to what was deemed inappropriate behavior in the capital city. For example, the conversion of

24. Harrison, "City of Rome," 52.

Roman elites prompted expulsions in 139 BC and AD 19. The Christian Jews expelled under Claudius in AD 49 returned to congregations that had been shaped and led by Gentile Christians for between five and seven years, and there are indications in Paul's Letter to the Romans that reintegration was not going smoothly. This is reflected in his careful elimination of Jewish privilege in God's sight in the opening chapters, his equal elimination of Gentile self-sufficiency and arrogance in chapters 9–11, and his urging of mutual acceptance and of making room once again for (and honoring) diversity of practice where foods, days of worship, and the like were concerned.

The wealth, luxury, and ostentation embodied in the public spaces of Rome and the semiprivate homes of its rulers were the prizes of conquest and political intimidation. They were spoils rather than wages or rewards. The Jewish community in Rome could swell through deportation of Jews from Judea as slaves, as in the case of Pompey the Great in 63 BC or Titus in AD 70, or be decimated through exile, as under Tiberius and Claudius. The temples dedicated to Rome's deified deceased rulers were the ultimate attempts to legitimate Rome's imperialism not just as the will of the gods but as the achievement of gods.

In such an environment, Paul's carefully nuanced words about the political authorities in Romans 13:1–7 would have been heard not only as promoting orderly submission but also as demythologizing the authorities. On the one hand, he wisely advises submission to Roman authorities and promotes such submission as an attitude aligned with God's will for ordinary people. On the other hand, and in keeping with his subversion of the imperial ideology of the emperors as divine sons whose accession to power was "good news for the world," he conceptually submits these same authorities to a higher authority—namely, the God of the Jewish and Christian communities. They are no longer gods in their own right but servants of the one and only genuine God (whether they are aware of the fact or not)—a point Paul seems to hammer home through threefold affirmation of the relationship (13:4–6). The mandate of the one God for the authorities is to promote virtuous conduct and to curtail vicious conduct. Paul does not himself raise the question of what should happen if the authorities fail in their mandate—that is, if they fail to reward the just and punish the unjust or if they should begin to do the opposite. That would fall to the more prophetically minded among the early Christians, such as John, the visionary author of Revelation.

The ruins of Rome are a constant reminder not only of Rome's greatness but of the fact that no empire forged by human beings endures. History proves the common epithet "Eternal Rome" to be a lie, now no more than tourist propaganda. The archaeological remains remind us—as Paul would remind his audiences—to look to the kingdom of our Lord and of his Christ if we are ever to find a truly stable homeland: "But our citizenship is in heaven, and it is from there that we are expecting a Savior, the Lord Jesus Christ" (Phil. 3:20 NRSV).

BIBLIOGRAPHY

Note: Resources particularly recommended for further study of sites relevant to Paul's ministry and letters are marked with an asterisk (*).

*Bakirtzis, Charalambos, and Helmut Koester, eds. *Philippi at the Time of Paul and after His Death*. Harrisburg, PA: Trinity Press International, 1998.

Bayhan, Suzan. *Priene, Miletus, Didyma*. Istanbul: Keskin Color Kartpostalcilik, 1997.

Beitzel, Barry J., ed. *Lexham Geographic Commentary on Acts through Revelation*. Bellingham, WA: Lexham, 2019.

———. "The Meaning of 'Arabia' in Classical Literature and the New Testament." In Beitzel, *Lexham Geographic Commentary*, 520–36.

Biers, Jane. "*Lavari est vivere*: Baths in Roman Corinth." In Williams and Bookidis, *Corinth*, 303–19.

Bonanno, Anthony. *Malta: Phoenician, Punic and Roman*. Malta: Midsea Books, 2005.

Bookidis, Nancy. "The Sanctuaries of Corinth." In Williams and Bookidis, *Corinth*, 247–59.

Bourbon, Fabio. *Petra: Jordan's Extraordinary Ancient City*. New York: Barnes & Noble Books, 2000.

Bowman, Alan K., Edward Champlin, and Andrew Lintott, eds. *The Augustan Empire, 43 BC–AD 69*, 2nd ed. Vol. 10 of *The Cambridge Ancient History*. Cambridge: Cambridge University Press, 1996.

Brélaz, Cédric. "First-Century Philippi: Contextualizing Paul's Visit." In Harrison and Welborn, *First Urban Churches 4*, 153–88.

Brocas-Deflassieux, Laurence. *Béroia, cité de Macédoine: Étude de topographie antique*. Beroia: Fondation Nationale de la Recherche Scientifique, 1999.

Browning, Iain. *Petra*. Rev. ed. London: Chatto & Windus, 1982.

Burnett, D. Clint. "Imperial Divine Honors in Julio-Claudian Thessalonica and the Thessalonian Correspondence." In Harrison and Welborn, *First Urban Churches 7*, 63–91.

Busuttil, Joseph. "The Chrestion Inscription." *Treasures of Malta* 62 (2015): 60–63.

Cadwallader, Alan H. "A Return to 'Peace and Security': The Parts and the Whole." In Harrison and Welborn, *First Urban Churches 7*, 93–122.

Camp, John M. *The Archaeology of Athens*. New Haven: Yale University Press, 2001.

*Claridge, Amanda. *Rome: An Oxford Archaeological Guide*. 2nd ed. Oxford: Oxford University Press, 2010.

Cochrane, Charles N. *Christianity and Classical Culture: A Study of Thought and Action from Augustus to Augustine*. New York: Oxford University Press, 1957.

*Connolly, Peter, and Hazel Dodge. *Ancient City: Life in Classical Athens and Rome*. Oxford: Oxford University Press, 1998.

D'Andria, Franceso. *Hierapolis of Phyrgia: An Archaeological Guide*. Istanbul: Ege Yayınları, 2003.

Danker, Frederick W. *Benefactor: Epigraphic Study of a Graeco-Roman and New Testament Semantic Field*. St. Louis: Clayton House, 1982.

Demirer, Ünal. *Pisidian Antioch*. Ankara: Dönmez Offset Basımevi, 2002.

deSilva, David A. *Discovering Revelation*. Grand Rapids: Eerdmans, 2021.

———. *An Introduction to the New Testament: Contexts, Methods, and Ministry Formation*. 2nd ed. Downers Grove, IL: IVP Academic, 2018.

———. *Judea under Greek and Roman Rule*. Oxford: Oxford University Press, 2024.

———. *The Letter to the Galatians*. New International Commentary on the New Testament. Grand Rapids: Eerdmans, 2018.

———. *A Week in the Life of Ephesus*. Downers Grove, IL: IVP Academic, 2020.

Dio Cassius. *Roman History*. Vol. 6, *Books 51–55*. Translated by Earnest Cary. Loeb Classical Library 83. Cambridge, MA: Harvard University Press, 1917.

Dumser, Elisha A. "The Urban Topography of Rome." In Erdkamp, *Cambridge Companion to Ancient Rome*, 131–50.

Ehrensperger, Kathy. "Between Polis, Oikos, and Ekklesia: The Challenge of Negotiating the Spirit World (1 Cor 12:1–11)." In Harrison and Welborn, *First Urban Churches 2*, 105–32.

Erdemgil, Selahattin, Adil Evren, and O. Ozeren. *The Terrace Houses in Ephesus*. Istanbul: Hitit Color, 1988.

Erdkamp, Paul, ed. *The Cambridge Companion to Ancient Rome*. Cambridge: Cambridge University Press, 2013.

Evangelogiou, Paraskevi. "Kenchreai." In Kissas, *Ancient Corinthia*, 31–38.

*Fairchild, Mark. *Christian Origins in Ephesus and Asia Minor*. Peabody, MA: Hendrickson, 2017.

———. "Paul's Early Ministry in Syria and Cilicia: The Silent Years." In Beitzel, *Lexham Geographic Commentary*, 494–519.

Fant, Clyde E., and Mitchell G. Reddish. *A Guide to Biblical Sites in Greece and Turkey*. Oxford: Oxford University Press, 2003.

Friesen, Steven. *Imperial Cults and the Apocalypse of John: Reading Revelation in the Ruins*. Oxford: Oxford University Press, 2001.

———. *Twice Neokoros: Ephesus, Asia and the Cult of the Flavian Imperial Family*. Leiden: Brill, 1993.

Galor, Katharina, and Hanswulf Bloedhorn. *The Archaeology of Jerusalem: From the Origins to the Ottomans*. New Haven: Yale University Press, 2013.

Geva, H. "Jerusalem, the Roman Period." In vol. 2 of *The New Encyclopedia of Archaeological Excavations in the Holy Land*, edited by E. Stern, 758–67. Jerusalem: Israel Exploration Society/Carta, 1993.

Graf, David F. "Aretas." In vol. 1 of *The Anchor Bible Dictionary*, edited by David N. Freedman, 373–76. New York: Anchor, 1992.

Guidobaldi, Paoli. *The Roman Forum*. Milan: Electa, 1997.

Hansen, Valerie. *The Silk Road: A New History*. Oxford: Oxford University Press, 2012.

Harrison, James R. "The City of Rome from the Late Republic to the Julio-Claudian Period: An Epigraphic, Archaeological and Numismatic Portrait." In Harrison and Welborn, *First Urban Churches 6*, 1–66.

———. "An Epigraphic Portrait of Ephesus and Its Villages." In Harrison and Welborn, *First Urban Churches 3*, 1–67.

———. "An Epigraphic Profile of Thessalonica from the Hellenistic Age to the Roman Empire." In Harrison and Welborn, *First Urban Churches 7*, 1–62.

———. "Excavating the Urban and Country Life of Roman Philippi and Its Territory." In Harrison and Welborn, *First Urban Churches 4*, 1–62.

———. "From Rome to the Colony of Philippi." In Harrison and Welborn, *First Urban Churches 4*, 307–70.

———. "Introduction: The Urban Life of Roman Corinth." In Harrison and Welborn, *First Urban Churches 2*, 1–45.

———. "Paul and the *Agōnothetai* at Corinth: Engaging the Civic Values of Antiquity." In Harrison and Welborn, *First Urban Churches 2*, 271–326.

*Harrison, James R., and L. L. Welborn, eds. *The First Urban Churches 2: Roman Corinth*. Atlanta: SBL Press, 2016.

*———. *The First Urban Churches 3: Ephesus*. Atlanta: SBL Press, 2018.

*———. *The First Urban Churches 4: Roman Philippi*. Atlanta: SBL Press, 2018.

*———. *The First Urban Churches 5: Colossae, Hierapolis, and Laodicea*. Atlanta: SBL Press, 2019.

*———. *The First Urban Churches 6: Rome and Ostia*. Atlanta: SBL Press, 2021.

*———. *The First Urban Churches 7: Thessalonica*. Atlanta: SBL Press, 2022.

Hellerman, Joseph H. *Reconstructing Honor in Roman Philippi: Carmen Christi as Cursus Pudorum*. Society for New Testament Studies Monograph Series 132. Cambridge: Cambridge University Press, 2005.

Hengel, Martin, and Anna Maria Schwemer. *Paul between Damascus and Antioch: The Unknown Years*. Louisville: Westminster John Knox, 1997.

*Holum, Kenneth G., Robert L. Hohlfelder, Robert J. Bull, and Avner Raban. *King Herod's Dream: Caesarea on the Sea*. New York: Norton, 1988.

Horsley, Greg H. R. "Appendix: The Politarchs." In *The Book of Acts in Its First-Century Setting*, edited by David W. J. Gill and Conrad Gempf, 419–31. Grand Rapids: Eerdmans, 1994.

Jipp, Joshua. "Paul's Areopagus Speech of Acts 17:16–34 as *Both* Critique *and* Propaganda." *Journal of Biblical Literature* 131 (2012): 567–88.

Josephus. *Jewish Antiquities*. Vol. 5, *Books 12–13*. Translated by Ralph Marcus. Loeb Classical Library 365. Cambridge, MA: Harvard University Press, 1943.

———. *The Jewish War*. Vol. 1, *Books 1–3*. Translated by H. St. J. Thackeray. Loeb Classical Library 203. Cambridge, MA: Harvard University Press, 1927.

Keener, Craig. *Acts*. Cambridge: Cambridge University Press, 2020.

Kennedy, David. "Syria." In Bowman, Champlin, and Lintott, *Augustan Empire*, 703–36.

Kissas, Konstantinos, ed. *Ancient Corinthia: From Prehistoric Times to the End of Antiquity*. Athens: Foinikas Publications, 2013.

Knibbe, Dieter. "*Via Sacra Ephesiaca*: New Aspects of the Cult of Artemis Ephesia." In Koester, *Ephesos*, 151–56.

*Koester, Helmut, ed. *Ephesos: Metropolis of Asia*. Harvard Theological Studies 41. Valley Forge, PA: Trinity Press International, 1995.

Koukouli-Chrysantaki, Chaido. "Colonia Iulia Augusta Philippensis." In *Philippi at the Time of Paul and after His Death*, edited by Charalambos Bakirtzis and Helmut Koester, 5–35. Harrisburg, PA: Trinity Press International, 1998.

*Koukouli-Chrysantaki, Chaido, and Charalambos Bakirtzis. *Philippi*. Athens: Archaeological Receipts Fund Directorate of Publications, 2009.

Koursoumis, Socrates S. "Corinth." In Kissas, *Ancient Corinthia*, 39–61.

Kraeling, Carl H. "The Jewish Community at Antioch." *Journal of Biblical Literature* 51 (1932): 130–60.

Kraybill, J. Nelson. *Imperial Cult and Commerce in John's Apocalypse*. Sheffield: Sheffield Academic, 1996.

Lassus, Jean. "Antioche à l'époque romaine." In vol. 2.8 of *Aufstieg und Niedergang der römischen Welt*, edited by Hildegard Temporini and Wolfgang Haase, 54–102. Berlin: de Gruyter, 1977.

Lavithis, Renos. *Paphos: Land of Aphrodite*. London: Topline, 2008.

Leon, Harry J. *Jews of Ancient Rome*. Rev. ed. Peabody, MA: Hendrickson, 1995.

*Levine, L. I. *Jerusalem: Portrait of the City in the Second Temple Period (538 BCE–70 CE)*. Philadelphia: Jewish Publication Society, 2002.

———. *Roman Caesarea: An Archaeological-Topographical Study*. Jerusalem: Hebrew University Institute of Archaeology, 1975.

Long, Fredrick J., and Ryan Kristopher Giffin. "'Every Knee Bowed': Jesus Christ as Reigning Lord over 'the Heavenly, the Earthly, and the Subterranean Gods' (Philippians 2:10)." In Harrison and Welborn, *First Urban Churches 4*, 239–90.

Longenecker, Richard N. "Antioch of Syria." In *Major Cities of the Biblical World*, edited by R. K. Harrison, 8–21. Nashville: Nelson, 1985.

Magness, Jodi. *The Archaeology of the Holy Land: From the Destruction of Solomon's Temple to the Muslim Conquest*. Cambridge: Cambridge University Press, 2012.

Maiuro, Amadeo. *The Phlegraean Fields: From Virgil's Tomb to the Grotto of the Cumaean Sibyl*. Rome: Instituto Poligrafico e Zecca Dello Stato, 1958.

Master, Daniel M., ed. *The Oxford Encyclopedia of the Bible and Archaeology*. 2 vols. New York: Oxford University Press, 2013.

McKnight, Scot. *The Letter to the Colossians*. New International Commentary on the New Testament. Grand Rapids: Eerdmans, 2018.

McRay, John M. *Archaeology and the New Testament*. Grand Rapids: Baker, 1991.

Mercieca, Simon. "The Proserpina Temple and the History of Its Chrestion Inscription." *Treasures of Malta* 61 (2014): 33–39.

Moo, Douglas J. *The Letters to the Colossians and to Philemon*. Grand Rapids: Eerdmans, 2008.

Muddiman, John. *The Epistle to the Ephesians*. Peabody, MA: Hendrickson, 2001.

Murphy-O'Connor, Jerome. *The Holy Land: An Oxford Archaeological Guide*. 5th ed. New York: Oxford University Press, 2008.

———. "Paul in Arabia." *Catholic Biblical Quarterly* 55 (1993): 732–37.

*———. *St. Paul's Corinth: Texts and Archaeology*. 3rd ed. Collegeville, MN: Liturgical Press, 2002.

*———. *St. Paul's Ephesus: Texts and Archaeology*. Collegeville, MN: Michael Glazier, 2008.

*Nasrallah, Laura Salah. *Archaeology and the Letters of Paul*. Oxford: Oxford University Press, 2019.

Negev, Avraham. *The Archaeological Encyclopedia of the Holy Land*. Rev. ed. Nashville: Nelson, 1986.

Netzer, Ehud. *The Architecture of Herod, the Great Builder*. Grand Rapids: Baker Academic, 2006.

Niewöhner, Philipp, ed. *Miletus/Balat: Urbanism and Monuments from the Archaic to Ottoman Periods*. Istanbul: Ege Yayınları, 2016.

Oakes, Peter. "The Imperial Authorities in Paul's Letter to Predominantly Greek Hearers in the Roman Colony of Philippi." In Harrison and Welborn, *First Urban Churches 4*, 221–38.

*Pescarin, Sofia. *Rome: A Guide to the Eternal City*. New York: Barnes & Noble Books, 2000.

Pfaff, Christopher A. "Archaic Architecture." In Williams and Bookidis, *Corinth*, 95–140.

Phillips, Elaine A. "The Geographic Importance of Antioch on the Orontes." In Beitzel, *Lexham Geographic Commentary*, 269–78.

Porath, Yosef, Kenneth Holum, Avner Raban, and Joseph Patrich. "Caesarea." In supplementary vol. 5 of *The New Encyclopedia of Archaeological Excavations in the Holy Land*, edited by Ephraim Stern, 1656–84. Washington, DC: Biblical Archaeology Society, 2008.

Price, S. R. F. *Rituals and Power: The Roman Imperial Cult in Asia Minor*. Cambridge: Cambridge University Press, 1984.

Raban, Avner. "Maritime Caesarea." In vol. 1 of *The New Encyclopedia of Archaeological Excavations in the Holy Land*, edited by Ephraim Stern, 286–91. Jerusalem: Israel Exploration Society and Carta, 1993.

Ramsey, William. *The Cities of Saint Paul*. London: Hodder & Stoughton, 1907.

Richardson, Peter. *Herod: King of the Jews and Friend of the Romans*. Minneapolis: Fortress, 1999.

Riit, Tullia. *An Epigraphic Guide to Hierapolis*. Istanbul: Ege Yayınları, 2006.

Robinson, David M. "A New Latin Economic Edict from Pisidian Antioch." *Transactions of the American Philological Association* 55 (1924): 5–20.

———. "A Preliminary Report on the Excavations at Pisidian Antioch and at Sizma." *American Journal of Archaeology* 28 (1924): 435–44.

———. "Roman Sculptures from Colonia Caesarea (Pisidian Antioch)." *The Art Bulletin* 9 (1926): 4–69.

Rogers, Guy MacLean. "An Ephesian Tale: Mystery Cults, Reverse Theological Engineering, and the Triumph of Christianity in Ephesus." In Harrison and Welborn, *First Urban Churches 3*, 69–91.

Romano, David G. "City Planning, Centuriation, and Land Division in Roman Corinth." In Williams and Bookidis, *Corinth*, 279–301.

Sarris, A., R. K. Dunn, J. L. Rife, N. Papadopoulos, E. Kokkinou, and C. Mundigler. "Geological and Geophysical Investigations in the Roman Cemetery at Kenchreai (Korinthia), Greece." *Archaeological Prospection* 15 (2007): 1–23.

*Scherrer, Peter. "The City of Ephesos from the Roman Period to Late Antiquity." In Koester, *Ephesos*, 1–26.

———. *Ephesus: The New Guide*. Istanbul: Ege Yayınları, 2000.

Schnabel, Eckhard J. *Early Christian Mission*. 2 vols. Downers Grove, IL: InterVarsity, 2004.

———. *Paul the Missionary: Realities, Strategies and Methods.* Downers Grove, IL: InterVarsity, 2008.

Smallwood, E. Mary. *The Jews under Roman Rule: From Pompey to Diocletian.* 2nd ed. Leiden: Brill, 1981.

Standhartinger, Angela. "A City with a Message: Colossae and Colossians." In Harrison and Welborn, *First Urban Churches* 5, 239–56.

Still, Todd D. *Conflict at Thessalonica: A Pauline Church and Its Neighbours.* Sheffield: Sheffield University Press, 1999.

Storey, Glenn R. "Housing and Domestic Architecture." In Erdkamp, *Cambridge Companion to Ancient Rome*, 151–68.

Sumney, Jerry L. *Colossians: A Commentary.* New Testament Library. Louisville: Westminster John Knox, 2008.

Tataki, Argyro B. *Ancient Beroea: Prosopography and Society.* Paris: De Boccard, 1988.

Thompson, Glen L., and Mark Wilson. *In This Way We Came to Rome: With Paul on the Appian Way.* Bellingham, WA: Lexham, 2023.

Trebilco, Paul. *The Early Christians in Ephesus from Paul to Ignatius.* Grand Rapids: Eerdmans, 2007.

———. "The Jewish Community in Ephesus and Its Interaction with Christ-Believers in the First Century CE and Beyond." In Harrison and Welborn, *First Urban Churches* 3, 93–126.

*Veleni, Polyxeni Adam. *Macedonia—Thessaloniki: From the Exhibits of the Archaeological Museum.* Athens: Archaeological Receipts Fund Publications Department, 2013.

Walker, Paul. *In the Steps of Saint Paul.* Oxford: Lion Hudson, 2008.

Walters, James C. "Egyptian Religions in Ephesos." In Koester, *Ephesos*, 281–309.

Weima, Jeffrey A. D. "'Peace and Security' (1 Thess. 5.3): Prophetic Warning or Political Propaganda?" *New Testament Studies* 58 (2012): 331–58.

White, Joel R. "'Peace and Security' (1 Thess. 5.3): Is It Really a Roman Slogan?" *New Testament Studies* 59 (2013): 382–95.

———. "'Peace' and 'Security' (1 Thess 5.3): Roman Ideology and Greek Aspiration." *New Testament Studies* 60 (2014): 499–510.

White, L. Michael. "Urban Development and Social Change in Imperial Ephesos." In Koester, *Ephesos*, 27–80.

Williams II, Charles K., and Nancy Bookidis, eds. *Corinth: The Centenary, 1896–1996.* Athens: American School of Classical Studies, 2003.

*Wilson, Mark W. *Biblical Turkey: A Guide to the Jewish and Christian Sites of Asia Minor.* Istanbul: Ege Yayınları, 2010.

Winter, Bruce. *After Paul Left Corinth: The Influence of Secular Ethics and Social Change.* Grand Rapids: Eerdmans, 2001.

MODERN AUTHORS INDEX

SCRIPTURE AND OTHER ANCIENT WRITINGS INDEX

SELECT SUBJECT INDEX